Moon Dance:

The Feminine Dimensions of Time

by

Sioux Rose

iUniverse, Inc.
New York   Bloomington

iUniverse books may be ordered through booksellers or by contacting:

iUniverse
1663 Liberty Drive
Bloomington, IN 47403
www.iuniverse.com
1-800-Authors (1-800-288-4677)

ISBN: 978-1-4401-2839-4 (sc)
ISBN: 978-1-4401-2840-0 (ebook)

Printed in the United States of America

iUniverse rev. date: 09/11/2009

Dedication

I am dedicating this book to my late father, Abraham, who taught me much about the archetype of Zeus; and to the wonderful women of Marathon Key, Florida, who have been my support circle for more than a decade, and have kept alive my television persona as celestial seer while the tide of a new Dark Ages swept over our land. Utmost respect goes out to those who paved the way to my spiritual growth and understanding. Many of these sources will be found sprinkled throughout this text, and acknowledged in the book's reference section. A few astrologers who refined my vision include Robert Hand, Alan Leo, Adrian Carelli, Alan Oken, Jim Lewis, Martin Schulman, Joseph Goodavage, along with numerous mystics. The ones that come to mind include: Edgar Cayce, Sun Bear, Merlin, Dick Sutphen, Joseph Murphy, Charles Fillmore, Baird Spalding, Sam Reifler, and the anonymous sages who left us the *I Ching* and its timeless wisdom. Special thanks to Jungian author Jean Shinoda Bolen whose articulation of the archetypes (*Goddesses in Everywoman* and *Gods in Everyman*) catalyzed a natural intuitive segue that gave birth to *Moon Dance*.

I wish to acknowledge my fiercely independent daughters, Gabrielle Alyssia Fernandez, and Rachel Nicole Fernandez; and my delicious dimpled grandson, Phoenix Merced who returns my heart to innocence. And new to this wild world, I welcome my granddaughter, Chloe

I also happily dedicate this book to the following individuals who brought the timeless personae of myth to life in ways that made them fascinating and accessible:

From Mars' domain: Shari Eve Rosenberg, Molly Jubitz, Aida Guzman, and my highly esteemed lifelong mentor, Vincent Procida, and Aunt Shirley & Uncle Milton.

From Demetra's earthy realm: Dennis Littleton, Mario Carabarin, Lori Webster, Darlene Nash, Ted Iseli, Arturo Molina, and Ron Lane.

From Mercury's winged domain: Estella Valles Acosta, Denei Morehouse, Luis Polo, Fancy Nanci Holtkamp, and Nelson & Grace Wee.

From Athena's realm: Frances Lear, Gerald Gould, Roberto Millian, Bob McKendry, and Jack Robb.

From the celestial sphere of Apollo: Leslie Artigue, Lee Sloms, Diane Covan, Susan Karen, and Millie Rivera.

From Hestia's Haven: Mirtha Castro, Carol Christine, Fred McCreedy, Suzanne Schwedock, and Bernice Rosenberg.

From Hera's Hideaway: Alan Maltz, Alexandria, Mary Prados, Axel Urbanic.

From Persephone's Province: Robin Margolies, Carlos Monteverde

From Pan's Play-lands: Bill Reed, James Caruso, Sandi Antonelli, Piquette Price & Nanci Porter.

From Chronos' Kingdom: Sandra Schindler, Jorge Vega, Valerie Ridenour, Millie Arango, Scott Campbell, Manny Casiano, and Lynne Knight.

From Artemise's Arena: Nora Casiano, Robin Matthews, Cynthia Civil, Lynne Sallot, Ron Weaver, Kevin Trudeau, Judi Roth, and Marnie (Key's Health Sage)

And from Aphrodite's amphitheatre: Chaun Muir, Anna Molina, Tim McCaulley, and Roberta Surina.

Table of Contents

Forward

"No problem can be solved at the level of thinking that brought it about."

Albert Einstein

If you have chosen this book chances are you are either already awakened, or are currently opening to the realization that there's more to life than what you have been taught by conventional sources. This book is going to challenge and hopefully change your paradigm beginning with the way you look at this nebulous "thing" called time. I am going to speak to you about time as no one ever has. To fulfill this promise, I must pull back the curtain that patriarchy has installed and ask you to look newly at the moon. She is kin to your soul and the keeper of time. Insofar as memory is concerned, she maintains the record of all those human endeavors that have transpired under her watch. The catalyst to all feelings, her journey explains why **your** sentiments flux, sometimes without any apparent cause. A powerfully sentient connection to the moon is specific to women; yet the analysis of human behavior has largely gone to men, many with status-bearing credentials that attest to all they are unequipped to recognize about women, particularly with respect to **the feminine experience of time**. A great many things uniquely encountered by women (especially those phenomena that run counter to the generalities agreed upon by men) are never entirely understood or genuinely explored. Established belief structures form our consensual reality and persist long after their raison d'etre has become obsolete. For instance, not long ago our earth was believed to be flat, nor was it considered sane to imagine that heavy objects could fly.

Mankind has officially arrived at the mind-boggling cusp of ages, a massive rare global transition phase. We cannot afford to live the fallacies of the past much longer. As the visionary pioneers of the World Social Forum attest, "Another World Is Possible." It may well begin with you. *Moon Dance* offers a luminous look at your place in time, time that's dynamically imprinted with thematic character as recognized by the Ancients. These timeless qualities never go out of fashion for their specific natures remain ageless. Fascinating archetypal signatures retained in the ethers form the basic components of human nature and operate much like "celestial D.N.A." *Moon Dance* will introduce you to the sacred twelve realms that are inlaid into Creation's blueprints. Getting to know these zones and the archetypes that dwell in each invites a new level of self-awareness.

As a professional astrologer (and established magazine/horoscope columnist) who has traveled the world to pursue a variety of esoteric disciplines, I wish to expand the understanding of those prepared to recognize the profound beauty inherent to the "As above, so below" Divine equation. How this universal relationship marks our destinies may seem farfetched to those accustomed to perceiving "reality" through an earthbound prism. Venturing to *Moon Dance* will bring you face to face with your own truth, one that transcends the limitations of orthodoxy. The experience of personal realization will speak for itself. Since women are biologically clocked to the moon we are destined to feel her cycle changes via our monthly menses. This rhythmic correspondence represents the uncharted feminine realm of time, a Divine heritage bequeathed to women. Our feelings are linked with the moon's passages through every one of the twelve zodiac signs due to a hidden (until now) resonance. The lunar journey recurs every month; thus our emotions relative to it can be both charted and predicted. A decade ago *Ms. Magazine* published a chilling article stating that twenty-five million Americans (mostly women, no doubt) routinely ingested anti-depressant drugs. That news served as my spiritual wake-up call. Clearly it was time to take *Moon Dance* out of the cosmic closet! Educating women would empower them. Never before had the moon's role upon female mood, behavior, and psychology been revealed. Apparently it was preferable to put a nation's female population to chemical sleep. Political repercussions are likelier when huge numbers of people reclaim their actual feelings. As an experienced astrologer sensitive to client-feedback, I can attest to the power of the moon. I now invite you to experience time as not only told by the moon, but also **felt** by her mutable character. Humanity has lived in accord with her tides and experienced these fluxes mostly on unconscious levels. By charting the nature of the lunar journey a revolutionary self-discovery process begins.

Moon Dance requires your participation. Utilizing a personal journal, a gradual familiarity with the astrological archetypes will emerge. You will soon be able to discern the qualities of time's characters and further recognize how they influence your moods, which in turn shape your various motivations. A convergence between myths and Zodiac signs will be established to sharpen your understanding. In order to grasp the impact of the moon, we will explore Luna's role in family life, and then examine her impact upon the mate selection process. We will review her operations by element and phase; and then probe the question, "Can men moon dance, too?" Moon Dancers will learn where to obtain an accurate copy of their birth charts, and how to code their journals. Equipped with a map designed to track the moon's passages through the twelve realms of time, you soon note correspondences. By examining what you feel when the moon passes through each sign-field a clear pattern will slowly emerge. You then can anticipate your internal rhythmic changes and essentially dance with the moon!

In Part II you will be introduced to the archetypes. The previously veiled components of time will take on shape, form, and character.

Should the initial chapters or thesis of this work prove inordinately complex, readers may advance to the final chapter of part I. There you will find instructions for setting up your personalized, guided lunar journal. This tool will enable you to come into synch with the hidden rhythm structure of time by recognizing the arc of your own inner journey. Themes intrinsic to time will be sensed instinctively with practice. After working with your journal you will never think of time in the same way again. *Moon Dance* provides the means to access your relationship to the great circle dance of the heavens. All orbital bodies pass through the twelve zodiac dimensions, and each lends specific character to time. *Moon Dance* guarantees unique personal insights, for you will discover that myths dance on the inside! Sentient beings inhabiting earth are cast into orb within a celestial sea that's imbued with silent, potent qualities. The timeless personae lend color and substance to the mysterious phenomenon we term time! Getting to know them will lead you to uncharted depths of your self.

Part I

Invitation to Moon Dance

Sioux Rose

A Word On Poetic License Of The Celestial Sort

It has been said that every new truth is first perceived as a heresy. Astrologers carry a colorful history and were prominent among the "first heretics." Ironically this book may attract consternation from some astrologers since it departs from conventional astrological theory to construct unusual hybrids. These designations result from the alchemy of marrying moon sign passages with ancient mythological archetypes. Certain combinations prompt a radical rediscovery process as they unmask the feminine realms of time and draw women to hidden interior places. An introduction to the twelve core archetypes invites readers to consciously integrate these personae into their life experiences. Peel back the veil of centuries of orthodox conditioning to fully embrace the nature of time as felt by the moon's dances inside of you.

It All Begins With The Circle

The modern world has us convinced that time operates uniformly. Our calendars depict the days of our lives as square slots of equal dimension set into straight rows, an entirely linear portrayal. This depiction is devoid of character. History contradicts by reminding us that not long ago the Indigenous counted time's passage by way of the moon. Her cycles of waxing and waning kept watch over mankind like an eye from the sky, plus her choreographic movements were predictable. The moon provided a living calendar set into the heavens for all to see as she moved from new crescent, to fullness, only to recede again into the celestial backdrop. The transition to a sun-based calendar constituted a strong patriarchal statement. It left the feminine-yin moon entirely out of the great celestial equation. Cloaked in mystery, the moon's influence was purposely obscured, if not outright denied. Why? The sun-based calendar introduced a masculine allegiance to the sun. This worked in concert with the induced worship of Jesus as **son** of God. With time engineered to move from a lunar to a solar count, the elite began its patriarchal programming of the masses. Part of the process involved formulating an antagonistic relationship toward the Divine feminine. This required a forfeiture of reverence and respect for the earth mother, along with the repression of female sexuality. Naturally relations between the genders became strained until outright gender inequality became the norm. Linear time is itself a lie! As is any religious teaching that excludes the feminine side of the Holy equation! Electing to box time into neat, segmented slots that march soldier-like toward the horizon suggests a future that is ever ahead and invariably reached by virtue of unconditional forward progress. Such a perception is absurd. It conditions us to see all days as standardized clones, and anesthetizes us to the rich distinctions presented by powerful, cathartic moments. We are expected to ignore the stark qualitative differences that separate one day from another. This paradigm divorces women from their biological clocks, and causes them to lose contact with basic instinct. So false a portrayal of time suggests that the influence of full moons, eclipses, and charged planetary interludes hold no significance. Yet stop anyone on the street and ask them if any date stands out, and they will likely remember events of both national and personal significance. Just as the weather changes to reflect alternating seasons, time is also designed to express diversity. Unnaturally linear time has become the norm yet earth clearly travels a circle as witnessed by our planet's orbital trajectory around the sun. The relative interplay and influence of our planetary neighbors (those companion planets each set into orb by the great cosmic clockmaker) imbue the field of time with undeniable character. We will discuss these qualitative distinctions in later chapters. To begin your *Moon Dance* journey envision time as a circle dance. Note the earth moving about the sun, the moon about the earth, and even our great sun about a central sun. Each is a whirling dervish set into a planned celestial orbit. Oscillating from the gravitational force of its own axis each of these stellar beings is endowed with specific energetic qualities. The same quintessential dance is evidenced by particles as tiny as electrons. These spiral movements reflect the great organizing principle of the cosmos: every entity spins around a larger central body. The circle is the preferred design of things as ubiquitous as the bird's nest to the woman's breast, added to the rings of trees. It is seen in the powerful rotation of wind and watery currents; and on an esoteric level Universal law demonstrates that all things are destined to come full circle. We humans were born to the circle of our mother's wombs, and live upon a planetary sphere that travels a circular orbit around yet another circling body. The circle is a core component of universal anatomy, and constitutes the blueprint of everything that spans from spinning atoms to entire galaxies. Strange that it's been left out of our reference to time! And just as water freezes at 32 degrees and transitions to steam at 212 degrees, there are specific numerical frameworks built into time's own processes. For instance, the earth requires 365 days to orbit the sun, while the moon requires 29 days to orbit the earth. Our world and its inhabitants share in a complex process of spiritual evolution that moves to the beat of the music of spheres. Einstein stated: "Matter could neither be created, nor destroyed." However it can be altered into energy. Our bodies, formed of that same matter, are as old as time. Thus human biology reflects the evolutionary result of eons of trial and error. We have become what we are in accord with the movement of the planetary spheres, most directly, the sun and moon. It is no accident that female menstrual tides directly accord with the monthly lunar cycle. To my knowledge, no study has ever been done that correlates the moon's phase changes with variations in female moods. Due to a male bias science prefers to dismiss the whole thing. Not long ago studies on heart disease exclusively featured men with generalized results applied to women. Needless to say the conclusions proved inaccurate. Female biology does not work on the same constructs as that intended for the male. Sigmund Freud, the "father" of modern psychology espoused views entirely circumscribed by biological determinism. Blind to the constraints placed on women he mistook their natural response to unwieldy restrictions for penis envy! He could not correlate the angst in female patients with the sociological constraints imposed upon them. Women in Freud's epoch did not have voting rights, could not legally own property, nor were they permitted to travel freely without chaperones. Few could select a lover or choose the marital partner she desired. The pain of such a narrowed existence explains the depression (or neuroses) a great many women experienced. Treated like children women were denied full participation in the societies in which they resided.

Darwin's theories remain challenged to this day, while Galileo was nearly executed for exposing flaws in the church's cosmological claim that the earth occupied the center of our solar system. Like the unfortunate astrologers of ages past, any who leveraged a viable challenge to the self-proclaimed immutable authority of the church had best beware. Neither should we modern women allow ourselves to be limited by the scope of science for it continually reflects a masculine image and likeness of the Creation paradigm. The eminent German mystic Rudolph Steiner said of science, "it represents the consensus of mediocre minds."

A New Feminism: Defining Time For Ourselves

Up until the feminist "revolution" as Virginia Wolfe lamented, it was rare for a woman to have a room of her own. No private domain offered her the sacred space where she might think, dream, read, or ponder the great questions of existence. For the vast majority of women life consisted of perpetual acts of servitude, endless responses to others' needs. Astrology maintains that human beings are not separate from the celestial field that enfolds our planet in a sea of radiant light. The moon, directly associated with the female experience, plays a significant role in the dissemination of that light. This phasing luminary serves as chief celestial medium for she transmits the energy received from the outer planets direct to our earth. The changing hues the moon takes on deeply affect women due to our biological link with her twenty-nine day cycle. In a very real sense the cycles of time flux through females and keep us connected to the Source. Conventional astrology links the moon with our ever-changing feelings. The lunar cycle directly impacts our emotions and energizes the collective unconscious, a pool that retains a heritage beyond our conscious cognition. Cosmic alchemy constantly impacts this collective bank of sentience. The moon is instrumental in invoking the Divine Archetypes for each is called to the heavenly stage in its due hour. Along with the sun, this quintessential pair gives birth to each of heaven's personae. Meanwhile established (patriarchal) experts of science, academe, and religion completely disavow this powerful concordance. For centuries the correspondences related by *Moon Dance* have remained an uncharted realm. Discovering the female side of time calls for a new psychology of the feminine experience, one that honors the exploration of inner space. Like archaeologists we must now dig deep into the abstract notion of time to locate lost relics of our larger identities. Profound celestial correspondence will emerge to liberate us from the deception that time marches in straight rows; and that we are intended to feel the same way everyday lest we be considered abnormal. Science is a domain where men have for centuries sought to remake the Earth mother in their image and likeness. First they co-opted all her vital resources to serve their own ends. Modern medical practices make use of a dizzying array of technological incentives to offset natural female processes beginning with menstruation and progressing onto menopause. Issuing from the false Biblical premise that "God" constructed Eve from Adam's rib, a deconstruction of the feminine to suit flawed male constructs has followed. Abducting the creative power allotted to women in their Goddess-given capacity to bring forth life, males have sough to control female reproductive powers along with a great many other expressions of the Divine feminine. Awakened women must challenge this agenda. How many women opt to fall under the knife by inviting plastic surgery to suit the specific metrics preferred by men? Perhaps a deeper understanding of the moon's relationship to our inner lives would merit a more holistic self-evaluation. Defining ourselves on a more enlightened basis may obliterate the "need" to mutilate our outer bodies to fit false ideals imposed by men.

Consider our ancestors: untamed women dancing uninhibitedly under the moon while watching her cycles wax and wane. Many loved nature and intuitively understood the silent language of herbs. They worked to heal the sick and mend wounded hearts. It was the power of the great Mother that guided their hands. It's reputed that millions of women were burned as witches for practicing rituals that connected them with the earth, the seasons, and the cosmos. This vast slaughter wrought against wise women constituted a spiritual assault the church has never sought to redress, no less acknowledge. How much wisdom was lost as a result? How much submerged upon threat of death? According to astrological theory the moon also cues into memory. Opening the door to *Moon Dance* may reawaken your own sentience and link you to powerful intuitive messages that reside in your soul. Some of these may trace back to former incarnations. Accessing this information by familiarizing yourself with the lunar cycle could play a cathartic role. You may be inwardly guided to recover suppressed awareness. As we will see later in this book, a process of feminine reclamation is vital to the birth of a new age for mankind.

The Sacred Conjunctio: A Marriage Of The Lights

Are actual archetypal stories embedded into time? How do they interface with the ancient myths? What power invokes the timeless ones back to life? Does a hidden rhythm structure endow time with specific qualities? These questions when vigorously pursued challenge the presumption that we should feel and act in the same manner every day. When societies force members to march lockstep by suppressing their feelings and championing logic alone, citizens forfeit empathy and compassion. A larger view suggests that each of us is a child of the cosmos, a miracle of the lights. We take on embodiment to actualize one of the twelve principles of Creation, each a Divine realm of sentience. Why do you suppose that persons born during given months express qualities consistent with specific sun signs? Pondering this enigma I've come to a romantic conclusion drawn from antiquity. The sun and moon are akin to cosmic father and mother principles. At each new moon the pair meets and bonds behind a veil of mystery. It's as if she, the feminine principle, gives herself to the male and thereby relinquishes her separate sense of apartness. No remnant of her light exists at new moon. The luminaries (sun and moon) meld forces and enter into a sacred marriage. This union holds the power to awaken the archetype that dwells in the sign-zone of their meeting. Each of the sacred twelve is invoked in due order from the vast celestial sea, thus given its chance to express specific qualities during its season of dominion. Exhibiting the qualities of a fertile marriage, each time the sun and moon unite their bond triggers an equivalent celestial birth. What is "born" is the archetypal entity that resides in the sign-field in which they merged. Apart from rare blue moons, the sun and moon blend once a year in each sign. These twelve conjunctions draw forth the appropriate astrological persona. Each new moon essentially joins the lights in an alchemical process of grand celestial significance. The fruit of the luminaries' "embrace" reactivates the progeny of time. Each one profoundly colors the quality of our experience here on earth. Whether the awakened archetypal imprint issues from the ethers or direct from the collective unconscious cannot be known. Mystical matters depart from those fixed boundaries recognizable on the physical plane. Thus one cannot say with certainty whether these principles exist in the outer cosmic realms, within our selves, or both. Regardless, they operate like celestial DNA, and are elemental facets of human nature. A great many aspects of human life accord with the cycles of the sun and moon. The twin luminaries engage in a magnificent cosmic dance that also profoundly influences human sentience and behavior. Let's examine the qualities stirred by the twelve zones of time where the great Lights recurrently meet.

When the sun and moon unite in the sign-realm of Aries, they invoke forceful Mars from the collective consciousness. Next they combine energetically in earthy Taurus to draw forth Demeter, the first of three distinct expressions of Venus. From there it's onto Gemini where the pair awakens Mercury from the universal tide-pool. The luminaries unite next in Cancer where the mythological archetype of Athena is summoned. The heavenly circle's sequence continues with the lights conjoining in Leo to draw Apollo from the ethers. Further engaged in the dance that animates time, the duo connects next in Virgo, where Hestia is brought to life. One lunar month later, sun and moon join forces in the realm of Libra to invoke Venus, now expressing a second set of characteristics as she assumes the form of Hera (also known as Juno), Zeus' influential wife. Progressing onto their next sacred union in Scorpio, Persephone is reborn. From there it's onto Sagittarius, where Pan is awakened from the ethers. And then the pair unites in Capricorn's realm, where old Chronos waits to be summoned from the pool of endless time. Uniting next in the rebel sign of Aquarius, they rouse Artemis; and finally the Lights commune in Pisces. (Although Neptune remains its traditional governor, given the sign's twin fish designation a second powerful archetypal presence deserves to be acknowledged.) In this last Zodiac domain Venus assumes her third persona in the form of Aphrodite. She has been granted the honor of exaltation in this zone, and clearly lends her influence to this final sign that ultimately returns the circle to itself.

The personae from ancient myth continue to imprint our world and inform our experiences. In electing to *Moon Dance* you will become the ultimate judge of your own lunar journey. This capacity matures as you take the time to observe how you feel when the moon makes her repeated crossings of each mansion of time, a process that recurs every month. Features described will assist you in recognizing each domain so you will not be left in the dark while learning to navigate these realms. You will soon find yourself familiar with the twelve Divine kingdoms that also reside on the inside! Their unique characters are regularly stirred by the moon's presence. As you *Moon Dance* you will notice personal patterns that emerge with the recurrent nature of these celestial engagements. Through observation you become your own guide as time's basic essences become recognizable. This knowledge constitutes a spiritual birthright, yours as heiress to the grand universal design. It is liberating and empowering to recognize your everlasting kinship with cosmos, and dance in accord with the music of time. Just as you are biologically shaped by the DNA heritage drawn from both of your parents, you are similarly shaped by the stories of time as revivified by the dance of sun and moon. These indestructible filaments of time constitute our celestial DNA! Human nature across the ages remains contemporary because the unseen forces that shape it are timeless. Anything that's ever really been true still is! We are star children linked to Creative forces that our earthbound intellects lack the imagination to understand. To deny these higher bonds is about as effective as challenging gravity; belief is not required to experience effects!

The amazing thing about the rotary nature of our solar system is that the twelve spiritual tribes take turns. Power is equally shared. Every principle gets its "hour upon the heavenly stage." Given that human births occur across the year, it's a cosmic given that humanity will remain peopled by individuals who represent all twelve kingdoms. Our world has been designed as a living mosaic. The inevitable interaction between the planned archetypal energies helps to refine and sometimes counterbalance the potential trespasses each is inclined to express. Sixties sensation Ritchie Havens penned these apropos lyrics: "That there is a great secret to life: there are only twelve of us." Most of us recognize our sun signs, but few realize the significance of their moon sign. Taken together, sun and moon reflect the state of our parent's marriage at the time of our conception. The relationship between the lights in your natal chart plays a significant role in your adult life mate selection process. We will examine this cosmic factor in a later chapter, *The Moon and Family Karma*.

The Twelve Faces Of God-dess

Whether we speak of Islam, Judaism, or Christianity, all represent long-established limbs from the same basic tree: that of patriarchal religion. A trait held in common by all three is a propensity to rob women (and society by extension) of equal status. All refuse to acknowledge the feminine side of the great universal equation. Some people feel that raising this issue constitutes a form of sacrilege. Really? What Divinity allotted religion the authority to shut women out of co-equal roles? Everything in the manifest universe is writ as a bond between supreme Yang and supreme Yin, that is, partnership! This fact is witnessed in the very structure of our DNA. Is it not a greater blasphemy that the church, mosque, and synagogue have denigrated women by closing off roles of power to them in service to their own ends? The Ages that have fostered male supremacy are coming to an end. However they leave behind enduring residue in the form of sexist behaviors etched deeply into cultural mores. Each Age is represented by a Zodiac sign and spans approximately 2200 years. The energetic overlay derives its character from the sign being transited by our entire solar system as it, too, orbits around a central sun. The Age of Aries occurred during the phase of Ancient Rome and it championed Mars, an inordinately macho archetype. Jesus entered as Avatar to introduce the next age, which as Pisces was intended to energize the feminine expressions of peace, compassion, and tolerance of differences. Unfortunately the higher plan was co-opted by "the old gods" who made sure that Mars/Aries still rules!

This factor has retarded mankind's spiritual progress. Currently humanity has arrived at the next age phase transition, that of Pisces into Aquarius. I chose Artemis to signify Aquarius (and by extension the promised new age) for several reasons. As liberated female her power can no longer remain hidden. Twin sister to Apollo (sun-god and symbolic **son** of God) she represents the Divine daughter, and prompts societies to recognize the need for gender balance. At this cusp of ages it is crucial that the expressions of Yin and Yang become evenly modulated. Both powers/perspectives must temper beliefs, behaviors, and lifestyles. While America arrogantly attests to its own progress a dangerous theocratic recidivism threatens the land and its alleged liberties. The ancient circle model designed with twelve archetypal expressions reflects a far more inclusive model than the God of limited access, the one that the churches, mosques, and synagogues demand we worship through orthodox channels and endlessly elaborate rituals. What have these patriarchal religious models done to ensure world peace or tolerance among tribes? In what concrete ways has the feminine estate improved over the centuries? The old patriarchal religions fueled by their fundamentalist sects are currently driving policies that veritably court Armageddon. Too many from within their folds champion of all inanities, holy war. This qualifies as a dark tribute to Mars! When only men are allowed to drive, vehicles inevitably go off course!

If we return to *Genesis* for a moment, recognizing that *The Bible* has been rewritten countless times to suit the preferences of ruling elites forced to negotiate with papal power to further their own flawed human desires, it's plausible that certain truths were left out or conveniently adulterated. Edgar Cayce addressed this issue clairvoyantly and revealed that references to reincarnation were deliberately expunged from the Bible during the command of Emperor Justinian in 553 A.D. He summoned the Fifth Ecumenical Congress in Constantinople to do the deed. The Bible read today has been altered many times. In relating God's first purported words "Let there be light!" I wonder could the original text be further elaborated upon? Perhaps "God" articulated a vision whereby the fullness of the firmaments would be divided into twelve rays, each endowed with unique qualities! Imagine this expansion of Creator's utterance: "Let

11

there be light! And I shall bear from its spectrum children born of light, each uniquely blessed upon entering this world direct from the twelve sacred realms. Every newborn shall be granted a special quality that reflects a facet of my nature that they remember their Divine source. Together, by virtue of their planned strengths and weaknesses, all will grow to serve the whole. Led by purpose each shall evolve; and so shall it be." The twelve quintessential energetic realms constitute the Zodiac. Is it mere coincidence that Jesus specifically chose twelve disciples; or that Abraham founded twelve original tribes? This number should give us pause, for taken in composite the twelve paths operate like an ingeniously crafted living mosaic. The individual sign-paths are designed to dovetail. When each functions according to plan it facilitates the optimal functioning of the whole. The long historical processes of time incline each to learn vital lessons from their astrological counterparts, i.e. fellow citizens. All twelve tribes/disciples/expressions are needed to make and sustain a balanced world! As the citizens of earth evolve the recognition that we are all part of a larger cosmos will arise. Thus it behooves us to study the full range of archetypal expressions that together reflect the essence of Creation. *Moon Dance* intends to provide readers with a keen understanding of those persons with whom they share their everyday lives, for each is a human extension of the original twelve archetypes.

It's probable that many of us dismissed high school geometry with its focus on seemingly useless angles we were forced to memorize. Yet there is an esoteric basis to this field of study. It's known as sacred geometry and recognizes these angular patterns for the powerful energetic alignments they symbolize. Within the circle exist hidden relationships that reflect mathematical principles, themselves the reflection of universal law(s). Certain positions share natural congruence, while others require reconciliation. As human beings we are given to argument and contention, and frequently assume positions that appear to be irreconcilably opposed to those of others. A mathematically based logic provides the means for transcending such polarities as was demonstrated by King Arthur. Ingeniously he sat his knights about the round table that all voices might be heard. The zodiac circle sets the template for true democracy. It is the perfect symbol of equality. All positions are inherently equal; and the circle holds no sides! A great many truths are best understood from within its context. The Initiate understands the circle as a composite of hidden relationships as it contains embedded magical formula. Additionally, the distance between any two opposing points found within the circle can be reconciled by a third position. This pattern essentially points the way to neutralizing all species of conflict. From the context of the Zodiac circle every perspective is valid; and all are necessary to the balanced functioning of the whole. "The case for twelve" represents a spiritual vision that honors human differences. Heaven's own model of democracy, this twelve-sign plan points the way to peace among earth's tribes. How differently might we treat one another if mankind moved beyond the notion that there is only one right way to be, believe, or behave? That there is only one chosen people? What if instead twelve types of humans were purposely cast from the heavens into the myriad cultures on earth? And suppose each is the chosen for her appointed purpose? Contrast this model of inclusion with the one promoted by enforced worship of a singular archetype, that of a punishing father-god? Allotted cruel features, in the **name** of this God wars have been launched, promoted and executed. Primitive martial impulses dominated societies pre-dating the birth of Christ. This phase in human history constituted The Age of Aries. The spiritual forces that guide mankind's evolutionary estate hoped that Christ's birth and teachings would open the way for a new consciousness. Christ arrived as Avatar to usher in the Age of Pisces. Unfortunately the Mars pattern for warfare was never overcome. Instead those who purported to be Christian too often applied Jesus' name to policies of vengeance and destruction. Monotheism arrived with the Age of Aries, and granted rule to Mars. The insistence upon one singular Deity subsumed the diverse qualities previously associated with specific gods and goddesses drawn from Ancient Greek & Roman legacies. The God envisioned by power elites of that time of transition came to resemble a hybrid: warrior-Mars crossed with stern father-Saturn/Chronos. Interestingly enough both Mars and Saturn are considered malefic planets by astrological standards. With this spiritual model operating it's no surprise that mankind has followed a path of destruction under the deluded notion it's been serving god's will all this time! This clarifying factor helps to explain why astrologers have been feared and despised by authoritarian cultures. The astrologer is well positioned to pose the question: "Exactly **which God** are you referring to when allegedly speaking for God's will?" The astrologer was disingenuously cast as heretic (a fate punishable by death!) because s/he held learned opinions, those capable of challenging the church's claim to immutable authority. By cleaving to Mars-Saturn religions have designed a deity that's rendered our world a zone best suited to violent tribes perpetually pitted against one another as each claims to speak exclusively for the one true God. Whoever is not cast among the chosen, too readily qualifies as the condemned. Given the limitations attendant upon our mortal status, we lack the intellectual wingspan to penetrate the great universal mysteries, particularly those that allege to define the nature of God. Our best shot comes from recognizing the twelve sacrosanct qualities etched into the filaments of time. This circle of personae invites far more diverse human expression. Out of conceit we insist that modern man is smarter and more philosophically sophisticated than his ancient counterparts. Yet the Romans and Greeks asked the same questions about life that we do. Why am I here? What is my purpose? What happens when I die? Is there a life beyond the one confined to the body? Encoded in their findings as the stories of myth is a legacy left to future generations that they need not get so locked into matter and its dense perceptual field of reference, as to lose sight of a quintessence that links our mortal experience with that of a larger cosmos.

Christianity, Judaism and Islam—The Abrahamic religions—retain the mindset drawn from The Age of Aries. According to the Bible, "God made man in **his** image and likeness." Accepted as fact, cultures have remained dominated by powerful men. The premise has been inverted: for it's truer that God has been cast in THEIR image and likeness! Wasteful carnage has beset the earth since this erroneous conclusion was drawn. It may not be politically correct to attack religion, yet when religions lead the charge toward war (presently courting Armageddon), it is timely to question the entire paradigm upon which they are based. What Creator-God would see in the destruction of Creation homage being paid? The only 'God' this type of behavior could satisfy is Mars, god of war. As we shall see when we examine the twelve archetypal components of Creation's Circle, there is a place for Mars in the celestial pantheon, as well as in our world. When honored, the circle's innate wisdom facilitates checks and balances to offset Mars' destructive trespasses. When conversely extended a disproportionate influence, Mars undermines the integrity of the holy circle. I believe this metaphor explains the current condition of our world. There is ample evidence that Mars is too much with us. My contention is substantiated upon examination of the U.S. budget. One cannot help but acknowledge the extent to which vast resources are bequeathed to war, weapons design, and production. These "industries" are fated to enact intentional harm on a massive scale. Such lethal priorities are not reflective of a life-sustaining model, and since mankind has now arrived at the cusp of ages it cannot continue in the old warring ways. Mars' grip over mass consciousness endangers us all. Ecosystems, the very webs of life, are on the brink of collapse. The Biblical concepts of "image" and "likeness" are better understood metaphysically. Human beings would be better served by the more expansive notion that they have been formed from the substance of cosmos that constitutes Creator's essence. In other words, everything is light-based! Our beings transcend the shell of the body and are composed of light. By studying the planets' emanations astrologers can explain the qualitative differentials attributable to light as diffused through the twelve Zodiac sign-fields. Each of these frameworks of experience expresses through a specific frequency. It's helpful to think of them as twelve unique spiritual pathways. Together these form a veritable wheel or dial of time!

In our mortal form we cannot hear a dog whistle, or see infrared or ultra-violet light. These examples demonstrate our sensory limitations. Thus how can we purport to grasp something as vast as the Infinite? A study of the Zodiac signs enlarges our understanding of the nature of Creator, who extends twelve fundamental qualities into our manifest world. The monotheistic premise of God as first and primary cause has given rise to a dangerous shortsightedness that fails to note the twelve key virtues that together reflect the "image and likeness" of The Divinity. Allow me an illustration through which to clarify: Each of us thinks of ourselves as a separate individual. The pronoun "I" connotes a singular person identified by a body that extends to an obvious boundary. Yet this body reflected in the mirror is itself composed of many hidden interior systems. Each one is assigned specific functions necessary to the optimal workings of the whole. We cannot see these separate systems or the organs they support from the outside; yet without their functions there could be no life. The premise of a Supreme Being who acts as central unifying cause doesn't negate the notion that Its nature is the sum of numerous distinct expressions. The many are included within the one. Returning to the ubiquitous "twelve tribes," this mystical design reminds us that the twelve archetypal expressions, each etched into the filaments of time, together make for wholeness (or holism).

Later in this book we'll discuss the reasons why many of us (women, in particular) don't feel the same way every day. Sometimes we scarce feel like the same person! It's as if a galaxy of selves resided within. Could it be perhaps that more than one "voice" operates your "control panel?" According to astrology, one's life experience mirrors their natal chart. This blueprint is based on the positions of all planets at the time of your birth. Metaphorically speaking each individual birth is an equivalent "cosmic Kodak moment." The imprint of each celestial ambassador is made manifest as flesh at the onset of each human being's first independent breath. The planets function like organs in the body of God. They reflect Creation's blueprint: "As above, so below." During the course of human history a number of oracles have been devised in an effort to explain our purpose and origin. These direct human activity to fall into congruence with its Divine counterpart. Ancient tools have been designed to assist individuals in meeting their fates while also instructing how to rise above their own worst reflexes. The tarot is one ancient yet contemporary oracle. Its visual depictions explain mankind's paradoxical estate. We are to an extent imprisoned in physical bodies where animal instincts and impulses run wild. However our souls reach for our higher spiritual counterparts. Each person grapples with the relative pull of these dichotomous interior forces. Astrology helps us recognize when we run the risk of falling victim to our lower impulses, and where we have the chance to transcend ourselves. It reflects the language of creation. Becoming familiar with time's planned cycles provides for profound personal realizations. This knowledge strengthens our faith in a benevolent universe, one that operates in accord with a magnificent organizing principle: that of Divine Order.

The beauty of the circle model is that no singular entity, position, or archetype is positioned to speak for all! And due to the rotary nature of our orbiting planetary sphere (adhering to its place within a system of synchronously revolving bodies), no single sign-realm maintains long-term dominion. The wheel of time constantly turns! And the circle provides an understanding of the unique differences planned among us. Enlightened by its cosmic context we discover ideological ways and means to transcend ancient feuds and overcome long-held antipathies that have turned tribe against tribe, race against race, nation against nation, and religion against religion for centuries. A model that shows us the ways and means to overcome our differences and rise above long-standing ism divisions was known to the ancients, and must now be rediscovered. Astrology is sacred to the sign of Aquarius, the Age now ascending. Currently it labors to be born, as it is "next up" on the great cosmic stage! Just as there could be no music without a variety of notes, imagine a world devoid of color? Earth was designed with twelve radiant hues in Divine mind! All tribes must freely radiate to produce that miraculous white light associated with saints and angels. The circle and its twelve Divine emanations express "God's" manifestation here on earth.

Do You Moon Dance?

Do you really feel the same way, or even like the same person everyday? Having observed the moon's dances as both a professional astrologer and woman given to a strong emotional range, I recognize that my inner being negotiates the voices of four dominant Goddesses. Aphrodite, who came to life boldly during the "free love" passage of the sixties, is still active and vital. (More so recently as a much younger man has been "sent" to me as lover.) She represents the "inner romantic" who yearns for powerful sexual communion. Given established positions on the great time dial, Aphrodite, the liberated lover opposes Hestia, the virgin goddess of the temple. (As we will see in Part II, Hestia accords with the basic nature of the sign of Virgo.) Not everyone will identify with polarized archetypes; but my life experience frequently swings between twin polarities. Past lifetimes dedicated to spiritual work incline me to periods of celibacy. These recur at the termination of intense love affairs. And as a writer, I require solitude to compose and finalize literary works. My "inner monk" resonates with Hestia, for this goddess salutes celibate rituals and a life based on service to others. Being a mother and recent grandmother (experiencing an exceptionally strong spiritual bond to her firstborn grandson), I also identify with Demeter, the great Earth Mother goddess. Completing the quartet, given my lifetime pursuit of the controversial, unconventional field of astrology qualifies me as a natural rebel. Artemis personifies that inclination. Therefore I readily identify with four predominant planetary personae! Lately Apollo has been coming through, too! As your own *Moon Dance* experience evolves you will learn which archetypes exist at your core to govern your nature and experience. None of us lives a life devoid of interior echoes. To those who devote time to inner reflection and consciously observe themselves, a chorus might seem to dwell on the inside! The personae of time speak through our souls. In all probability mentally ill people hear these varied voices but experience antipathy as the distinct principles seem to vie for prominence within. Such persons effectively experience their own versions of an interior civil war. Each "utterance" and its resonant motive can be linked to an astrological sign (which in turn answers to a ruling planetary principle). *Moon Dance* gives voice to the long silenced Moon, the great feminine counterpart to the widely worshipped Yang sun. She is the primary conveyor of tide cycles (celestial and mundane). As we shall see these bear a direct relationship to our changing feelings. The female's indisputable biological connection to the moon, a phasing entity, grants women passage to the moon's journeys through all twelve signs or realms of light. While patriarchy in accord with its academic institutions has defined "norms" for both genders, its position on what is natural is taken exclusively from the masculine experience. It denies any viable relationship between the moon's cycles and women's moods. During each twenty-nine day sequence (a lunar month) as the moon travels across all twelve sign-realms, the sun remains in only one. Essentially Divine Yang awaits its reunion with Divine Yin at each new moon. Once united their joint energies usher the next sign principle into its awakened state. This process repeats month by month, and year after year as the pair draws each of the twelve Divine principles perpetually back to life. Our cosmic parents, the luminaries, engender a cosmic conception each month.

Moon Dance recognizes predictable fluxes to the fabric of time, and thus takes the frequently asked question "How are you?" beyond its conditioned response. The answer as dictated by society's minuets of protocol is: "I am fine." *Moon Dance* encourages you to search deeper. Remember, your body's outline suggests a singular being while its interior workings include the shared input of a number of systems: digestive, reproductive, hormonal, endocrine, etc.! Just as our physical body relies upon integrated functions, our spiritual being reflects the workings of a collection of unseen energetic entities. We don't feel the same way everyday because the cosmos lives inside us! And just as weather constantly changes (mystics believe it reflects the projection of collective human emotions) so too does our interior clime.

I hope I have established that women are cosmically wired to the moon. Luna spends slightly more than two days in each sign, and crosses all twelve zones within the course of the month. Women **become** the moods the moon travels. Pay attention! Become **present** to your feelings; sit with them, listen to them, and make note of what each has to offer. Given 21st century marketplace values feelings may soon find themselves on the Endangered Species list! These days when not ignored or stuffed they are increasingly medicated away. To observe your true self and ponder the question, "How am I?" can yield evocative results. I believe your answer will vary in response to the moon's transits (her rotating sign positions). While the scientific community is prepared to accept the moon's influence over the oceanic tides, it doesn't appreciate the link notable in that our bodies are primarily composed of water. Naturally the night's luminary exerts a palpable pull over our inner "tides," too. Astrology correlates the water element to feelings, instincts, and intuition. The Bible guides the prayerful person to "get thee by the still waters." Poets, mystics, romantics, and sailors have always felt an irresistible urge to commune with the sea. The ocean and seashore hold a timeless allure, perhaps because these locations inspire our connection with our deepest feelings. The moon also imbues the ethers with character, so when she crosses fiery Aries, we tend to feel more agitated, independent, or aggressive. And when she proceeds onto Taurus, we identify more fully with our desire to nurture or be nurtured. These transitions are not haphazard. In Eastern mysticism the premise of being at one with the Tao is equivalent to harmonizing our interests to accord with prevailing trends. The moon holds the key to aligning our actions with the trends of the times.

Modern society as shaped by patriarchal protocols generally expects citizens, especially workers, to deny feelings. This "male model" applauds the functions of the left-brain. It's oriented toward logic, reason, and rational thought while powerfully resisting more diffusive emotions. Persons are expected to adapt and march lockstep in the direction of order, conformity, and control. Although women are more keenly tuned to the functioning of the right brain, society has largely cordoned it off and effectively denigrated this realm of sentience. This helps explain why intelligent, highly trained academics find it difficult to believe that something as remote as a planet (since it exists outside their immediate personal sphere) holds any bearing on their lives. Things are seen as separate and distinct when logic writes the rules of engagement. The right brain in contrast senses the innate, inviolate connections among things. In mankind's past, it was the chosen venue of mystics and shaman. During earlier epochs people accessed and utilized portions of the brain that modern society has left to atrophy. Strongly developed intuition enabled the medicine woman to recognize which plants could be used to treat specific ailments. In my circle of spiritual acquaintances there is a Taurus woman with an exceptional connection to the earth who intuitively senses where large crystals are buried.

Orthodox psychology has no way to explain the special aptitudes individuals are born with. Nor can it define why children born into the same families exhibit widely differing behavioral traits. Arguments over nature (genetics) versus nurture (family conditioning) do not meet the burden of proof! Qualities of character are attributed to good genes, or otherwise dismissed as fate's game of Russian roulette. Karmic astrology offers the contrasting view that any existing talent was developed in one's past, that is to say during a past lifetime. Each of us meets our own legacy. We will expand on this basis for endowment in upcoming chapters.

The important thing to remember is that as a child of cosmos, your sentience was designed to move with the moon. By virtue of an empathetic resonance you take on the features of the zodiac sign the moon crosses, each one in due succession. Cycles of time are recurrent and fascinating. Getting to know this hidden "alphabet" can prove immensely rewarding and empowering. The female connection with the moon presents a gift unique to our gender. It renders us sensitive to the changing hues of time. As mothers and social creatures it's important that we understand the planned range of human expressions. This knowledge enhances our tolerance of personality distinctions, which in turn helps to facilitate unconditional love for our partners and offspring! In Shakespeare's tragedy *Romeo* asks his newly beloved *Juliet* to swear not by the moon, for it is an inconstant witness. Because men are clocked to the sun, they do not understand the ways women alter to rhythmically accord with the moon. Creator devised a built-in strategy that's key to redirecting the covert male tendency toward infidelity. (We will uncover this mystery in: *Men Can Moon Dance, Too!*)

According to the ancient mystery schools each Initiate was first directed to "know thyself." A key Hebrew credo, Tikkun Olam, espouses the view that we are embodied to help heal the world. How can these two premises best work together? In future times those women willingly prepared to express the **full** range that femininity is heiress to may be perceived as the healthiest. Such women will assist our world as it transitions to its next phase, a planned interval of spiritual revolution spanning the globe!

Just as no two snowflakes are alike, yet all possess six symmetrical sides, the planets follow consistent orbs but never form the same configurations twice! Therefore it is absolutely true that no two days are alike. We can and will discover patterns if we pursue an understanding of our relationship to the larger cycles of time. We've been looking for answers in countless places; yet for many women the secret to a more satisfying life lies within. As we open the door to examine the phases that reside on the inside, liberating realizations will follow. A foreknowledge of personal cycles allows us to wisely plot our activities knowing when the character of time best supports these initiatives.

Where We Are In Time: Aquarius Rising

It came as something of a surprise to learn that not only do earth's planetary neighbors revolve around our sun; but that our entire solar system, sun directed, revolves around a central sun. Its full voyage runs approximately 25,000 years allotting just over 2000 years for passage through each constellation or zodiac sign. Astrologers understand that these intervals synchronize with profound cycles known as the great Ages. Our planet (along with the entire solar system) has come to a major Age transition phase, and it's utterly disorienting. To the fundamentalist Christians, this passage is perceived as End Times. That perspective recalls the mindset that beheld our world as flat centuries ago. Since this is not the first Age phase transition mankind has undergone, it is unlikely to be the last; lest Mars, champion of war, succeed in fully undermining the great balance wrought into the Divine circle plan. To the extent Mars continues to step out of his appointed role as protector of the weak, and increasingly uses his power to propagate violence, marks the degree to which life systems will face collapse. Creator designed twelve positions intended to interact in ways that support the varied strengths and weaknesses of the parts in order to preserve the integrity of the whole. When any singular persona assumes a disproportionate representation, not only does the model fall out of alignment, it becomes seriously disabled. No single god or sign can speak for all! The very premise undermines the celestial order! Later in this volume we will examine the formation of an ingenious Yod allotted to Venus. Her influence over three particular Zodiac realms forms a marvelous triangle that encapsulates Mars to curb his projected forceful expressions (via his sign of dominion, Aries). Venus not only serves as Mars' romantic counterpart, she is also positioned to act as counterbalance to his dangerous impulses and aggressive overtures. Mars is the Zodiac's agent of naked aggression and stands for the human ego in its raw unmitigated state. The Yod provides for a divine measure of balance. It is a device intended to constrain the violent god's darker impulses. Tragically Venus has been undermined, and this higher plan corrupted. How was Mars able to engineer his current position that operates with such awesome power and catastrophic influence over our world? Apart from the massive human anger that feeds this archetype, the historical answer draws us back to the previous Age phase transition, that of Aries morphing into Pisces. The birth of Jesus, fisher of men, signaled the onset of the Piscean Age. This holy avatar entered our world to demonstrate the transformational teachings of forgiveness, compassion, and turning the other cheek. The old powers watched their authority slip away as Jesus' miracles swayed the masses. He introduced a belief system that transcended the fear and control utilized by authoritarian systems of governance. Those elites that have profited from constraining their fellow citizens realized they could insidiously adopt Jesus' name while still maintaining their old warring ways. This deceit has gone on so long that it explains why citizens in the 21st century still countenance pious religious groups defining themselves as Christian while they ferociously clamor for war against what increasingly resembles a fictitious enemy. A war against terrorism? Against a nation (Iraq) that did nothing to warrant so blatant an attack on its people? Deception runs inordinately high now that mankind has arrived at the cusp of Ages and Aquarius, the sign that champions truth, endeavors to rise. This fledgling consciousness must overcome the hypnotic spell cast by falsehoods that keep too many minds under thrall. Humanity is exiting the Piscean Age as symbolized by fish opposing fish. Our current interval hovers in a veritable twilight zone set between the sign of Truth and that of deception. Twenty-two centuries under the aegis of Pisces conditioned mankind to behold the world through a marked polarity (as symbolized by two fish swimming in opposing directions). A prominent strategy used by elites to divide and conquer involved manufacturing an unholy rift between the genders. Patriarchal religions exclusively called for a worship of God the father while casting the Mother out of almost every spiritual equation. This deletion has led to asymmetric belief systems with respect to the nature of Creator as well as our selves. The allegory of the Garden of Eden turned sexual communion into "original sin," and thereby set a spiritual chasm between men and women. This break in the fundamental weave (which I term "the great wound") has spawned a spellbinding array of sexual dysfunctions ever after. Prior ages and religious traditions were not built upon extreme notions of polarity. The Ancient Greeks and Romans acknowledged an original **trinity** endowed with management powers direct from Olympus. Their Creation myths held that earth was to be governed by three brothers: Zeus (Jupiter), Poseidon (Neptune), and Hades (Pluto). In other words, their worldview was not shaped by polarity.

Since each age lasts approximately 2200 years, presumptions become encoded and over time pass for consensual reality. In other words traditions rest unchallenged. Our notions of intelligence are shaped by the cultures in which we reside. The vast majority presumes the "way of things" to be inevitable. Indeed events recur like a photographic negative duplicating its embedded image. Erroneous programming recapitulates what most take for unchanging reality, a testament to the innate foibles of human nature. These conclusions ain't necessarily so. The retardation of the human spirit has occurred largely because mankind has been playing with half a pack gender-wise, and as a result seen its purpose, passion, and possibilities crippled. Currently as our world sits at this cusp of ages many of us confront powerful personal tests to our faith, health, and pocketbook. It's precisely at such a time that we're internally motivated to re-examine the assumptions we've taken for granted. How else can vital new expressions of personal, not to mention mass consciousness arise? One by one as we shift, so does the old template. The dominant paradigm that has granted false witness to the Creation plan falls away making space for new options! The Age of Aquarius ascends on the basis of this shift. It gains momentum every time a citizen casts off the chains of self-limiting, passé beliefs along with the narrow thinking processes that shaped them. A promised age of peace and affinity among tribes requires human beings to play a co-creative role. Truth is the **power** sacrosanct to Aquarius. It's been said that the truth shall set them free. What currently hinders this development? An answer may be found in the "mutual reception" now operating between the two planets that represent the signs of Pisces (fading) and Aquarius (rising). Currently the pair is enacting a veritable "changing of the guard" in higher spheres. Time is marked by planned intervals as our universe operates in accord with a Divine order.

Given that the phenomenon of mutual reception is currently underway we note that Uranus, ruler of Aquarius, requires 84 years to orbit the sun. It is destined to spend seven years in each sign, and entered Neptune's sign of dominion, Pisces, in 2003. It will remain there until 2010. Meanwhile, Neptune, adhering to its orbit of 165 years began its crossing of Aquarius (Uranus' sign) in 1998, and will remain there until 2012. That means that Uranus is navigating across Neptune's home sign, while Neptune likewise crosses Uranus' home sign. These interchanges are not uncommon among planets; but this one is extremely significant because it specifically involves the two planets directly associated with the current age-phase transition. It's as if heaven's torch was being passed from the age struggling to maintain power to the one asserting a new claim to it! Uranus (and by extension the Aquarian Age) represents the most evolved expression possible to air's elemental trinity. Encoded with the imprint of the eternal verities, Uranus operates like a compass directing human souls towards Creator's laws and ideals. Inviolate principles do not alter, nor do they adapt with time to conform to those fashionable fictions peculiar to any given era, especially those dressed up and marketed as viable norms. How can Uranus fulfill its Truth mandate while transiting Pisces, the sign of dreams, escapist behaviors, and delusion? Adding to the complexity of current celestial events is the fact that Neptune, planet of duality and deception, currently fogs the atmosphere by obstructing clarity in the sign-realm of epistemology. Thus with the planet of deception passing through the zodiac's kingdom of Truth, while the planet of Truth transits the kingdom of deception humanity is not experiencing a great cosmic fit. Hardly surprising that so many things have departed from their stated purposes and intentions. Only those individuals possessed of a firm grasp of innate Truth (the basis of integrity and strong character likely developed in previous incarnations) can adequately separate the wheat from the chaff. Given the powerfully pervasive nature of modern media, it owns a 24/7 capacity to utilize varied venues to relay false information. Aiding and abetting this compromised communications climate is the worship of a dark god, mammon, as seen in an overt widely celebrated love of money. In the U.S. greed has been given a facelift! Fiscally endowed corporations make full use of the media to develop desires in people where there were none. The profit motive has been unapologetically allotted a free pass. On a mission to drive appetites in every conceivable way it makes use of sinister props to manipulate peoples' lives. All aspects of how we live, down to the sacred, have been commercialized. The din created by advertisers is now inordinately dense, and shuts out all voices except those carefully groomed (so-called experts) to ensure that people adapt to the "expert judgments" of the marketplace. Clearly too many souls have lost the capacity to judge the tree by its fruit. That's fairly understandable given the tainted nature of the prevailing cultural climate. Remember that Aquarius is an air sign, and mass media makes direct use of this element. Fundamentally its use of the airwaves to project its wares non-stop means people are being conditioned in ways they don't even realize. And popular pundits, those I term "the programmers," do no service to humanity's evolution by insisting that individuals adapt their lifestyles, predilections, and behaviors to suit the norms of an increasingly unnatural and denatured—to the point of ecological overload—world. That world, and the worldview it was founded upon, is coming asunder. Earth mother cannot further support the model of rabid consumerism. Clearly our fulfillment must come from less tangible sources. We have forgotten that we are not just bodies, but spirits temporarily embodied. Our essences are closer to light. As the highest octave of the air element, Aquarius reminds us that we all breathe and share in a universal unified field. What kind of atmosphere is generated when mass intention trained like Pavlov's dogs focuses solely on gross materialism? Alarming rates of resource depletion coupled with inordinate population growth pits tribe against tribe to further the prospect of a modern day Armageddon. Possibilities beyond this paradigm exist if we can cease and desist from investing our resources and belief systems in effete divisive models. Aquarius is the sign of friendships. It practices calm detachment and upholds the motto, "live and let live." This enlightened sign makes room for differences since all are welcome at the circle. The Mars model in contrast champions one right way to do things, one role model alone to follow. It insists that only one tribe represents the chosen unto Creator, whereas the circle envisions a world based upon Divinely devised diversity. A high price is paid in offering homage to a god of exclusion when we could lift our outlooks and behold a blessed vision of inclusion instead.

Astrology presents a perspective that like Al Gore's film, *An Inconvenient Truth,* challenges our habitual behaviors. The vibrant insights revealed by its cosmic sign language never go out of style even if people find accountability to a system of karmic justice inconvenient. Given the prospects of global climate change, worldwide trafficking in increasingly dangerous arms, and the rise of authoritarian institutions it is borderline suicidal to argue for the mindset that got us here. The wisdom drawn from the Logos, an ancient yet contemporary field of inquiry expands our understanding and leads us beyond previously held fictions. By looking higher for meaning we can correct our collective vision, and it is imperative that we do so. Why take this view? Perhaps because so much is out of joint, and even more at stake. Between statistics on eating disorders and rising obesity rates (related to a growing Diabetes epidemic), rampant alcoholism and drug abuse, massive prescriptions for anti-depressant drugs, unspeakable violence and child abuse, our society resembles the shrieking canaries responding to lethal gas escaping into the old mineshafts. We're indeed being shafted! We have been conditioned by academe to look at aberrant behaviors as separate unrelated categories of affliction. In sum they tell us that something is very wrong with our land. Our pro-war policies reflect the misguided leadership of Mars. When Mars rules a "Venus deficit" results, and it's seen in the lack of reverence and respect shown toward the natural world, the one our bodies and senses rely upon as vital source of nourishment. Nor is there regard for future generations in the random way resources are wantonly used and discarded; or the way militarism lays entire regions to waste. Ours is a society of irreverent wastefulness. Allied with Mars, Mammon holds high stature in the modern world too. Individuals have been conditioned to believe that fiscal transactions alone seal deals. Unquestioningly they lay homage to the marketplace and its artificial allocations of worth. Meanwhile nature is dying along with something precious to a great many people. The life of the inner spirit is drained out of them as they're forced to lead robotic lives that trade their mortal time for trifles built in honor of Mammon. I know women who ingest anti-depressant drugs daily just to maintain the requisite composure to fulfill their job demands. Emotions are not allowed in the workplace. What does it do to a society when so many are prompted to place feelings aside or otherwise suppress them? The vast majority finds itself divorced from the actual state of the world. Sentiments, drawn from the diffusive right-brain hemisphere are rendered essentially worthless by academe. Logic exclusively runs things. This cold approach to the myriad conditions our world faces causes a lopsided sentience. It resembles mankind navigating its "vessel" with a singular oar. Technological progress may result, but little can be said for a healthy humanity. The wisdom of using both brain hemispheres (symbolizing equal gender representation) can be seen in the example of that vessel. Ultimately it requires the utilization of two complementary oars. Only when both jointly navigate does it attain forward momentum. Since men have claimed the sole right to determine humanity's course, our collective estate—much like that vessel—circles endlessly and fails to demonstrate genuine progress, particularly when it comes to matters of the spirit. Clearly the female side of sentience has been cordoned off too long! The architects of the patriarchal church-state (academia emerged from these venues) see no flaw in this design plan thus they have no onus to change anything. Well paid "experts" do all they can to convince us that things are right and fine just the way they are. Conventional thinking has brought the world to the brink of despair. Increasingly it countenances everyday acts of destruction, what one author termed the banality of evil. This is not okay. Presumably thoughtful people take this hell bent scenario as a representation of God's will! What we're actually witnessing is the sum of false belief systems programmed so thoroughly for so long that lies and dismal fictions are taken for true. Established religions, academic institutions, and even the scientific community limit conjecture, especially of the esoteric sort. Arrival at the cusp of Ages now serves as mankind's wake-up call. We either continue to grant allegiance to Mars and allow wars of increasingly grave nature to plunder our existences; or we learn to balance both oars and return to the circle. There a basis for peace among tribes can be recovered. Humankind must prepare to enter the larger universal family. To do so we must transcend previous definitions. That is to say a global quantum leap in the form of an increment to understanding is required. New social paradigms will encourage individuals to integrate logic with feelings. Societies will respect the unique perspectives and contributions offered by women as emissaries of the Divine feminine.

Part II will introduce Artemis, archetypal counterpart to Aquarius. Significant at this cusp of ages, she represents the Divine daughter, twin sister to Apollo, the zodiac's Divine son. Mankind could do much better than squander its considerable fortunes on war if given better tools of awareness. What we take for inevitable appears as such to the degree we adhere to the same outdated ideological feedback loops. Remember: all new truths begin as heresies. That statement could qualify as Aquarius' mantra! As the age of higher reason emerges individuals who access the full range of intrinsic archetypal expressions will prove the healthiest and most creative! It's like being free at last to paint with all colors, to make music with every possible note! I invite you to welcome the new dawn by exploring your own innate personae. Truly the heavens reside within you!

Transitions R'Us

How do we know that we've come to the final phase of the Piscean Age? One considerable cosmic clue comes by recognizing Pisces is governed by Neptune, the god of the sea kingdoms. That's where all those fossil fuel deposits originate. Our "president" recently admitted the U.S. has an "addiction" for oil. Experts believe the rapid industrialization of Asia is hastening the "end of oil." Since Pisces is linked with both oil and patterns of addiction, turns out that our dependence on the black stuff, which the Arab world terms "a soft loan from Allah," is being celestially phased out. In addition Pisces "rules" prisons, drug companies, and hospitals. These constitute chief "wealth building industries" in this odd era of "disaster capitalism" as noted by author Naomi Klein. In other words a premeditated creation of catastrophes constitutes the new business model being practiced by a number of corporations that clearly lack conscience. Pisces, sign of illusion also plays a significant role in Hollywood and its elaborate productions. The big screen functions as a highly efficient mechanism for "catapulting the propaganda." Few people are paid better than Hollywood's manufactured stars. And thanks to those dubious fish swimming in opposing directions, Pisces is no stranger to hypocrisy. The "war on drugs" comes to mind. Although youngsters hear the mantra, "Just Say No!" A plethora of pharmaceutical advertisements cross their television screens. Most amusing is the fanciful names given to these chemical aberrations, titles that intentionally simulate states of imagined splendor: Elantra, Allegra, Lunestra, and Viagra, to name a few! In our modern world drugs have entered the mainstream to manage and direct every stage of a woman's life from menstruation through fertility to menopause. Many things are not what they seem, since Pisces traffics in semblances. The loss of the authentic added to the busy pace of our lives leaves a hole in many of us. Modern practices have too often lost contact with meaning and purpose. Aggression is championed in the name of religion, with patriotism the mask used to silence dissent. Freedom (in name) is intoned while civil liberties are widely suppressed. The "fish not taken" suggests a path based on spiritual practices, those that align the individual with the numinous. Few attempt this path. Instead the pervasive emptiness acts like a vacuum that many people seek to fill with substances. What passes for the norm in our twisted culture frequently includes endorsed harmful behaviors. Media hacks and conservative pundits assert that one's quality of life is a direct result of her personal choices as if the larger factors of culture, economics, and government policy play no role. A society that invests in and supports the best in each person's untapped potentials would make real growth possible. Instead, we have engineered a nation where people compete rather than cooperate. They carry guns (millions are on our streets) and show suspicion rather than trust towards fellow citizens. The atmosphere is divisive to the point of toxic! We cannot afford the old definitions and questionable standards we've been taught to live by. A healthy society is incompatible with every man/woman out for them self. The Aquarian Age asks more of us, and offers more in return. The intended age phase transition is best fueled by spiritual synergy. Aquarius signifies the 11th house and sign principle. (For many it feels like the 11th hour!) It celebrates the adage, "When two or more come together and ask in my name, so shall it be." Awakened individuals must bypass the walls fear has built in order to rejoin humanity's intended circle. Here the best of what we were designed to be can at last shine radiantly. It is time to summon dreamers into an awakened state. So dare to dance to your own drummer by learning to respond to the powerful rhythm structures of time. They are intended to move you.

(Readers who wish to learn more about mankind's age phase transition can check out: *Neptune and The Final Phase of the Piscean Age*, available at: www.iUniverse.com).

"The laws of nature are not forces external to things, but rather represent the harmony of movement immanent to them. That is why the celestial bodies do not deviate from their orbits, and why all events in nature occur with fixed regularity." The Chinese *I Ching*

The Moon And Your Basic Blueprint

The moon is an important Zodiac ambassador. She evokes a steady stream of human emotions. Luna additionally provides us with a means to access our memories, while drawing us into environments that suit our natures because they feel familiar. She cues us into basic instinct. In conventional astrology the moon is associated with home, family life, one's mother, motherhood, and long-term bonding choices and behaviors. Anatomically the moon represents the stomach, thus emphasizing a direct link between what we eat and how we feel. It also provides clues to what may be "eating" at us. Psychology has never studied the role the moon plays with respect to changing moods or the patterns of sentience these give rise to, especially in females. Having utilized astrology to counsel hundreds, the importance of this luminary is quite clear to me. It's evident that each of us responds to the moon's cycle in her own unique manner. That's why *Moon Dance* outlines a journey both personal and unique. Astrological data accumulated over the centuries provides evidence of predictable themes, specific patterns to watch for because they recur with regularity. Our responses to these cues become individualized, and that's where *Moon Dance* comes in. Because the moon's phases occur with regularity, we can learn from them.

Since it's helpful to understand how the moon operates, in this section we will note her behavior by sign, house, phase, and key aspects. This material is based on conventional astrology and some readers may find it complex. Assimilate the information at your own pace since *Moon Dance* intends to elicit a self-discovery process. Part II will introduce you to the twelve Divine personae and thereby your personal encounter with the indwelling archetypes of time will begin. Each is ultimately a part of you!

Moon Times: How Does the Moon express in each of the Twelve Signs?

Just as there are twelve sun-signs, there are twelve corresponding moon signs. As the lights dance in their respective orbs they generate 144 possible combinations. When you know your moon sign (and ideally the moon signs of persons close to you) evocative clues to character and motivation emerge. Amazing grace has been lent to women by virtue of their biological link with the lunar cycle. We actually **feel** the twelve phases of time. This sentience presents an enhanced tool for empathy. In a very real sense we "become" the moon in her varied passages and are able thus to feel what others feel. It's the cosmic equivalent of walking in someone else's moccasins! Every woman is extended this opportunity to expand her awareness of human nature. Given her link to the moon she is granted virtual passage through each of the twelve kingdoms every month. As we grow familiar with these distinct expressions of time we will come to instinctively recognize them! The following defines the basic energies and expressions generated by each sign realm. We begin with Aries, first sign on the cosmic dial.

When the moon crosses **Aries**, where Mars holds dominion, she incites us to become more assertive, independent, and potentially aggressive. The latter emerges proportional to the degree we feel our desires thwarted by others. Root responses derived from the primal self dominate personal behavior when the moon transits Aries. Physical sex can be rough. <u>Keywords</u>: impulsivity, self-centeredness, self-realization, thrust for exploration and potential personal discovery. Here the soul learns sovereignty and works to develop an independent sense of self. Ask yourself: Is my anger an excuse for creating personal space? Am I pushing someone away that feels too close for my present comfort?

Next the moon enters the domain of **Taurus**; and here the role of nurturer comes to life. Many become natural comforters to their children, or unconsciously play the role of "guardian Mother" to others in need. <u>Keywords</u>: Security, practicality, sensuality, also enhanced artistic/sensory attunement. Many spend on luxury items. Taurus (thanks to its Venus connection) draws us to fine scents, fabrics, tastes, and beautiful objects. This moon prompts us to learn the ways and means for securing roots and establishing solid foundations. (Home and its comforts become especially important since this position constitutes the moon's position of exaltation.) Ask yourself: Am I really hungry for a specific food item, or looking for a way to stuff unexpressed feelings?

Then the moon passes onto **Gemini** prompting us to take up multiple projects at once. We find ourselves busily running errands, checking information, reading, studying, writing, teaching, spending extra time on the Internet, or promoting projects since a hefty dose of celestial salesmanship kicks in. The "interior dialog" (as Carlos Casteneda's teacher Don Juan termed it) intensifies as the mind's inherent twins (left and right brain) debate whatever issues stand before us. Duality is projected and the world mirrors back the polar perspectives of good versus evil, logic versus feelings, etc. <u>Keywords</u>: curiosity, a great need for discourse, communication, debate, and discussion. Enthusiastic volleying of ideas leads to new personal choices. Here the soul explores options, and in the process learns to listen for and express flexibility. Openness to learning greatly assists the retention of youthful features. Ask yourself: Does my belief and stated intention match my present action or agenda?

Progressing to **Cancer**, the moon's home domain, Luna triggers our birth chart's natal pattern. Ultimately Cancer, sign of the family and its past conditioning opens our memory banks. Events from the past unconsciously sway our present mood. We tend to repeat old behaviors, and this happens unconsciously. Loved ones and relatives pull our strings, perhaps inadvertently. Personal security waits on red alert; so if someone violates it, we coil into our shell, crab-style. If filial bonds are strained, our emotions reflect that stress. Some people cope by creatively directing their angst; others find themselves over-eating, closet drinking, or acquiring novel ways to self-medicate. Keywords: Subjectivity overwhelms logic. Prepare for "auto-pilot" replays of past scripts that reflect your family system's operational features. There is an authentic need to secure one's place within the group/family/tribe, accompanied by a converse reflex to hide in our shell (especially if filial encounters prove painful). Ask yourself: Are old habits preventing me from growing and changing?

The Moon's entrance into **Leo is** often accompanied by a cycle of high drama, lest an actual visit to the theatre (where we vicariously experience intensity) occur. Actions result from feelings of increased romanticism or quixotic yearnings. We find it's easier to bond with our children since we connect with that place of childlike innocence that still resides on the inside. (Some luckily retain this quality into adult life.) Here we find awakened the power of the Divine spirit that's planted in our hearts. Keywords: celebration, festive mode, romance, showmanship, and generous gestures stemming from the open heart. Here the soul seeks to live from passion. Courage is required to pursue such a course in a world that increasingly values status objects over feelings. Ask yourself: Where am I stepping out of Divine will into my ego to project my script onto others?

You'll sense the moon's visit to **Virg**o as you suddenly find yourself gripped with a need to clean in places usually forgotten, or otherwise elect to catch up on laundry, make a grocery list, or organize your domestic or office ambiance. Mending what is broken asserts like a psychic clarion call telegraphed to all things Virgo. Keywords: Urge to organize, indulge in clean-up efforts, critical analysis, medical diagnosis, and enhanced awareness of health concerns prompt a keener dietary focus. Here the soul is compelled to take care of the body temple, and serve as an example (teacher, healer) to others in that regard. Part of this process results from recognizing the ways one's personal issues act upon their tissues. Ask yourself: What now requires healing, cleaning, purification, or more efficient organizing with respect to my life or lifestyle?

The moon's **Libra** transit inspires diplomatic dialogs, teamwork, the goal of fairness, and a marked capacity to work towards compromise. It's public relations time! For many there is a marked yearning for a partner. A balanced partnership begins first with how we regard our self. Keywords: partnership, social justice ideals, fair play, enacting Feng Shui to balance our domestic sphere. Here the soul quests to find a companion with whom harmonious intimate sharing is possible. Ask yourself: Am I practicing the letter or spirit of "the law?"

The next stop the moon makes is **Scorpio** where former grievances resurrect to haunt us, and taunt us to indulge our darker reflexes to even scores. Some do take up arms or act out vengeance. It's far better to work on personal healing, and cast thy net to the other side. Since Scorpio relishes privacy as well as secrecy, if you can't schedule a mini-vacation then consider turning off your phone. Enter solitude's cocoon without the threat of interruption. Scorpio promotes the powers of rebirth, renewal, and regeneration. As Marvin Gaye sang, "Sexual Healing" may prove the best medicine during this interval. Keywords: secrecy, research, bouts of jealousy and vindictiveness. Here the soul grows as a result of practicing forgiveness, and it's prompted to mend past wounded places. The Scorpio moon demonstrates that we can learn ways to heal or experience an equivalent rebirth. Forgiveness functions as alchemy for the soul. Ask yourself: What must I release to acquire the magical alchemy of transformation?

The moon **Sagittarius** is playful, and stirs people to expand their worldview. Some make travel plans or embark on trips; others attend seminars designed to open their minds; still others join groups that expand faith in spiritually empowering ways. Many get physical and enjoy the great outdoors given that Sagittarius is the sign of athletic expression as well as The Olympics! Keywords: Spiritual renewal, physical exertion, inspiration, risk-taking, plus musical expression that speaks in universal rhythm to touch all souls. Sagittarius is associated with "higher mind," and favors activities that stir the grander portions of our intellects. New discoveries result. Ask yourself: Is my faith an excuse for not taking action to improve my shortcomings?

When the moon enters **Capricorn** it's "get back to business" time, generally accompanied by a heightened sense of self-discipline. Projects avoided at other times now become manageable. Personal accountability is emphasized. Keywords: duty, responsibility, ambition. Guard against feelings of guilt during this interval as a marked tendency to play accountant (with self or others) may warrant the "taking of inventory." Here the soul learns to manage personal affairs. Some assume the larger concerns of the community by accepting leadership roles. The ego's self-interest comes up against Machiavellian temptations. These must be leveraged against the higher ideal of honorable service. Responsible stewardship competes with this sign's "ends justify the means" prerogative. Ask yourself: Where does my need to manage impede my capacity to be present to feelings, whether my own or those of someone close to me?

Then the moon progresses to **Aquarius** where she opens perceptual gateways wider to intuition. We may be drawn to offbeat activities, and take spontaneous detours in a wish to more fully explore our world. Some experiment with new routes to work, or lunch in colorful ethnic restaurants. If you pay close attention, you'll note where serendipity guides present events. I call this evidence of "behind the scenes cosmic choreography." Our guides seem more active as they set up specific "accidental" meetings and encounters. Keywords: Friendship, group associations, offbeat activities, and an inclination to court the unconventional. Here the soul catches a glimmer of the Divine present in persons met through ordinary encounters. Fellowship inspires people to work together in joint efforts to attain shared aspirations. When two or more align with higher truth in mind, they frequently find themselves the channels through which amazing possibilities (some that benefit the human race) arise. Ask yourself: How can my ideals further the greater good, or benefit a cause I believe in?

In **Pisces**, the moon stirs duality. Think: two fish! Empathy runs high and we unknowingly pick up on others' emotions, and if we are struggling with personally charged emotional issues, it's easy to feel sorry for ourselves during this interval. Some fall into victim-mode and then indulge in the reflex to self-medicate the pain away. Watch what you get attached to at this time. Pisces encourages the path of "the fish less navigated by," a course that may lead to deeply imaginative or spiritually oriented activities. A concert attended plucks sensitive inner chords. And you can always swim. Water purportedly acts as medium clearing the emotional burdens we cast into it. This explains the origin behind Baptismal rituals. Keywords: Dream, cry, dance, attend a support group to stave off addictive behaviors before these abduct your will. Pisces closes the circle. Some believe it's an amalgamation of all previous sign experiences. In any case the soul currently feels all that can be felt: all the music echoing from the scales, and all the colors radiating from the spectrum. This wide sentience can open the floodgates to boundless compassion and invites a near magical connection with all living beings. Ask yourself: What does surrender of the spirit mean? Or am I evading the responsible utilization of free will?

Now we will examine how the natal moon operates as it transits the twelve actual **houses**. Consider this "advanced Moon Dancing." If you find the following material too complex, you can skip ahead. However it's advisable that you spend time learning the method for designing your guided lunar journal as offered at the conclusion of Part I. You will need a copy of your birth chart. It can be calculated gratis on-line at this wonderful site: www.astro.com where you will be guided through the procedure. If you do not know your time of birth, use sunrise. That way the houses will follow a natural sign sequence. (This is the method used when the astrologer pens generic horoscope columns for mainstream magazines. Having written hundreds of columns using this system, I can attest to its accuracy.) Equipped with your birth chart, you now can locate the sign and house position of your moon. You may calculate the moon's position for family members as well. This information is your key to unlock the secrets of the enchanted *Moon Dance*!

How Does the Moon Express in Each of the Twelve Houses

The following references apply to your birth moon's position. However, these analyses also elucidate how the moon operates when she crosses these sectors each month.

<u>Natal moon in the first house:</u> Your feelings will be unmistakably revealed to the world. For better or worse, your appearance now reflects how you feel about yourself. Emotions arise from a narrow context of self-interest. When found as a natal signature, a strong family resemblance may be in evidence coupled with behaviors unconsciously mimicked from the family heritage or ethnicity. For instance, you may look like your mother, or laugh like your father. The first house operates like a showcase to the world. With your moon found here, your emotions will be on display, like it or not.

<u>Natal moon in the 2nd house:</u> This position is considered the accidental exaltation of the moon, and indicates the type of person who focuses on personal security, moneymaking, and establishing a stable home foundation. Emotional security is strongly associated with fiscal well-being. Such persons often provide stability or foundation for others. They function as veritable "Rocks of Gibraltar" to relatives or friends in need. Gardening may come naturally. This chart signature often brings a marked capacity for decorating, even when it's forced to operate on a modest budget.

By (monthly) transit, one's focus will center on money as a basis for gauging personal security.

<u>Natal moon in the 3rd house:</u> This individual will be very talkative, always inclined to seek explanations for the way she feels. She may have an especially strong intuitive link with an aunt, uncle, brother, sister or cousin. Knowledge is pursued in an effort to gain an understanding of frequently changing emotional states. Moon in the 3rd house often indicates a savvy salesperson, or one otherwise endowed with the gift of gab.

By (monthly) transit one experiences a marked urge to be out and about; is more talkative and given to making lots of phone calls, or engaging in numerous emails.

Natal moon in the 4th house: This position represents the natural domain of the moon, and it locks the individual into the family system, karmic patterns and all. Where the individual grows up and what type of home environment she is raised in plays a huge role in her outlook on the world. Even in adult life, the home remains a strong near organic extension of who she is. This person would prefer to be a stay-at-home Mom, or work from home.

By (monthly) transit one feels the urge to cocoon, or get their home base in order.

Natal moon in the 5th house: Due to the phases the night luminary undergoes, those born with this influence are prone to many changes of heart, or shifts in romantic partners. There also is a strong identification with children. Many educators hold this chart signature. The 5th house can ignite star quality. Some with this position may claim their five minutes of fame, perhaps by performing in local theatrical productions. A delightful connection with the "inner child" is retained throughout the lifespan. Some with this position unconsciously court drama. Others simulate celebrity status by acting like visiting royalty.

By (monthly) transit one either looks for drama or finds it inadvertently. Romantic longings are heightened.

Natal moon in the 6th house: This moon holds an affinity with the natal Virgo moon as both suggest a susceptibility to health challenges brought on by stress, dietary factors, or internal tension. The inner prompt to strive towards unrealistic, perfectionist standards puts a strain on the body. Healers often hold this signature as they are compelled to learn what isn't working and in the process educate themselves on the varied therapeutic techniques available to alter or mend the condition. It comes down to "Physician, heal thyself!"

By (monthly) transit one is more in touch with their body language. It's a wise time to listen for cues as prevention is indeed worth pounds of cure!

Natal moon in the 7th house: This individual was designed for marriage, although major chart afflictions will undermine efforts to maintain a satisfying state of union. The 7th house holds an affinity with Libra, and here the moon fosters balance. A 7th house moon naturally defers to their partner's wishes, and can prove a substantial helpmate, whether operating behind-the-scenes or directly. These individuals also make caring counselors. Their emotional lives are invigorated by direct interaction with others.

By (monthly) transit one is more interested in sharing activities with a partner, or seeking and finding one.

Natal moon in the 8th house: This individual is a natural psychic and may function as a conduit capable of intuiting languages from the spirit world. S/he may be intrigued with sex, death, as well as others' resources from a young age. If the chart holds planets in earth signs, the 8th house moon may incline towards banking, accounting, or the more mundane applications associated with this otherwise occult and mysterious chart sector. A difficult experience in early life (if not treated with forgiveness) can cause the individual to build a wall against intimacy. Such persons must learn how not to nurse grudges.

By (monthly) transit, one may experience marked sexual tension that seeks release. If there is a feud underway, one must curb the ego's reflex towards avenging slights.

Natal moon in the 9th house: Since the moon directly refers to the home life, while the 9th house points to long-distance travel (often in pursuit of a "higher" education), this position inclines its bearer to dwell in a foreign land. Soul memory becomes activated, and the individual resonates with a distant zone familiar from another lifetime. Often the initial purpose for the journey stems from an educational goal. Those destined to travel far from home often form bonds too compelling to release. Marriage to someone of a completely different background is plausible. This position favors writers of renown.

By (monthly) transit, the mind is activated and there is an intensified urge to learn more, see more, and expand one's usual boundaries by breaking free of constraints.

Natal moon in the 10th house: This placement catalyzes ambitious drives. It suggests the type of individual who will consciously discipline her personal life so that career plans can be satisfied first. Such a one may put off family life until her professional life is firmly established. Others with this signature will marry powerful mates involved with politics, law or the corporate world. There is a potential for hardened emotions and an "ends justify the means" approach to life as well as people!

By (monthly) transit, ambitions are galvanized and efforts normally avoided become manageable. Work goals take on a crystal clear focus.

Natal moon in the 11th house: This individual is naturally gregarious and probably loves people of all sorts. Akin to the Aquarian moon, such a one can love humanity but might prove rather detached when it comes to close, intimate ties. There is a great need for freedom and spontaneity. Few bonds allot such liberty. Therefore the 11th house moon requires an open marriage or a mate with liberal beliefs. Friendships, or a significant ally, play a major role in the life plan.

By (monthly) transit, convivial urges intensify and we're more open to participating in activities that lay outside our usual sphere of interest. Unusual events "click."

Natal moon in the 12th house: Many with this signature are natural psychics due to inherent empathy. Given the moon's connection to soul memory, this position suggests a previous lifetime spent in retreat, possibly one dedicated to religion in a peaceful cloistered order. The 12th house is reclusive and needs to periodically turn off the world. When the spiritual inclinations of this position are not duly noted, this sensitive soul may otherwise imbibe in bottled spirits, or seek a chemical means for turning down the "volume" emanating from our angry, abrasive planet. Emotional overload can cause this individual to periodically become ill.

By (monthly) transit, reclusive tendencies kick in. Those with addictive personalities must now struggle against these inclinations.

Now that you have been introduced to the twelve mansions that mark the moon's monthly voyage you are on the path to conscious enlightenment. Family members can also be charted to note their natural emotional fluxes. When you really master *Moon Dance* you'll want to understand the lunar rhythms that influence those around you.

The moon, like all planetary dignitaries, is consigned to an orb designated by the great Cosmic Clockmaker. Taking into account her twenty-nine day revolution, intervals of intensification occur with regularity and fall into synch with the "law of seven." The moon's dance is punctuated by acute phases that happen to occur every seven days. The cycle itself is akin to an endlessly undulating (if hidden) tide. The pattern is easily plotted, and should be since it profoundly colors the emotional lives of women (and some men).

Let's observe her cycle: Luna is destined once every twenty-nine days to meet with the sun. Their unified estate constitutes **new moon**, the sacred conjunction. Seven days later she assumes her first **quarter moon phase**. At the mid-point of her twenty-nine day cycle (fourteen days after the new moon) she reaches her farthest distance from the sun. Great tension results from her opposition to the sun for this polarity constitutes the **full moon phase**. Police departments and mental institutions report increased levels of volatile activity. Weather patterns often reflect the antipathy between the luminaries. Continuing her journey Luna forms a **waning square** seven days after full moon, or twenty-one days from her initial new moon stage. From this point in her trajectory she progresses towards the inevitable reunion with the sun that once again signals the next new moon cycle. With the exception of the blue moon (this event takes place if a full moon occurs at the beginning of the month so that a second one will follow at month's end. Operating like a celestial echo the same Zodiac sign-field is activated twice) she progresses from sign to sign to join with the sun in each domain, a dance of time that follows the natural sign sequence. For instance during the span of March 21 through April 20, the sun and moon meet in Aries, and thereby invoke Mars from the celestial ethers. Their next meeting will take place (between April 21 and May 21) in Taurus, thereby invoking Demeter, and so on. The transitions they share not only keep their "relationship" exciting, but also trigger tempo changes to time's themes. Serving a Divine purpose this dance between the lights reveals that Creator did not intend for each day to prove a facsimile of every other! Recurrent dramas engaged between the luminaries charge the mundane atmosphere and trigger a wide array of human emotions. Our natural feelings are not supposed to be diluted, chemically treated, or suppressed. The sun and moon represent the primal pair, the quintessential union between supreme Yang and Yin forces. By Divine design they also represent men and women, particularly our actual biological fathers and mothers. Even though these stellar bodies orbit space, they direct life cycles here on earth in profound ways!

Polarities: What Can Full Moons Teach Us?

Every sign is positioned to perpetually dance (or intensely interact) with its opposite. These configurations as we shall see reflect specific lesson plans activated during full moons. Given that there are twelve signs, six primal sets of polarity recurrently come into cosmic play. Each constitutes a mandatory lesson plan for students enrolled in "Earth School 101". Tensions between the Lights impact all humanity, although some people demonstrate the effects more overtly than do others. One theory explains that a greater tidal pull is exerted by full moons as witnessed through the movement of ocean currents. The premise may be analogized to the human body as it's composed of a high water content. Astrologers fine-tune this explanation by ascribing discernible themes to specific full moon cycles. Each one energizes potential conflict between signs that are already opposed. Many people experience pressure as left-brain logic inwardly argues against right brain intuition. Since men and women are projections of these dual planetary forces, they relate poorly during full moon intervals. If new moon signifies the primordial **marriage of the lights** (via the cosmic union set between yin and yang), then full moon implies their temporary divorced status! Fortunately what can't be resolved with reasoning can be sensually negotiated during these intense intervals. (That's an ancient recipe for neutralizing lunacy!)

Let's take a closer look at core themes that full moon polarities animate:

Aries-Libra: Here lies the great battle between self-interest and making conscious concessions towards a partner in order to sustain harmony in a close tie. How can the individual prove true to herself without denying the benefits and duties that partnership entails? This polarity tests commitment. We can neither lose our self utterly into another, nor necessarily appreciate life without someone significant to share it with. Two whole persons can unite to form the best of partnerships; whereas two wounded persons will likely exacerbate each other's problems, a trend this full moon can easily catalyze.

Taurus-Scorpio: Sharing is keynoted here, both in the sensual sphere of the body, as well as in the practical realm of joint assets. Where does one best draw the line between mine and ours? Both signs relate to bodies as well as bank accounts. Discovering boundaries that make good sense is a sound idea. How then to mark turf and practice the ideal of fairness without hurting your partner or shutting him out? During this interval financial differences may emerge that rattle trust and intimacy. The key is to share what you're comfortable sharing, not what's offered on the basis of sexual bribery or coercion of any covert sort.

An interesting fact worth noting is that issues that arise during the full moon that polarizes Aries (Mars) and Libra (Venus) recur during the following month's full moon polarity play-out since Taurus (Venus) and Scorpio (co-ruler Mars) are energized! Essentially the same opposition is invoked by both sets of lunation cycles. Thus themes that directly correlate with the functions of Venus and Mars come to life in spring as well as autumn. That's when the Zodiac "flips gears" and new moon signs reverse to become full moon signs. Four of the year's twelve lunation cycles bear lessons that pivot the twin stars of passion and romance. The cosmic lesson plan evidently stresses a "karma-yoga" between the genders for a reason! Until mankind arrives at a state of balance where grace is found in conjugal relationships, intimate relationships will continue to pay the price.

Gemini-Sag: Here the individual's personal belief system is apt to be challenged by the larger society, or a group s/he identifies with. One either reconciles personal beliefs within a supportive group context, or otherwise moves on in search of more compatible associates.

Events prompt a fine-tuning of personal ethics, religious beliefs, or adherence to cultural norms. Is truth merely convenient, or does it come from the depth of the soul? Can honesty occur between two persons if they maintain hidden agendas? Without compromising the integrity of personal values, one must make every effort to accept another's uniqueness.

Cancer-Capricorn: This polarity addresses the traditional gender roles adhered to by mainstream culture, particularly those attributable to the mother and father. The individual may experience a conflict between domestic duties (the mother) and those simultaneously demanded by the career (the father). We unconsciously enact behaviors learned during our early childhoods. Who wears the pants in any given tie? Self-protective instincts buck up against obligations imposed by others. One may wall off to protect personal security against this onslaught, or complete tasks that require absolute self-discipline.

Leo-Aquarius: Romantic love sometimes turns the ego into a monster. Learning to experience love without believing you can control your partner is keynoted here. Aquarius promotes detachment. Its ideal involves a love of humanity. Aquarian inclinations rebel against the quixotic call to get lost in the comfort zone of a lover's arms. The message, "if you love something, let it go; if it's yours, it will return" comes to life. A beautiful lesson conveyed by Kahlil Gibran in *The Prophet* is that lovers must put spaces in their togetherness. Leo seeks the swept-away rapture of romantic love, whereas Aquarius resists it! Relationships require times of togetherness, as well as healthy spaces apart. Arriving at a satisfying rhythmic interchange between these opposing inclinations can take a toll on the ego. That's what's at issue during this intense lunar interval.

Virgo-Pisces: This interplay is especially difficult as it exacerbates the lessons mankind at large now faces at our current age phase transition. Where Virgo seeks order through an elaborate labeling process, Pisces courts potential chaos by dissolving the categorical references previously utilized to define the (illusory) boundaries between things. Hypocrisy arises as one meets her own inner resistance as a battle between adherence to the letter rather than

45

spirit of The Law ensues. Both signs relate to health matters, and the various modalities instituted for addressing them. The human body functions as a message system. Often it conveys through our tissues causes that originate from our issues. Is there a lifestyle practice one should reasonably implement to enhance their well being? Could an ounce of prevention be worth a pound of cure? Earth mother may respond to this lunar cycle by sounding her own alarm. Weather events pose risks. The spiraling nature of Pisces often expresses as cyclonic activity, including tornado outbreaks. Gaia appears to be calling out for us to assist her healing process.

Quarter Moons: Cosmic Crossroads:

If you happen to have been born with the moon 90 degrees (3 signs) away from another planet, quarter moon cycles will exacerbate the lessons associated with this natal chart configuration. I call it a "cosmic traffic jam." Additionally if you happen to live with someone whose moon or sun is 3 signs (square) away from yours, the quarter moon agitates these placements and will likely give rise to conflict. Involvement in such bonds (explained below) qualifies for the heading "karmic ties." For instance if one individual's sun or moon is found in square to another's, the nature of this alignment produces life-altering lessons and potential realizations. Basic identity (along with personal needs) is pivoted due to the intensity inherent to such interaction. Since the moon (like other planets moving at slower paces) will repeatedly cross these charged zones, the issues represented will be regularly activated. In other words there's no escape from the lesson plan! Do not look to place blame. It's wiser if the involved parties seek an understanding of the differing motivations at work. The traditional view that there is **one** right behavior or approach belies the higher truth: that Divine Intention has established twelve basic models, each with its own characteristic distinctions. By interacting tolerance of these differences is expected to emerge. Whether we study mythology, the writings of Plato, Shakespeare's dramas, or the Astrologos, ancient themes remain contemporary because they reflect inborn aspects of unchanging human nature.

Human beings incarnate on earth in order to evolve. The spiritual journeys we encounter here allot specific opportunities to integrate Divinity's full expression. Perhaps in the fullness of time we each incarnate to walk all twelve quintessential paths, and thus receive the gifts each has to offer.

Let's take a look at the challenges likely to arise during **quarter moon phases.** These conflicts will be felt internally if your natal chart holds planets in signs that square. Otherwise these potentially charged issues may arise among persons who have their sun or moon signs involved in these naturally conflicted arrangements.

Aries-Cancer: How do I reconcile my independence (acute sense of self will) with the need to belong to a family or group?

Taurus-Leo: When does my personal need to possess (or mark territory) thwart my wish to act in a truly loving manner? In what way is hunger (sexual and/or digestive) being confused with a displaced need to express something vital from the wellspring of my soul?

Gemini-Virgo: Does my need to label something or define it intellectually impede true understanding and thus limit my capacity for discovery? Is focus placed on intellectualizing rather than putting into practice that which would determine a real test of efficacy?

Cancer-Libra: What patterns accrued on the basis of family conditioning/programming preclude me from having an honest genuine partnership now? Where do personal insecurities bar my capacity to recognize my partner's point of view, thus undermining the basis for fairness and mutual acceptance within our tie?

Leo-Scorpio: Am I using my power or sexual prowess to control another? Am I acting out of genuine concern, or in the interest of fulfilling my own powerful desires? Is sexuality being bartered to obtain other things? Lust disguised as the urge to merge can result in bonds clutched tightly. These may die premature deaths due to suffocation. Fate may prompt the lesson of setting free.

Virgo-Sagittarius: Where does my focus on detail undermine my capacity to recognize the big picture? How is the greater truth being obscured by a myopic tunnel vision? How can the facets best serve the whole?

Libra-Capricorn: How does my ambition conflict with my need for a fair and balanced partnership? Am I unconsciously applying the professional standards of an accountant in determining the quality of my relationship? Different systems of collateral are necessarily applied to each. Is Judgment getting in the way of caring to undermine my capacity for unconditional love?

Scorpio-Aquarius: Am I allowing wounds from the past to impede trust, or seeking a covert cause to impede another person's freedom/free will? Am I acting out of good will, or unwittingly manipulating another's choices? Is possessiveness choking the bond's spontaneous expression? Are secrets preventing open sharing? Trim the sails if you like smoother sailing!

Sagittarius-Pisces: Is religious orthodoxy interfering with my ability to accept another as s/he is? Is analysis impeding genuine compassion, the basis for true spirituality? Am I stating a set of objectives while acting to undermine them? How can I live the credo, "To thine own self be true," when more than one voice seems to speak to me from interior planes?

Aquarius-Taurus: Is money the yardstick upon which I measure my contribution to the world? Can I reconcile my desire for prosperity with a call to accept altruistic service that benefits humanity? How do I fulfill my high ideals in a mundane, materialistically driven world?

Pisces-Gemini: Watch closely for signs that imagination not be mistaken for actual truth. Be astute enough to recognize where you become the victim of your own con game. Are you becoming dangerously self-sacrificing, or otherwise succumbing to passive aggressive tactics? What impact does worry, or a habit of negative thinking have upon your body? Is your coping mechanism self-medicated? Are you depending on chemicals to offset the sorrow logical explanations cannot remedy?

Now that you understand the key dynamics that accompany the moon's changing positions, let's take a look at your own chart "dialogs." First you'll want to know if your natal moon is involved with another planet. The most intimate bond is known as the conjunction. It indicates that the moon and another planet continually combine respective energies. (Generally the pair is found in the same sign.) Examine your birth chart to see if your moon is found close to another planet. These natal moon mergers represent lifelong interior dialogs and operate like celestial Siamese Twins! Across your lifespan the moon will contact, and thus simultaneously activate both entities every single month! Depending on the nature of what's bound together, responses to the moon's monthly transit may prove dichotomous. Luna is by nature a "mediumistic" entity because she possesses no innate light of her own. Instead she readily takes on the "persona" or quality of whatever planet she connects with. She also assumes the character of the sign-field she crosses. This awesome luminary collects "the force" and distributes it back to earth as psychic fuel. By this process she activates each realm and dramatically influences our moods. Everyone feels Her contacts with their key planetary players. That's because every planet in the birth chart essentially operates like a sensitive satellite receiving apparatus. Each has its own intended range. For instance there are marked distinctions between the mandated functions of Mercury and Venus. Every planetary body receives and radiates a specific range of energetic properties. It goes beyond the purpose of this book to explain all of them and the degree to which each may configure with the moon. However, it is important to make note of the conjunctions. The insights drawn from this discussion can help you in that you will learn a great deal about your own emotional wiring or basic nature. Not everyone identifies with their sun sign, nor do most know much about their moon sign(s). Suppose your natal moon is found in calm Taurus, but you're not especially even-tempered. A closer look at your chart reveals the moon conjunct volatile Uranus or perhaps in square to aggressive Mars. These planetary overlays explain the variance. A powerful alchemy is at work. When its dynamics are brought to life you're prompted to observe **the way you feel**. Suppose your natal moon is found close to Mars in the sign of Gemini. Each month

49

when the moon returns to Gemini you will experience potential anger (due to Mars being simultaneously triggered) until you learn to modify your own behaviors. In contrast if you have no planet in Gemini (or whatever sign the moon is transiting) then this monthly transit will prove a neutral realm, and operate like a blank slate.

The following references will emerge as heightened effects that last for about two days each month. Let us take into account one more interesting factor. The five outer planets make extended stays in each of the Zodiac signs. For example, everyone born between 1939-1956 has Pluto in Leo. Therefore when the moon transits Leo every month, she meets the Pluto position of millions of persons! By studying the Moon-Pluto explanation offered below you will gain deeper insight into this recurring two-day interval and how it impacts your peer group. The alchemy at work also impacts the everlasting tango of human relationships. Allow me to elaborate. Suppose your birth moon is located in the same sign as your best friend's Jupiter? Then the following account of Moon-Jupiter will provide insight into the nature of that bond. Your friendship is likely to benefit each time the Moon crosses this auspicious shared domain. If this material sounds complicated, keep this in mind: Astrology is like music except that planets replace the notes. Or think of it as an alphabet. Once you understand the sign language derived from the twelve original positions, added to the messages of the ten planetary bodies that govern these, the rest becomes a cosmic piece of cake! Indeed it is astro-logical! A little study and families could benefit greatly from color-coded *Moon Dance* calendars. Hung prominently in "high traffic" domestic zones these would specify dates of probable tension among relatives, while conversely noting days of exceptional promise. As an example, my natal Moon is found in Leo, as are the moons of both my daughters. The moon represents the mother, extension of the Divine feminine, and in our filial case it reads literally to form a powerful basis for connection. This position suggests that both daughters have inherited the mother's dramatic emotional nature. Yet both hold air sun signs (apropos since their father is an air sign) to wisely configure logic into their stellar heritage.

Across a span of thirty-years of astrological counseling, in those instances where clients ask to see the charts of family members analyzed, recognizable "fusion zones" show up. These planetary hot spots clearly identify the snags as well as rewards bound to impact those involved in close filial interaction. And because related individuals often share related planetary positions, their destinies are jointly shaped by those planetary passages that cross over these common "chords." Shared lessons will find themselves periodically triggered. The study of inter-chart planetary fusion zones is most revealing. Among the players the moon is responsible for rousing our instinctual feelings. She directs us towards those bonds that will resonate with our lifetime's karmic lesson plan. It appears that Creator designed the Zodiac as a didactic apparatus fashioned in such a way that mankind would learn on the basis of interaction set among the twelve quintessential tribes. Human beings are akin to minute particles in the body of the Infinite, the planets like ganglia occupying a portion of Creator's nervous system! Can the spinning electron envision the entirety of the whole? Can we?

Remember, to master any dance requires practice. As you familiarize yourself with the rhythm of the moon's phases, you will begin to sense the regularity of her tempo transitions. *Moon dance* allots the capacity to gradually sense the interior tides as they wax and wane in accord with the lunar cycle. In particularly stressful birth charts (the moon found under affliction) individuals may find solace in the understanding that they are meeting in the present a karmic debt carried over from a prior incarnation. Newly armed with self-knowledge aids personal efforts, and assists one in efforts to overcome past conditioning or a current self-defeating pattern. Scripture reveals that we are never given more than we can handle. Often there is something to be found within our birth profile that acts providentially to offset or otherwise defuse the soul wrenching planetary tension found elsewhere.

Dialogs Of The Moon
(For Advanced Moon Dancers)

Let's explore the following dialogs to shed light on themes destined to recur since the moon returns to reenergize each of these positions every single month! It's worth noting that these descriptions are general templates. Since nothing in our universe is static, each moon cycle will vary somewhat from prior ones because the other planets that contribute to her field of responsive resonance continually shift positions, too. In other words the big picture constantly alters, and provides a changing stellar backdrop for the moon's varying projections. The lunar cycle plays a pivotal role in articulating the Biblical promise: "There is a time for every purpose under heaven."

New Moon in your sun sign: This constitutes an empowered personal phase where you can hone in on your emotions and become better centered. You find that you're clearer about what you want, and more equipped to face your usually hidden needs. It's a time of heightened self-awareness. An interior sense that life can begin anew is felt on a visceral level. The strong elemental blend underway between yin and yang elucidates the true state of your union or intimate tie. If you are solo you may now strategize the means to alter that status.

New Moon in your own moon sign: Emotions will run high while logic will be temporarily placed aside (unless your birth moon is found in Libra or Capricorn). You may long for someone or some aspect of your past, or otherwise view a previous experience with new eyes. It's a powerful time to reenergize your living environment. Clear away items that no longer nourish who you are. Home cooking proves therapeutic. Listen closely to your feelings as these will guide you towards the fulfillment of your true calling.

New Moon in your Mercury sign: Here the planet of feelings is united with the agent of analysis, for Mercury constitutes the winged god of communications. There is a great need to intellectually understand personal feelings. You will want to talk these out until you become clearer about what's internally motivating you. This alignment favors writers, researchers, teachers and personal coaches.

New Moon in your Venus sign: This "fusion zone" energizes Yin virtues that support or nurture your senses. You will be more interested in beautifying your home, preparing delicious foods that draw family and friends together, or enjoying other sensual expressions. If your natal moon is afflicted, then satiety is difficult to discern. A lifelong task may include learning to identify when you've had enough, the psychological equivalent of essentially rewiring an old house. Since the arts essentially feed the senses, it's a great time to court your muse. Enroll in a cooking class, get a facial or massage, or lose yourself in the pages of a romance novel.

New Moon in your Mars sign: There may be angst, tension, or conflict felt now. Independent needs buck up against duties imposed by family members. Personal space may feel crowded or else under siege. The ego fights to preserve its boundaries against the encroachment of others' claims to your time. Because there is a heightened need to express independently, impatience resists the "usual routines." Find a creative way to harness or process your anger. How you handle this transit reveals the relative state of your ego: healthy or otherwise?

New Moon in your Jupiter sign: Joy is often naturally experienced during this interval as is a tendency to view life in a big way. Many people over-spend, while others overeat. There is a desire for plentitude and related wish to live prosperously. (If your birth moon is naturally afflicted, then curb impulses that will ultimately tax your budget, weight, or well-being. Gambling, in particular, is a no-no under this influence.) Try to set wise limits on all forms of self-indulgent behavior. It's an ideal time to open your mind to new thought. Visit a bookshop or attend a seminar on a topic you have not delved into previously.

Outer planet convergence zones: Saturn remains in a sign for thirty-months, Uranus for seven years, Neptune for fourteen years, and Pluto for fourteen years or more. For this reason, these outer planet convergence zones represent experiences shared with your entire peer group. Anyone whose natal moon is found closely conjoined with one of the slow moving planets will feel the monthly effect amplified, for this factor constitutes a permanent part of her lesson plan. Let's review how the moon behaves when she bonds each month with one of the four outermost planets, as follows:

New Moon in your Saturn sign: This combination makes a person feel old before their time, or weighed down by heavy responsibilities.

Saturn's connection with karma can summon feelings of guilt. We feel compelled to take on jobs that we'd ordinarily shy away from. A sense of restriction or gravity surrounds family life and its demands. Willpower is needed to stand up to life's challenges. Some will be drawn to older or more serious mates. Life events test our sense of self-discipline. For all of us, destiny has a way of periodically sending reality checks our way. This may prove such a time. If bonds have outgrown their reason to exist, they may splinter or show signs of a beginning dissolution.

New Moon in your Uranus sign: Expect the unexpected in or around the domestic sphere. This combination bodes ominously for climate change and its increasing threat to domestic stability. On the plus side, lively Uranus favors social activity and can render your home a monthly meeting place for unusual types. Perhaps you will elect to take in a foreign exchange student, eccentric aging relative, or foster child. Life can stun you through a radical discovery. Personal wiring is easily agitated; therefore you are not a particularly good candidate for indulgence in caffeine, sugar, or stimulants. At this time if a relationship or domestic pattern has become stale or automatic introduce spontaneity. Strained ties that do not yield to growth may come apart. (This influence acts as trigger, while true causes may have been brewing for some time.)

New Moon in your Neptune sign: At this time the plane of dreams speaks loudly and the world's abrasive tone can feel overwhelming. Many thus retreat into their own inner sanctums. Unfortunately due to Neptune's association with addictive behaviors, self-medicating (via drugs or alcohol) becomes reflexive. For spiritually balanced sorts, this combo favors meditation, dance, Tai Chi, Yoga, and Tantra. Personal boundaries easily diffuse warranting a sensual meltdown into a partner. One woman I know describes this as feeling like jelly. Sentience opens to communion with forces few ordinarily come into spiritual association with. Neptune is the enemy of realism; so do not buy a house or sign legally binding contracts at this time. Leave the fiscal facts for another transit!

New Moon in your Pluto sign: Watch the plumbing! And bear in mind it's not only snakes that molt their skins. Old family issues that have left scar tissue in their wake require spiritual (applied forgiveness) mending. We must let go to release elements of our past that tether us to outmoded responses. The inner life enters a phase of endings that eventuate in a potential rebirth. Butterflies emerge from long cocoon passages. It is often by releasing a behavior, person, or object from the past that psychic space is provided for new growth. That's the proven recipe for transformation. Such activity invites in the therapeutic power of the proverbial Phoenix. Since Pluto loves a mystery, you may feel unconsciously drawn to play a detective role at this time. If you fail to respect others' rightful needs for privacy, you could cause problems. Sexual healing is possible and can neutralize conflict felt elsewhere in an intimate bond.

The Moon And Family Karma

Should you make the effort to study the moon signs of family members, you will learn many useful things. First, you will see solid evidence of astrology at work. Armed with the knowledge of the moon's expressive range you will recognize what motivating distinctions guide the actions of relatives and loved ones. A rudimentary understanding of zodiac signs enables you to read heaven's intriguing language and note its unmistakable impact on others. Astrology speaks in a magical dialect that reveals the unspoken needs and desires of all human beings. How individuals differ on the basis of inborn sign-proclivities is lost on a society (Mars ruled) under thrall to the dominant fiction that "one size fits all." Creator drew up the ingenious living mosaic of our world so that its planned parts would ultimately evolve the whole. As author Paul Brenner eloquently termed it, *Life is a Shared Creation*; or as the American Indian proverb relates: "We were born involved in one another."

The moon and sun not only symbolize the **abstract** parental archetypes known as yin and yang, they also reflect our parents' actual relationship. Specifics are revealed through the positions occupied by the luminaries in our birth charts. And here's the unique thing: one's brothers and sisters, arguably raised by the same parents within the same filial environment likely possess quite different sun-moon alignments! Call it cosmic chemistry. Orthodox psychology engages in a debate over the relative impact of nature (genetics) versus nurture (how your family raised you) in its attempt to explain why different personality traits take shape and form. Neither explanation can account for the marked dissimilarities found among siblings. If only nature and nurture figure into the personality equation, why then do brothers and sisters demonstrate such diverse traits? One option considered is "birth order," but it hardly satisfies this otherwise unfathomable conundrum. And while it's true that enlightened persons can be found in every field, psychology continues to deny the veracity of astrology. It also fails to recognize the karmic implications of past life conditioning and how this legacy bears upon the present lifetime. Each natal chart is a portrait and reflects in its unique blueprint those experiences garnered from former incarnations. Like a seed its potentials ultimately unfold to accord with time's embedded rhythms. No two charts or persons share the same pattern. This cosmic fact of life helps explain the innate differences witnessed among brothers and sisters.

I believe each natal chart constitutes a bona fide legacy. It reflects aptitudes and deficits the soul has picked up in earlier times spent on earth. Psychology examines personality formation as if each of us begins as a generic blank slate. That's like observing the tree from where it meets the surface without ever studying its deeper root structures. Answers to life's enduring mysteries require pursuing those depths! Ancient adepts have done so and relate how life's continuity reflects the workings of the law of karma. Divine order is built into this premise! Noted mystic Edgar Cayce whose work broadened my consciousness often related that, "Entity is meeting self." Amid thousands of readings channeled from The Akashic records, one theme stood out: that conditions in the present lifetime reflect actions, beliefs, and behaviors enacted in previous lives. The astrologer's tools grant witness to how this dynamic operates. It is based on the natal blueprint where evidence of the strengths and weaknesses of character can be found. These unfold as personal destiny. No chart factor exists due to sheer caprice; rather each reflects traits (even conditions) inherited from prior incarnations. While psychology asserts that our parent's relationship dramatically colors the person we grow up to become, the particulars of who they are and how they relate also show up in our birth blueprint! This is symbolized by the moon's angular relationship to the sun, added to secondary dimensions afforded by the outer planets. (These give rise to sub-themes that add texture and nuance to the essential dynamic presented by the sun and moon.) Cayce had much to say about the importance of the home and family ties. He offered: "Family life is the hotbed of karma," which substantiates author John Bradshaw's claim that probably 90% of American families are dysfunctional. Individuals destined to dwell together are forced to confront lessons that cannot be walked away from. The contrast between difficulties in the home and the picture painted by popular television sit-coms where relatives congenially resolve differences and genuinely show love for one another is a poignant one. How viable were early media models that shaped my generation as it came of age, and still does? Do these portraits reflect actual norms? My childhood was marked by the loss of my natural mother, an event indicated by harsh aspects made to the moon in my natal chart. Similarly both my daughters' births corresponded with the moon in square to Uranus. This signature presages the breakup of the family, which indeed proved the case for my offspring as well. The *Bible* states: "the sins of the fathers will be visited upon the sons." More aptly, the choices we feel compelled to make as parents on the basis of our own unhealed wounds imprint our children. Thus the karmic lineage passes from adult to child and so on. It's counterproductive to place blame on parents for they too are part of this lineage. Besides, if the chart blueprint defines the quality of family life the individual is set to experience, then the legacy begins at birth, and must be fulfilled across their lifespan. This birth map appears to reflect what we have earned on the basis of our own past experiences. The Buddhists see this endowment as something akin to a spiritual bank account.

In addition to the personal slings and arrows of outrageous fortune, each of us contributes to history and is a beneficiary of group karma. Who would argue that history's character is not stained in blood? Thus with respect to the greater paradigm our separate lives reflect in part its long legacy of redundant carnage. As will be elaborated further in Part II, human relationships suffer on account of a veritable chasm purposely set between the genders. Real and lasting love is relatively rare in our world. Could a pervasive sexist disequilibrium have anything to do with that? The notion of sin wedged between men and women abrades uncomfortably against their natural lust for one another. The ensuing tension has led to wounding behaviors that have been passed from generation to generation. This antipathy also contributes to the redundant history of warfare. A great many intelligent persons have observed mankind's past and deduced that aggression is inevitable, bound to endlessly recur. How then to escape this seeming inevitability? One answer offered by the world's master teachers is that forgiveness acts as a powerful cathartic tool for transformation. I would argue further that at this cusp of ages, mankind can ill afford the fictions celebrated by and through religious traditions. These ultimately hold minds hostage to old gods. The search for catharsis leads many people to conventional therapists. Some become dependent on their counselors. However, the practice of looking backwards glues consciousness to the past where it remains focused on mistakes made by parental custodians. This approach too often freezes intended personal growth. It is far wiser to ask yourself: "What did I elect on a **soul level** to work out by allowing this lifetime's family as basis for experience?" While some of what is met is choice, many influences and conditions exist to satisfy karmic debts. These predestined factors often compel us to live with incompatible people; thus we face an exceedingly difficult set of lessons on a daily basis. Therefore charged domestic environs call for recognizing the lunar cycle since the moon's transits foreshadow predictable periods of increased tension. (Given high statistical levels of domestic abuse this astrological data could prove lifesaving, operating as the lunar equivalent of the unique forecast protocol portrayed in the film *Minority Report!*) Conversely it's advantageous to anticipate beneficial cycles since they're apt to favor our personal affairs.

The individual who never looks inward to understand her own cause factors neglects an arena ripe for personal growth. Astrology provides us with the cosmic weather report; but ultimately the responsibility falls to the individual to make informed personal choices. Person by person, group by group, and civilization by civilization the much anticipated Age of Aquarius will rise to the degree we change how we live, interact, and relate to effete belief systems. Enlightened options must be role modeled by courageous individuals until trends build that impact entire communities. Together we can change the channel that consensual reality has been playing. (I'm sure I'm not the only one tired of brute macho contests like war monopolizing the globe and the experience of too many living upon it.) Astrology, sacred unto Aquarius, holds substantial keys that can expand our knowledge and understanding. Most amazing, its clues are writ into a universal language that's elemental and thus easy to learn!

Life is largely based on chemistry, so let's examine how the moon operates in the **four elements**. This brief course in "cosmic chemistry 101" will demonstrate why we are magnetically drawn to bond with certain persons and not others. The four directions honored by Indigenous tribes represent the foundation blueprints of the manifest world. Analogous to the four season changes, these point to the root motivations people feel internally directed to pursue. Sexual attraction also accords with this elemental design plan. It's shown in the way fire signs easily connect with air signs (since fire is fueled by air). Whereas water signs respond to the magnetic pull of earth signs since water epitomized as the great ocean finds itself inexorably pulled to the shoreline. This union also facilitates the growth of earth's harvests. A pattern is seen in that three signs fall under each of the four elements. Taken in pairs six signs form two-overlapping triangles and symbolize the mystical signature known as the Star of David. It connotes harmony. Thus Aries, Leo and Sagittarius (the fire trinity) relate amicably with Gemini, Libra and Aquarius (the air trinity). Taurus, Virgo and Capricorn (the earth trinity) blend harmoniously with Cancer, Scorpio and Pisces (the watery trinity). These interchanges foster compatibility, and are quite fortunate when found in the following combinations: sun to sun, moon to moon, moon to sun, or Venus to Mars. These pairs forge satisfying bonds. However, given the likelihood that relationship karma must be faced, many of us are inwardly compelled to form relationships with persons who are not so naturally compatible. Just as the grain of sand finding its way into the sensitive oyster shell causes the irritation that ultimately builds a pearl, marital discord overcome can facilitate genuine love. Tolerance, understanding, and self-discipline are requirements. Another tricky factor bears mentioning. Most peoples' charts own fault lines, implied tests of varied sorts that must be negotiated if personal growth is to occur. For instance if the natal chart holds a hard angle between the sun and moon or its romantic surrogates Mars and Venus, the likelihood of sustaining a harmonious relationship is suspect. It's a metaphysical given that close ties act as mirrors. We tend to meet ourselves in projected form through our intimate bonds. Rare individuals whose charts hold harmonious indications between both sets of romance "stars" bear the promise of happy unions. Chances are their auspicious fates are the result of having mastered tough lessons in close bonds during former incarnations. While the vast majority pursues bonds on the basis of physical attraction or financial benefit, there is no guarantee these mundane enticements do much to offset the indications of their birth maps. Besides, it's often the case that those endowed with riches or fine figures are not always lucky in love. Too many people chase wealth to the point that their relationships suffer. Yet an interesting study done by Professor Emeritus Robert E. Lane revealed that more people place value on satisfying loving ties than accumulating wealth.

The celestial facts of our existence are overlooked by orthodox sources, especially those that purport to be experts on human behavior. Academe follows the mistaken notion that mate selection stems from the sound rational realm of the intellect. That we **choose** who we love. Hardly. Is love a choice when it's compelled from an inscrutable place within the soul? This force is so compulsive that often when our minds **can** determine that the intended is not necessarily what we need (or even good for us) our inner being cannot relinquish its hold on this object of desire. Inner restlessness drives us until some form of commitment or denouement ensues. So-called soulmate ties seem inordinately intense; yet generally burn out, consumed by that which they were once nourished by. Any two people who share a strong sun-moon or Venus-Mars link are apt to feel a magnetic connection regardless of whether their lifestyles, bank accounts, ethnicities, or family plans concur. As Shakespeare stated in *Hamlet*, "There are more things in heaven and earth than dreamt of in your philosophy, Horatio."

Cosmic Chemistry Moon Style

The Zodiac begins with Aries, season of spring; so we'll first examine the moon's qualities when she is found in **fiery signs**. These include Aries, Leo, and Sagittarius. If you simply tap a match you'll notice that flame appears instantly. This helps to explain why fire signs are simply not given to patience. The fire sign nature is cued to immediacy with spontaneity their modus operandi. In family life fire sign moons will experience friction when forced to live with earth or water moon counterparts. Quite simply they operate at different speeds! When a fire sign moon (or sun) gets an idea, they prefer to quickly act on it. Their responses and moods are hair-triggered. Besides, fire cannot hide its light under a bushel; so its emotions readily show. If the fire sign is angry, s/he may let loose in a show of verbal fireworks. These soon blow over (and unlike earth or even watery moons fire sign moons seldom carry or hold grudges). The sensitive water moon may wonder why the fire sign acted out at all since they **do** harbor hurt feelings! The impulsive tendencies of fire sign moons can be mitigated if there are strong planetary placements, such as Mercury (for intellect and decision-making), or Mars (for action) found in slower moving earth signs. Fire moons generally live for the moment. They are not equipped to consider how today's gestures will impact tomorrow's five-year plan. Plus fire sign moons fall in love quickly. Their emotional range spans the gamut from anguished displays of temper to innocent childlike enthusiasm. The fire sign moon is likely to grow up in a family where she is the life of the party, the exciting relative that all wish to be around. Even if the fire sign does not seek attention, like stunning fireworks, their presence is tough to ignore. Too many fire signs in the same family spells competition as each vies dangerously for attention. Serious sibling rivalry can spur some to great achievement. It can also induce lasting resentment if ill-considered choices taken in youth leave emotional scar tissue behind. On the whole, fire sign moons need lots of room to do their own thing. Most gravitate towards occupations where they can enjoy creative freedom, autonomy, exotic travel, or even confrontation with danger. In terms of adult bonding, the fire sign moon is generally attracted to exciting persons. However the *I Ching* offers an intriguing explanation that maps the path to reconciliation between fire and its more stable earth "cousin." If the earth partner consents to acting like wood the fire will continue to burn. This adaptation could cement a workable union taking shape as a quiet domesticated mate acting behind the scenes to support his fiery partner.

Air sign moons include Gemini, Libra and Aquarius. These positions strengthen reasoning faculties and tend to be thoughtful. Here the direct experience of emotion is siphoned through the intellect's filtering process. The air moon wants to understand what she feels, and will apply herself to study in an effort to discover answers. Sometimes the need for explanations precludes the actual experience of the emotion itself. Often air sign moons grow up in families where knowledge is valued over the less precise and fleeting realm of feelings. Parents may hold high academic degrees and emphasize the importance of a quality education. Of course the converse may also prove true. In a family system that is constantly thrown into chaos, the air-moon learns to detach in order to survive. Such a person will retreat into their mind and safely view their feelings from an artificially controlled distance. Air sign moons are very comfortable with logic, analysis, and creative ways to interpret information. They make terrific attorneys, sales representatives, educators, and public speakers. Air sign moons never rest, for there is always something they wish to read, study, learn, express, or understand. Communication is their forte. Due to innate salesmanship some excel in entrepreneurial enterprises. They function well in the social sphere. Just as our satellite signals and cell phone messages traverse the airwaves, conversation is the oxygen that animates air moon natives. Logically they require mates they can talk to. If you've ever noticed a couple that seems physically incompatible (she's beautiful and he's grossly overweight or vice versa) it's likely that their union is based upon a mental rapport, communion via the air element. Theirs is a meeting of minds. The air-moon feels at home with a partner who understands her thoughts. Shared belief systems act as bridges for persons who are celestially designed to meld through air. In addition, air moons will enthusiastically support educational opportunities for their offspring.

The **water sign moons** include Cancer, Scorpio, and Pisces and predispose natives towards deeply feeling intuitive natures. If you've ever placed water in the fridge next to an inadequately wrapped item, the water will soon taste like it. That's because water is a natural medium. It literally receives molecules (or energy) from other items. In astrology water represents natural sensitivity enhanced by direct empathy. Water moons can enter a bar in a perfectly good mood and leave feeling anxious, angry, or unstable. Unknowingly they have picked up the emotions of others standing by. Water moons often feel genuine sympathy for others' plights in life, and for this reason make excellent psychologists, nurses, psychics, and social workers. Many prove exceptionally patient when it comes to assisting children who suffer from emotional, physical or mental abuse. Water is capable of experiencing vast transitions. It can quickly move from a frozen state (32 degrees) to hot steam (212 degrees). Symbolically similar alterations occur within the psyches of water moon natives. Yet they may not evidence what they feel. Therefore turbulence consistent with their powerful emotional range lays in wait beneath the surface of appearances. In my practice as astrologer, I've noted that water sign moons prove the likeliest candidates for eating disorders, alcoholism, drug addiction, and other escapist behaviors. This does not mean that everyone born with a water sign moon will self-medicate in a maladaptive manner. Much depends on the aspects made to the moon (i.e. the chart's secondary dialogs) along with the relative willpower of the individual in question. The propensity does exist in part because water sign moons pick up and carry others' unprocessed emotions. They must take special care when it comes to choosing environments for work and social affairs. Sensitive by nature, if someone hurts their feelings the scar tissue may never fully heal. Water moons may grow up in families where emotions are stuffed away by eating, or diluted in booze. It's equally possible that an impressionable water-sign moon will live among relatives who hail from the air element. This pushes the water moon further into the depths of her self as in the cold, logical emotional clime she may feel like an alien. Such a one may grow up utterly convinced she's been born to the wrong family. Remember: Edgar Cayce identified family life as the hotbed of karma. Home is not necessarily where we meet all those delicious strokes the healthy ego craves. Often the family environ is where the soul meets its toughest tests. As a result life could become a journey in pursuit of recovery. Part of the therapeutic process may draw catharsis by helping others discover ways to heal. Water moons do best in partnership with earth moons since water requires a solid container to hold it steady. The earth moon makes the water moon feel safe, protected, and secure thanks to its unmistakable boundaries. Reciprocally, the dry earth benefits from the nurturing qualities of water. Each brings to the other what is missing. Without the inner "climatic" vicissitudes inherent to the water moon, the earth moon's existence proves bland.

The **earth sign moons** include Taurus, Virgo, and Capricorn; and as the saying goes, they function as the salt of the earth. When you're in the hospital and need someone to feed your cat or collect your mail, the earth moon will respond to the call of duty and responsibly fulfill those tasks. Earth signs are closest to the tangible realm and value material things. They have trouble imagining how things as distant as planets can influence their lives, feelings, or basic biology. Earth sign moons identify with substances like their stock portfolios, real estate investments, bank accounts, kitchen cabinet contents, or job status. Someone's got to deal with the nuts and bolts of the physical world, and that task fits comfortably with the contours (and emotional orientation) of the earth sign moon. Emotional responses of earth-sign moons configure with their physical needs first and foremost. Therefore the earth sign moon can find itself marrying an individual with an impressive income because she realizes what it will mean for her quality of life, along with that of future children. Most important to the earth sign moon are stability and security, not that riches aren't sought after or appreciated. Given that earth relates strongly to the physical senses, earth sign moons love to indulge in life's sensual pleasures. They are frequently gifted in avenues such as interior decorating, massage therapy, sculpture, gourmet cooking, weaving, fashion design, and real estate. If the earth sign moon grows up in a dysfunctional family (or one given to substance abuse), she will likely become the breadwinner or family caretaker. A marked sense of responsibility prompts many earth moons to make sure the practical logistics of daily life are covered before loftier passions are permitted or pursued.

In addition to element, there is another fascinating qualitative feature that bears mentioning. It is represented by the moon's **mode** of expression; think of it as attitude! Creator designed the twelve zodiac positions so that each would remain cued to its own celestial rhythm and expression. Each planet's distinct orb can be likened to the specified courses of pieces moving across a grand cosmic chessboard. Because human life (along with its biological relations) is profoundly influenced by the planetary personae, the debate cast between fate versus free will remains unresolved. Great thinkers have contemplated this conundrum for centuries. Astrological theory suggests a mysterious third force at work which counters the notion of absolute polarity. It's represented by the three modes of expression constituted by the cardinal, fixed, and mutable signs. The cardinal signs (Aries, Cancer, Libra and Capricorn) directly correspond to the earth's four season changes. These correlate with the premise of "free" will. The fixed signs (Taurus, Leo, Aquarius and Scorpio) suggest the role fate plays in our affairs. The resulting interplay between fate and free is something akin to a dance. Neither on its own determines a specific outcome. As Christian mystics pray to the Holy Spirit by invoking the Divine **trinity,** a mysterious third factor influences the play-out of actual mundane events. This elusive force is represented by the zodiac's mutable (which is to say chameleon-like) signs which include: Pisces, Gemini, Virgo and Sagittarius. The inherent duality of these signs (all but Virgo are symbolized by a dualistic symbol) suggests more than one possible play-out since the element of chance is ever at work.

Conditions in the earth sphere reflect not only the interaction between fate and free will, but also the unpredictable, ever-changing results of their ongoing engagement. Therefore the mutable mode can be likened to luck, chance, mutation, and permutation! Let's examine the three modes to gain further insight into the motivations of persons close to us.

Cardinal moons (Aries, Cancer, Libra and Capricorn) express as strong-willed natures. The cardinal moon seeks the ways and means to attain personal desires, and can operate in a Machiavellian fashion. The exception here is Libra because it is deeply interested in pleasing its partner, or arriving at win-win situations for all concerned parties. For Libra personal will extends beyond self-interest to accommodate what suits significant others. Moon Aries is committed to life as discovery process; Moon Cancer strongly identifies with its domestic environment and family ties therein; while moon Capricorn will frequently put off family matters to establish a satisfying career status first.

Mutable moons (Gemini, Virgo, Sagittarius and Pisces) change like chameleons. One way the pattern expresses is through frequent changes of residence or location. Since the moon governs our inner lives, flux may be felt internally without any evident outward projection. Mutable moons are given to multiple marriages, and possibly children resulting from each union. Inasmuch as the moon acts as barometer to inner feelings, the mutable moon is so changeable that the individual is left to wonder what genuine authenticity actually feels like. This individual will probably learn from an early age that adapting to her environment is critical. Perhaps the family model was unstable or volatile, and survival required putting on a happy face to hide what was really going on inside. As an adult mastery of one's outward demeanor to suit circumstance may dangerously obscure inner truth. Such persons are fortunate in their ease of adaptation; however they pay a price for this adroitness. Their inborn propensity to adapt to all occasions raises the question of loyalty. Given the Sage advice that one should follow her heart, the mutable sign accustomed to wearing many disguises cannot easily recognize the calling issuing from her own core self. A person divided against her self cannot necessarily stand firm in a committed union. If a mutable moon bonds with another mutable moon and their charts generally align, they luckily discover someone who dances to their same drummer. In this instance the pair's constant vicissitudes will match; and they may find it quite natural to remain steady together.

The **Fixed moons** (Taurus, Leo, Scorpio and Aquarius) bond deeply with other persons. Like ocean liners set on a specific course, once embarked upon their "emotional route," any capacity to change gears becomes nearly impossible. Such persons may remain longer in relationships than their mutable moon counterparts would; however to their credit they possess a strong internal stamina that enables them to see matters through. The toughest lesson to confront the fixed sign moon occurs when their modus operandi clearly isn't working to bring them the results they desire. Can a fixed sign moon truly change her emotional pattern? Owning this signature myself I ponder the question. Should one adapt the adage, "to act as if" in the interest of creating results? Or does such a premeditated strategy (even if it warrants "success") represent a fundamental counterfeit of the true self? Are we expected to transcend our own blueprint or instead learn through the specific lesson plan it generates? Or put another way is it ultimately wiser to be true to one's self (even if anticipated outcomes do not arrive) or create a surrogate self that attracts more beneficial results? In following the arc of one's own instincts the intangible reward is spiritual growth. Every human being must sooner or later face the task of learning to tame her emotions. By making that effort grace can arise in the face of life's most poignant tests.

The Moon remains a key player throughout our journey on the earth plane; yet her power and influence have been given bad press for centuries. She utterly deserves spiritual vindication. And while powerful insights can be drawn from the moon's sign, element, and mode, she is not the only factor that drives character and destiny. Ultimately the chart must be taken as a whole. To benefit from *Moon Dance* you are invited to work with this fascinating, magnetic luminary and see where her journey takes you... likely it will lead to places charted along with those yet to be discovered.

A Word On The Moon And Group Karma

The moon directly impacts memory both on a personal and collective level. She draws us to familiar tribes. What makes anyone feel familiar? Esoterically speaking, a bridge drawn from shared experience carried over from a former incarnation provides the answer. Modern America celebrates concepts of personal power, individual responsibility, and free choice. The notion of group or family karma isn't even within the realm of consideration. External appearances suggest that collections of people meet by caprice; but on higher planes these souls have been directed into each other's lives to share specific purposes. These same individuals may have worked in concert on similar projects in previous lifetimes. The moon provides the "cosmic glue" that binds people together so they can fulfill their missions, even when those purposes are unknown to them!

One way we can chart the operational instructions connecting persons is through the outer planets. Each one is mandated to fulfill a specific purpose, and because they remain in signs for years at a time, their influences bind huge groups of people together. Uranus, for instance, remains in the same sign for seven years, while Neptune spends fourteen years. Furthermost Pluto transits a given sign for twenty plus years! The countless millions born into each generation therefore celestially face shared lesson plan specifics. It is not the intention of this book to elaborate further on these secondary factors other than to provide background for the moon, as lead performer. Astrology as a complex system of correspondences recognizes that each planet's attributes lend specific character to every birth chart. *Moon Dance* will guide you to identify more directly with each of the archetypal energies. These personae animate the twelve zodiac signs. Some of you will immediately recognize the ones that speak loudest for who you are, while others will need time to align their awareness with the archetypes of time. Unless you are adept at reading the aspects made among the planets as drawn from your natal chart, you may not understand why, for instance, your sun sign is Aries, but you identify most intimately with Artemis, the energetic "ruler" of Aquarius. A skilled astrologer would probably find Uranus (ruler of Aquarius) active in your natal chart, or your moon in Aquarius. It is not necessary to understand the entire chart framework to benefit from a knowledge of the moon's cycles.

We're all in this thing called time together; and as earth's motion relative to its neighboring planets suggests, we're natural participants of an amazing cosmic dance!

Men Can Moon Dance, Too!

One of the greatest wounds to a woman's self-esteem results from sexual betrayal, the knowledge of her mate's infidelity. In extreme cases persons have been known to commit suicide, or die of broken hearts. Ironically, studies on human sexuality relate that seventy-three percent of married couples (the numbers apply to both genders!) report having indulged in an affair during the course of their marriages, usually during a stressful interval. "You've come a long way, baby" demonstrates gender parity given these statistics! Of course what society condemns is not improved upon by the fact that nice girls do it too! Some may reasonably ask if monogamy constitutes a natural state at all? Bible literalists believe prostitution to have been the oldest profession. Research aimed at the lifestyles of senators from Ancient Greece and Rome recall a caste of women, high-class escorts known as Hetaera. The Japanese had their "comfort women" during the great war; and Latin men act like legendary Don Juans aspiring to maintain as many mistresses as their bank accounts allow. Thus we see a penchant on the part of men of varied cultures to access a sexual pool of diverse conjugal possibilities. Allow me to propose a radical theory. Perhaps Creator understood the wanderlust the male psyche was Divinely heir to and devised a strategic countervailing plan. Casting the male's intended feminine counterpart into alignment with the changing moon, she would take on the personae of each Goddess and thereby assume a dazzling array of expressive roles, each sure to tantalize her man. (For all we know the moon plays a part in keeping the sun adhered to his orbit!) Because the sun, associated with the male experience, stands at the center of our solar system, masculine experience largely views the world likewise. It's as if unconsciously the male expects everyone (just like those planets) to encircle him (or his imagined throne). He perceives himself the

69

natural center of attention; some even take this expected modern homage for their due! With his female counterpart equipped to take on the character of each of the twelve celestial realms (since she virtually travels along with the moon in Its passages) the male by "stellar extension" is afforded not one, but twelve partners in marriage, not to mention the bedroom! What a plan! However, as societies have largely clipped the wings of feminine expression to curb the feared sexual wantonness of Eve (alleged to carry the stigma of Original Sin direct from the Biblical Garden of Eden) this vast range has never been tolerated! Patriarchal societies have betrayed the higher plan. The majority of societies across the centuries have permitted the female an astonishingly limited array of acceptable expressions. Naturally intuitive acumen stemming from feminine sentience was inhibited on threat of death, as indeed proved the case for millions of women living in Europe several centuries ago. Even today female sexuality is brutally thwarted by the crude practice of clitorectomy. This cruel tradition is still underway in West Africa, while dowry murders are widely reported in India. The sex trafficking of children thrives in the underbelly of Southeast Asia. These are only a few egregious examples of repressing female sexual identity. Along with the high powers drawn from the Divine feminine, varied mundane expressions of women remain controlled, degraded, and/or marketed in far too many regions on our globe. Regardless of man's attempts to usurp the innate powers that belong to his female counterpart (while also violently co-opting what belongs to Mother nature), modern women like their ancestral counterparts remain sensitive to time's hidden nuances. The beauty associated with our intended, interior wingspan is all but lost on today's females who conform robotically to marketplace culture. A great many unwittingly follow the overt and covert dictates of men. Given the dominant patriarchal model how much have women departed from the fate of being taken for extensions of Adam's primordial rib? Is it merely coincidental that we find the masculine pronoun applied to processes that belong exclusively to women? **Men**opause, **Men**struation, **hys**terectomy, and hy**men** come to mind? A female is not a male without a penis (though that would be news to those who still respect Freudian psychology). Men have through time sought to render us into **their** image and likeness. Thank the Goddess they are unable to obliterate our connection to higher forces! They do however discredit, first by the authority of the church and now by virtue of academe, our intuitive link with the moon. This powerful endowment of instinctive knowing is our feminine birthright and entirely discredited by both patriarchal camps. Never underestimate the myriad strategies used by modern patriarchs to keep women in the dark regarding their own Divine heritage. The tragic irony of this scenario is that by crippling the full-intended range of feminine expression the male reciprocally succeeds in crippling himself. As will be explained later in this book, men have been taught to identify with Mars. The vast majority serves time in the military, and few among our fathers, brothers, husbands, lovers, and sons are not left with blood on their hands, stains on their karmic accounts. Expanding the range of masculine archetypes would go a long way towards taming the overt martial impulses that render of civilization a study in unending war(s). When the female freely reflects back to the male his own inherent possibilities, he is at last free to grow!

Regardless of the various and sundry societal taboos devised to curb human sexual behaviors, people find ways to fulfill their urges. Nor can authoritarian agencies (in spite of attempts to flood our bloodstreams with antidepressants) disable the powerful cosmic chords that tie women to the moon and men to the sun. What do these links actually mean to people today? Dr. John Gray recognized distinct behavioral trends attributable to each gender. The popularity of his books and lectures proves his insights hit a massive chord. Yet we cannot say for certain if gender-based distinctions are a product of society's socialization mechanisms or a biological fact of destiny. To this binary equation I would add evidence to substantiate the more subtle cosmic links. Fifty years ago Margaret Mead shared groundbreaking research. As an enlightened anthropologist she sought to study gender roles in societies uncorrupted by the modern world. Her results challenged a great many sexist presumptions, a good number now being reconstituted by an insidious fundamentalist religious backlash.

Dr. Gray noted that women wish to be listened to when they become angry, sad, or frustrated. Men, he argued, are action-oriented, and less inclined to fulfill the function of nurturing listener. They are wired to respond with an urge to **do** something to solve the problem. For a woman, the "problem" can just be a mood. Among male peers, a guy may tell his friend, "I don't understand her. Yesterday she was nice and couldn't get enough of me. Today I'm a stranger. She wants me out of her way." What the unenlightened male fails to recognize is that the female must *Moon Dance,* and is merely acting out her intrinsic natural range. This is exactly where a "lunar education" comes in handy, for the true feminine norm is neither natural to, nor easily understood by males due to their being biologically clocked to a luminary with its own quite different rhythm structure. Because men are linked to the sun (which remains in the same sign during the whole twenty-nine day month as the moon goes off gallivanting from one sign to another) the male range is slower, and some might argue steadier than that of his feminine counterpart. Women truly experience mood changes that by Divine intention respond to the moon. She reflects back at her male counterpart the changing nature of Divine light as it is dispersed through the heavens from twelve quintessential realms. Astrologers believe that men generally project their emotions onto their partners. In this way men can detach themselves from the direct experience of feelings. By and large societies have taught males to suppress emotions. Feelings are considered inappropriate responses for "real men," with the notable exception of anger! A friend of mine convinced her hostile husband to seek counseling. For every descriptive circumstance the counselor utilized in an attempt to elicit feelings from the reluctant spouse, the only response he could identify with was anger. This emotion is quite useful, given its association with Mars, god of war. If a society wishes to maintain within its population pool a ready fodder for war, then angst functions as a key psychological tool! It's hardly accidental that the repressed sexuality enforced upon young Muslim men (the women they would date if they lived in more liberal societies are kept under strict cultural wraps) becomes the lure to recruit would-be suicide bombers. Young impressionable males coping with natural hormone surges are taught that by becoming martyrs to Allah they will be allotted virgins to attend to their every wish in the afterlife. The equivalent exists in modern America. Youths sworn to abstinence no doubt feel these same surging hormones. Nature sends these swirling chemicals during that ripening phase when human bodies are most vibrant and attractive. To bottle up nature's intended expression invites aberrant responses. When love is not allowed, its polarity is generated. For readers who wish to study this dynamic more directly, Dr. William Pollack's book, *Real Boys: Rescuing Our Sons from the Myths of Boyhood* is a good place to start.

Is it possible in a society where women were freely encouraged to take on the glamour of diverse Goddesses (thereby thoroughly intriguing and enticing their mates) that infidelity would disappear? The best answer to that question is it's never been tested! If put into practice, we might conclude that were women to express more celestial archetypes, their male partners would be inspired to reciprocally answer to cues other than those preferred by Mars. For that shift alone, it's worth a shot!

So men can *Moon Dance*, too, but have they the incentive to do so? Given that the male, as sun, sees himself as the center of all archetypes' attention the task facing the woman who wants him for her partner is daunting. She must seduce his frequently oversized ego and retain his affection. She is not alone in her cause for the moon lends magic suitable for securing a mate (after all the biological continuity of the human family depends on this) by rendering each woman mutable enough to reflect the semblances of all realms. Every woman is born with a biological connection to the moon that allows her to virtually move through the mansions of time and at essence mesh with each one! Inspired author Marion Zimmer Bradley refers to a related alchemical process whereby an empowered female "takes on the glamour of the goddess." Does this potential only belong to mystical adepts? I consider it a faculty **inborn to the feminine experience**. Men benefit from this mysterious alignment that ties females to the dance of time. Since the moon cyclically awakens each archetypal expression, what's extended to women is an unconscious capacity to merge with every one; thus a feminine partner virtually offers her mate a diverse set of personalities, or personae! In other words through a celestial process of reciprocity (that takes place on organic as well as elemental levels), she invites him to dance to a more expansive set of drummers. We are designed to function as cosmic partners. With the male's life experience clocked to the sun and the female's calibrated to the moon we were born locked into a cosmic tango. Imbued by qualities inset into time itself, the female lures the male in a perpetual mating dance. This dance between the luminaries is mirrored in other celestial "engagements" based on attractive polarity, or magnetism. Consider the manner by which slews of negatively charged electrons encircle each atom's positively charged nucleus. Or look to the poetic DNA molecule constituted by dancing doubled helixes. When society elects to limit the female it also limits the male because we are energetic extensions of one another. To the degree civilization has cordoned off Divine feminine expressions, men have been crippled. One side of creation alone cannot dance, neither can it make for or sustain life. Shared communion is intended between two co-equal Divine counterparts!

As women learn to move with the moon they carry their partners along for the ride. The lunar connection experienced by women on inner planes is subtle, yet dynamic; and like alchemy bears a magical effect. Carlos Casteneda conveyed the teachings of his Toltec mentor Don Juan in a number of fascinating accounts; but it turns out he was not the only student. In *The Sorcerer's Crossing* Taisha Abelar explains how she, too, became an unwitting student of Don Juan. Further, she reveals that her first key exercise consisted of sitting in a cave to painstakingly enact a complex breathing exercise known as the recapitulation. Its purpose was the gradual clearing of chords left inside her by the men she'd slept with! (Once I became aware of this enduring energetic connection, I was far more selective about who I invited inside!) Beyond tangible intercourse there is a process of alchemy that occurs when a man moves inside a woman. Mysticism associated with early matriarchal societies wisely correlated the female body with a cave. Such places likely served as early temples. Similar in function to this naturally occurring geological phenomenon, women were designed to absorb the essences of all sacred encounters that occur within their contours. These are retained energetically within the cellular folds of their interior cavern. When a lover enters we absorb him, and although bodies return to their separate stances, he leaves something intangible behind (lest you conceive a child). It can neither be defined nor possessed. Sexual intimacy itself may prove temporal, yet the experience remains encoded into memory, cellular memory in fact. Ancient alchemy sought a means to turn dross into gold. Could it be that through our interior caverns, the dross of raw male expression is through love, patience, and spiritual intention altered? Shifted into a purer substance?

Female priestesses of ancient times recognized caves as holy places, especially if they bore springs. Great gemstones form slowly in these cavernous zones. The cave is a place where unseen magic happens, and serves as apt symbol for our vaginal cavity. In its liquid folds who can imagine what deep processes of alchemy await the male that enters? Within the female dwells an ocean of vibrant possibilities; and the male finds himself compelled repeatedly back into its immersion. The universal process of ongoing creation is extended to the female through sharing this fusion zone. With the exception of rape, that lover invited into our sacred cave experiences a hall of mirrors. Prior lovers who previously visited our temple left something of themselves behind, and on subtle levels, the current entrant meets those impressions. From a mystical perspective each lover encounters the variant of alternative archetypal masculine expressions imprinted inside of us. Through this process, albeit unconscious, our intended may discover a new persona for himself. As channels of birth and rebirth women are extended the power to transform their intimate partners by virtue of this sacred sexual alchemy.

Up until the present the acceptable range of feminine expressions has been restricted, and by extension this has unduly limited the fabric of maleness. In contrast the astrological model draws from the holy circle **six yin**/Goddess roles magnetically devised to complement **six yang**/god counterparts. The mating dance insures that not only will the male exit the birth canal at birth; he will be perpetually drawn back to it for repeated rebirths! The tides that course with the moon also wax and wane inside of us. The varied personae these fluxes invoke compel us to bond with different men across the spans of our lifetimes. Once a chosen lover enters our gateway his identity melds with whoever arrived on the scene prior. In a mystical manner, each man meets all men inside the fusion chamber of a woman's vaginal cave! This constitutes a bona fide Initiation process! Since virginity has been championed across the globe for centuries, many men have only encountered their own image and likeness in this mysterious coital well. But as women have increasingly claimed their liberation and opened their sexual wingspans, the vast majority has coupled with multiple partners. To those that champion celibacy, abstinence for youth, anthropologist Malinowski revealed a significant lesson in his work, *The Sex Life of Savages.* He noted that in those societies that permitted young people to freely choose initial sexual partners, long-term fidelity followed. Those youths grew into persons mature enough to make good, solid mate selections. Can anyone choose a viable partner without a basis for sound sensual comparison? Of course that freedom is precisely what insecure men, bent on the control of women want least. Sex can and should be an extremely beautiful way to know creative inspiration as well as The Creator. Tantric sex provides the path to heightened states of spiritual atonement. Rajneesh wisely related, "And lovers have often known what saints have not." Both partners may be altered through the sacred alchemy of sexual fusion. This magical potential is not only not taught, it constitutes **the** great taboo. What is gained by arguing against this mystical prospect when world societies risk forfeiting their very souls to war and gross materialism? Could the denigration of sex or demeaning of women play a role in this compromised estate? Perhaps it's time for men and women to reclaim the great gifts implicit to a sensual Eden, and at last disavow the disfiguration of sex into sin. What has so gross a distortion and focus on alleged debasement cost mankind?

In summary, the moon and sun are the quintessential archetypal duo. They are parent figures to the love stars, Venus and Mars. Both sets reflect the sacred binary code as writ into Yin and Yang, the quintessential cosmic language. Males and females on the earth plane function as its metaphorical extensions. There is a Divine plan at work as seen in the cosmic clockworks. Each planetary body holds to its own orbit, yet all interact and remain inextricably connected in their voyages through time. We are all fellow lovers, travelers on this sacred, mysterious journey called life. We need each other--men and women--and the gift of rebirth each can offer the other. The prayerful communion of two can light the world. Perhaps it can counteract this latest Dark Age where war is too casually courted. Shall we celebrate lovers or fighters this late in mankind's intended evolution? Besides, in the budding new age of Aquarius, men are invited to own their own moons by learning to honestly feel and express a full range of emotions! This is a celestial tradeoff since women have reciprocally come to own their sun-sign expressions by acquiring valid identities outside of the home in professions that once belonged exclusively to the so-called "man's world." Men now access their feminine side, or moon sign, by identifying with the domestic sphere where women are quite happy to assist by sharing the endless tasks that belong to this realm!

How To Moon Dance: Designing Your Personal Lunar Journal

Now that the theoretical case has been set for *Moon Dance*, the real excitement gets underway as you "engage the process," and watch as patterns begin to emerge from your lunar journey. *Moon Dance* claims no expert testimony over the lunar landscape; rather it's intended to provide a guided tour for you, the informed reader. Be mindful that the moon's dances elicit unique patterns of response in each of us! The very premise that you are your own authority presents a radical departure from the patriarchal context wherein collective programming becomes the established norm! *Moon Dance* turns us into budding Artemis-goddesses, rebelling against standardized labels and behavioral assumptions to arrive at our own personal truths. Before you meet the archetypes and embrace their rhythms consciously, it's helpful to draw up a guided journal. I suggest that you spend twenty minutes crafting as prop the following dial, for it will visually assist your perception of the female dimensions of time! As visual cue it will demonstrate how the archetypes rotate, so that each one gains their hour upon the grand cosmic stage.

Making Your Dial

The art of *Moon Dancing* is designed for the Goddess realized woman who has experienced the flux of her own internal rhythms long enough to sense that there's an underlying "music" animating these mood changes. We all dance with the moon. Every woman is biologically wired that way! So let's get your steps into synch. Assemble the following: Two sheets of heavyweight blank paper, a straight edge or ruler, a scissor, 2 different colored magic markers, and a twist tack that can be purchased at any office supply store. You will also need either a compass, or may substitute two circular plates of different sizes. Trace the larger plate (or compass open to 4 inches, so as to create an 8 inch radius) on one sheet of paper; then repeat the process with a smaller dish so that on the second sheet your circle's circumference will be 4-6 inches. Cut both circles out. Next with your ruler, divide each circle into twelve equal sectors. If you place the smaller circle atop the larger one, the lines of division from each should align. At this point it's fun to color the circles in. Use two colors alternately as you go around the wheel. This sets up the visual reference for "yin" and "yang." I like to use yellow and purple. Choose whatever colors you like. When you've completed this process place one wheel over the other, and then tack them together at the middle. The larger circle will function as your sundial. Its twelve delineated positions represent the twelve zodiac signs. The inner circle represents your moon dial, and it symbolizes the twelve moon signs. Now code the outer circle using numbers one through twelve to designate the natural sign succession. Repeat this process using letters A through L to code the lunar circle. You can mount your time dial on a piece of cardboard. It helps you relate to the truth about time, that everything comes full circle!

Refer to the graph below to note that the sun's position in Aries is symbolized by the number 1, while the moon's position in Aries is signified by the letter A. Since there are twelve possible positions for both the sun and moon, they form 144 combinations, each indicative of a different "relationship." (You can read a thorough analysis of these combinations, although all alignments were delineated through interactions between Venus and Mars, in *Starmates*, which I co-authored with Zolar.)

Here are the designations:

Sun sign	number	Moon sign	number
Aries	1	Aries	A
Taurus	2	Taurus	B
Gemini	3	Gemini	C
Cancer	4	Cancer	D
Leo	5	Leo	E
Virgo	6	Virgo	F
Libra	7	Libra	G
Scorpio	8	Scorpio	H
Sagittarius	9	Sagittarius	I
Capricorn	10	Capricorn`	J
Aquarius`	11	Aquarius	K
Pisces	12	Pisces	L

These are the codes that will be used inside your journal. Depending on your taste you can purchase anything from a large hardbound Mead composition notebook, to a fancier bound journal. Bookstores sell the expensive versions, yet I have found a wonderful assortment in shops like T.J. Max and Marshall's in their gift departments. Your first pages will compose chapter 1 and will be devoted to the first sign, Aries. The second chapter will represent the following month when the sun crosses Taurus. Your third chapter will coincide with the sun's passage through Gemini, and so on. Each chapter requires a minimum of twelve pages to establish a full sum of 144 page entries; so it's best to have a journal (or two) large enough to accommodate that task. If you set your journal up as recommended the deeper qualities of time will slowly emerge as personal observations enable you to recognize how you feel when the moon makes her regular crossing of each of the twelve signs, a process that recurs every month. New and ever-changing alignments color the lunar cycle as the sun complements her journey as he too progresses through each successive sign. During the course of each month the moon transits all twelve Zodiac signs. However, since your *Moon Dance* may not necessarily begin in April (given it relies on when you receive this information and choose to put it to active use), it's a good idea to code your entire journal. Then your starting place will anticipate the appropriate journal entry.

Coding your journal is easy. Page one will be depicted by 1-A to represent your personal observations when the sun and moon meet for new moon in Aries. The next page would be 1-B, and it would represent the sun-Aries combined with Moon Taurus. The next page would be 1-C, to represent the sun-Aries and Moon Gemini. When you finish labeling the first twelve pages, you move to the next chapter, which is Taurus-Demeter; and begin your pagination starting with 2-A, to represent Sun Taurus-Moon Aries. It will be followed by 2-B, representing sun-moon (this indicates new moon) both in Taurus; and then progress to 2-C for Sun-Taurus-Moon Gemini, and so on. Once again, when you reach the 12th page, which should be designated 2-L, for sun Taurus-Moon Pisces, you progress to chapter three indicative of Gemini/Mercury's realm.

This coded journal will function as your map. It will reveal your own inwardly shifting landscape. The rhythmic, episodic shifts of the moon depict the female side of time. You are now invited to explore its mysterious topography. At the onset you're apt to feel like a neophyte, but you will learn the value of charting her course by discovering its parallels with your own interior shifts. Begin where you are. Knowledge will emerge from the process itself. Suppose you begin your *Moon Dance* journal when the Sun is in Leo and the moon in Scorpio. You would turn to the fifth chapter of your book since Leo is the 5th sign, and thus represented by the digit five, your journal's fifth chapter, while Scorpio is connoted by the letter H. You locate the page designated 5-H. Write down what you feel, that's it. Add any observations about your relationship to key relatives, a loved one, or the world. For the most part during your **first year** the process of *Moon Dance* will remain in its formative stage. However, after several months, as you respond to the same moon sign, you will begin to see a pattern emerge. After your first year, you will return to the page you began on to again make your notations. By this time you should begin to experience that exhilarating "Aha!" moment having recognized where specific lunar passages elicit the same reactions and responses on your end. Of course the longer you retain your practice of self-observation the more you will learn about yourself, which is to say the rhythmic nature of personal recurrent feelings. It could be said that you've begun to mine your own archaeology. Treasure of a sort awaits your efforts!

Let me share what *Moon Dancing* has revealed to me. Please remember that because I am a fire sun/moon person, my wiring is not the same as yours. Therefore my personal impressions in response to the lunar archetypes may not match yours. We're not all meant to feel alike, respond in the same manner, or receive dynamic universal energies in the same way! Honor your uniqueness!

Sioux's Moon Dance Personal Impressions:

Moon Aries: I sense amplified levels of aggression on the road, and tangibly feel the presence of Mars in the way people drive. They push past speed limits to get to their destinations first. And while I recognize a strong fundamental sense of self, I also feel greatly isolated. Everyone seems ram-like in his "me-first" orientation which pushes me into a cocoon of solitude.

Moon Taurus: I instinctively prepare or gravitate towards great, nourishing food. My appetite increases; yet this exalted expression of the moon allots enough patience to prepare a fine meal from start to finish. It's also my favorite time to receive a massage.

Moon Gemini: Tons of email heads my way. I always receive money (my natal Jupiter, the prosperity principle is found in this sign), and I find conversation exceptionally stimulating. Just like Gemini's twins, my capacity to multi-task kicks up a notch, and I usually find myself executing several projects well at once.

Moon Cancer: I get quite moody, and like a Cancer, tend to opt for hanging out in my personal shell. It seems this position directly activates scar tissue drawn from my family life. (That may be due to tough planets found in this sign in my birth chart.) Others may respond nostalgically to past conditions or find themselves drawn into fond memories.

Moon Leo: My self-confidence rises. I often write love letters or scripts that bear highly romantic components. The inner child comes alive, and I spontaneously encounter, create, or find myself seduced by quixotic adventures. I love this time of the month.

Moon Virgo: Two significant themes emerge. First, I do laundry; then I make up a list of things that need to get done or better organized. These reflexes occur so organically that I can tell when the moon enters Virgo without checking the ephemeris or lunar calendar! I also find that my writing capacity is profoundly enhanced. I never have to search for the right word. Virgo retains a link to Mercury, the messenger, and in this sign of precision, it's clear that acumen is sharply honed.

Moon Libra: An unmistakable craving for chocolate asserts, and that's how I know the moon has left Virgo for Libra. Normally I know what I want to wear, as if an intuitive sense of color determines the day's choice without any second thought. I tend to plan ahead, too; but when the moon crosses Libra, its reputation for equivocation takes over. I find myself hesitating, wondering if taking action is necessary at all. Decisiveness is not on the menu!

Moon Scorpio: Although I am given to celibate cycles as pauses between lovers, I find the practice of Yoga deeply sensual and profoundly centering at this time. I can sense my body's issues, as if they speak direct to me from my tissues. People seem less willing to talk openly, as the secrecy principle associated with this sign asserts.

Moon Sagittarius: My travel urges explode. I often make plans to take off to some distant horizon on this lunar cycle. Otherwise, I have a strong need and desire to be outside. I love biking, hiking, or kayaking when the Moon is in Sagittarius. For me, it's the absolute worst time to be cooped up anywhere. The wild horse has to run freely!

Moon Capricorn: This is when I morph into Ms. Efficiency. Since there is no earth in my chart, I rely on this moon cycle (its reflexes come naturally, they are not imposed) to deal with life's annoying logistical tasks, the ones that require patience. For instance, if I have a credit card charge that's incorrect, this is the time of the month I can deal with phone bureaucrats or those awful automated systems. Traffic seems to move unbelievably slowly, as if a patience test is directed at me. On the plus side, it's my best time to deal with mundane duties.

Moon Aquarius: Added to the Virgo moon, this is my favorite phase for metaphysical writing or doing readings for clients. I tap into higher mind with ease and often take notes since profound personal insights seem to channel; they just "come through." Some of my most abstract thinking (including concepts for movie scripts and children's books) has come to me when the moon crossed this vitally imaginative and inventive sign.

Moon Pisces: I tend to get the blues and mull over regrets when the moon transits Pisces. I dated a dancer in college who had a Pisces moon. An excerpt from one of his poems fits its mood: "Sweep up all the broken hearts and pour them into me." Pisces is so deeply empathetic, and it trends toward martyrdom. Spiritual teachers and light-workers naturally pick up on others' sorrow during this interval. I feel for humanity and often cry without provocation at this time.

Some of my readers may be advanced *Moon Dancers* who know their moon signs, along with other key planetary positions from their birth blueprints. If you do not have this information you are fortunate that we live in the computer age where generous sources on the Internet provide this data gratis. To assist you in charting the moon's flow (as you develop your own intuitive sense of her passages) you can purchase the Lunar Calendar published by Llewellyn; or log onto the highly recommended astrology website: www.Astro.com. It will provide you with the means to view and print your birth chart (or anyone else's); progress your chart (for advanced *Moon Dancers*), and learn where the moon is on any given day. Just log on and follow the site's cues.

Riding the Edge

Even when one is forearmed by knowing the "inner weather report" that *Moon Dance* illuminates, it is impossible to avoid rough times altogether. For instance Saturn, the planet that articulates our toughest karmic lessons not only crosses our sun sign once every twenty-nine years (for a period of about twenty-eight months); it similarly spends two years contacting our moon sign(s). During these powerful, life-changing intervals that simulate what author Kurt Vonnegut termed "heavy gravity," the density of Saturn's world-weary projection is added to our own cyclic highs and lows. Needless to say this factor can exacerbate the emotional vicissitudes we experience. It's likely that many who opt for anti-depressant drugs are undergoing a major Saturn transit. This is a natural process and while anything but joyful, it's been inlaid into the cosmic clockworks for a reason. The Biblical, "A time for every purpose under heaven," is made manifest through the planetary cycles. It's been reported that depression peaks around the Christmas holidays. This happens to constitute Saturn's hour of power, for Capricorn, the sign of its dominion then assumes its term on the cosmic dial. Skeptics counter that dark moods are best explained by the lack of sunlight one experiences in winter due to the shortened span of daylight. There is a dreary cast to Saturn, who embodies as Chronos, the keeper of time in *Moon Dance*. Whatever the source or sources, none of us feel joyful and sunny every day. And it would seem that these emotional variances are part of the learning process here on this blue-green spinning sphere.

Before I crossed the big "50 yard line" my menses were as predictable as Old Faithful. I knew when the moon storm (as lyrical author Anais Nin termed it) was approaching. Not any more! The edgy feeling associated with the rapid shift in hormones added to the moon's crossings of personally vulnerable stellar sectors tests my inner sense of balance. Even though the menstrual cycle has completed its course, a "ghost dance" apparently continues that links inner processes with the cycles of the moon. It's natural to feel edgy, especially when conditions in the world are blatantly off-kilter and add a serious component of stress to our lives. How many live lives free of stress at this final phase of the Piscean age? Inner agitation also results from dietary sources and is exacerbated by elemental incompatibility. It's an astrological "given" that a natal fire sign moon will not feel especially comfortable during a water sign moon passage. (If the chart as a whole bears planets in earth-signs this would act as a counterbalance.) It's well and good to remember that there is a method to the lunar "madness." Each month She traces the path of all signs to give each its chance to shine. This system ensures that no single archetype can ultimately dominate. Through the variance in sentience imparted by the moon we are lent the capacity to feel and empathetically relate to others. Mystically speaking women "travel" with the moon; thus we meld with each of the twelve distinct Divine realms along with the personae that dwell there.

We should take "the edge" for a given and learn personal strategies for how best to negotiate it. The moods that come over us can feel scary. I once described the sense of inwardly losing control to a friend on anti-depressant medication as "all our balloons taking off at once." She asked me how I knew? That image defined it for her. Society, under the clasp of tight-reined emotions tolerates little in the form of public displays of feelings, especially when these appear to be "off balance" or inappropriate. In answer to the question, "Are you out of your mind?" *Moon Dance* responds: "Depends **which** mind (i.e. personae) you are referring to." The edge is not a comfortable place to be. The anxiety associated with it suggests a deeper implication. The fear of falling off the edge may have been carried forward via genetic memory, a legacy from our flat-earth ancestors. In their day no one dared to venture out past the evident horizon for fear of falling off a world considered by the greatest minds of their time to be flat. Later, when the realization emerged that the earth was round (a true revelation for it opened the way to expansive exploration and colonization) a new epoch began for mankind. In a sense, death remains the final edge we feel awaits our inevitable fall. If life is lived from the soul's perspective following the course revealed by mystics, then even **that edge** becomes an illusion. Given the rotary nature of time, the edgy feeling that drives a great many women towards anti-depressant drugs, alcohol, or what Mick Jagger termed "the mother's little helper" can be remedied. The truth is that even the darkest mood will soon pass. Thus the question should not be how to medicate out of it, but how to work through the energy, which itself is fleeting. When Carlos Casteneda's teacher Don Juan noted a penchant for dark moods in his budding student, he prescribed a natural remedy I put into practice: "Seek and see the marvels around you, and you will grow tired of dwelling on yourself so much."

My point is that there really is no edge to fall off! Moods roll over us like the tide, especially when we learn to roll with the lunar cycle, as she moves from sign to sign, and phase to phase. At times an atmosphere may come over us that suggests something akin to a lingering low-pressure system as graphically depicted on *The Weather Channel*. The good news is we are never left long in a dark or difficult place. However if action is taken from a compromised mental or emotional state it tends to undo us, and that can cause problems that last! The antidote is to understand your personal cycle with respect to the organic system in which time itself operates, while observing the wise Chinese adage: "If you can control yourself in a moment of anger, you save 1000 days of sorrow."

Each of us may see fit to utilize different strategies for riding the edge. My best friend Leslie recommends: "Be very good to your self." That advice has served me well. Even when my personal budget (life can be tough on us mystics) was limited, I still took myself out for dinner, preferably on the water facing a scenic horizon. Too many people waste inordinate sums on cigarettes, junk food, and cable TV. Then they complain there is no money for indulging in a holistic meal served with wine in a setting that's pure therapy for the soul. Small, simple life-affirming actions can do wonders to speed along a difficult if fleeting mood. Some women may jog or get physical to ride out the force until they (or it, given its temporal nature) become exhausted. Others may opt for a trip to the shopping mall, beauty salon, day spa, or psychologist's office. Anyone can rent a funny video since laughter is always good medicine, or call a friend, especially if you think you could be dangerous to yourself if left alone. Take a walk by the sea, or among people who seem joyful.

Remembering that our feelings follow the rotary course of the moon is useful; and it serves us well when our moods approach that ominous edge. Observing ourselves in relationship to these larger cycles provides ample evidence that we can rapidly regain our inner balance, "This too shall pass" style. Energy shifts quickly! As you become familiar with your inner moods and their resonance with the lunar cycle, you will be able to anticipate "dangerous" times.

Ultimately, you will recognize the arc of your own journey as its design emerges from the landscape of time itself imprinted by a twelve-fold character. And while feelings do prove fleeting they can be plotted. By making the effort to watch for correspondences, a great mystery is revealed: you discover the underlying rhythm structure to time.

There are those who prefer to succumb to "big pharma's" prescriptions for their mood swings. I believe such a coping mechanism comes with a price: the loss of fundamental knowledge about the self. From a spiritual perspective, opting for drugs that desensitize suggests an avoidance of intended growth. Life is not easy; it often consists of pain to foster growth. When we work to overcome and transcend our life lessons, our personal karma is improved. The Buddhists uphold a strategy that I personally applaud. Call it the "law of spiritual economy:" that you improve your own lot in life by consciously being helpful to other people. That axiom occurs by reflex when we feel at peace. An understanding of the lunar cycle and its tidal pull on our inner lives assists us in sustaining equilibrium. The knowledge of natural cycles empowers us because it allows us to anticipate those timeframes that will likely challenge us, as opposed to those that will support our aims and intentions. Armed with powerful insights, we better accommodate to our place in time. Since *Moon Dance* is an inter-active journal, your role is to observe yourself. Watch for recurrences of feelings, responses, and behaviors each time the moon returns to the same sign. Don't cheat! Just make your journal entries, and allow the truth of your responses to evidence themselves in due time. As witnessed in mastering any skill, the time you commit determines the expertise you gain. For earnest *Moon Dancers*, it will not be long before her rhythms become an integral part of your life experience.

Our next step (Part II) involves getting to know the archetypes. I have expanded the vocabulary of astrology's twelve traditional signs by merging their essences with those of key personae drawn from ancient mythology. These timeless entities are invoked by specific lunation cycles. You now embark on an amazing adventure: an encounter with **the ancient archetypes of time**. Remember, time does not just happen outside you as an abstract clause, it also happens within you by virtue of a universal tide that courses through you. You are part of it all, and it's all part of you! Don't let the outer boundary of your body fool you. Delight in the fact that your human form was designed as the instrument through which to experience the dance(s) of time. Since our anatomy consists of 75% water content, there is a profound resonance between the celestial sea and our biological immersion within it.

Part II

Meet the Archetypes

Sioux Rose

Prelude to Venus and Mars: Exiles from the Garden

There is a perfectly Divine reason why our earth is set between Venus and Mars, two complementary planets. To penetrate the full symbolic meaning, consider the law of balance. Just as the sun and moon act as pair to represent the parental dyad, Venus and Mars reflect a second planned union functioning as the Zodiac's love stars. These predictable astrological interchanges reflect a symmetry consistent with the Divine law of balance. It works through celestial polarity. One notable example is seen in earth's annual orbit whereby two specific equinox points are crossed. One occurs on March 21 to signify the onset of spring. This season of beginnings is associated with Aries and ruled by Mars. Six months later the complementary equinox takes place in Libra to signify the onset of autumn, and it's ruled by Venus. These correspondences and the powerful life cycles they warrant connect to Venus and Mars. Other powerful recurring rhythms accord with the sun and moon, and both sets portray characteristics resonant with Yin and Yang. The influence of dual elements working as complements mirrors our own genetic make-up which draws an equal sum of chromosomes from both parents. Evidence of the undeniable interplay between Divine Yin and Yang might inspire human beings if they recognized the concurrence. Mankind stands witness to a "sacred binary code" for it animates human life as well as complex planetary systems. In fact, with earth placed between the planet of love (Venus) and that of war (Mars) its inhabitants are destined to find their own balance between aggression and cooperation. If civilization learned from and elected to integrate the lessons drawn from "the higher model" into its social organizing principles, the majority of our values, actions, and perceptions would not cleave to Mars. The intended symmetry has slipped so far off course that violent combat is too often championed over art, culture, peace and diplomacy. Mankind must recover the equilibrium that's been dangerously forfeited. For several millennia church-state policies motivated by the selfish interests of elites have maintained relative order by using gender as a basis for societal division. Across the world women have been treated as second-class citizens, and scant references to God, as Mother, are ever uttered.

With emphasis solely placed on the masculine side of Creation (Sun/Mars) the equally Divine attributes of Venus (and the moon) have been forgotten, when not devalued or merely taken for granted. To live by grace, to restore our world's ecosystems to a semblance of homeostasis requires the process of "learning to balance both oars." There are fundamental distinctions between the operational instructions that govern the genders, in addition to the brain's left and right hemispheres. As appropriated to our planet's design-plan each gender has specific gifts and aptitudes, and both are intended to act as complements. Western culture and belief systems derived from the Bible have opposed this Divine symmetry by catering exclusively to patriarchal prejudices, presumptions, and predilections.

Researcher/author Dr. Alberto Villoldo rejected conventional medicine to study with the Incan shaman of Peru. His expansive adventures among Indigenous peoples led to the realization that the Judeo-Christian myth of creation is the only one that throws the lovers out of the garden. This is a very powerful message. It promotes an antithetical relationship between men and women, and human beings with nature. It also directs the powerful mojo of sin toward healthy mutual sexual attraction. The Greeks and Romans were not conditioned by this mindset since their civilizations preceded the Piscean Age. Instead of viewing the world through the divided lens of polarity their worldview involved a trinity as basis for Creation. Recall that separate, but equal powers were allotted to three brothers: Zeus/Jupiter, Hades/Pluto, and Poseidon/Neptune. Among today's faithful, brave voices like Matthew Fox challenge the church's stance regarding "Original sin." Granted the castigation of heresy, Fox sought to enlighten followers by suggesting instead a basis for "Original blessing." Although fundamentalists take Biblical text as the direct word of God, Bibles have been rewritten countless times over the centuries to suit a variety of rulers. In the process much original content has been tainted. A viable question worth posing is why the church's powerbrokers elected to distort the holy equation. (It's rather schizophrenic to define sex as a sin, but then permit it within the "sanctity" of marriage.) What authority extended to the church gave it the right to usurp the Divine equilibrium by turning intended lovers into perpetual antagonists? And what has this depraved deception cost the world? So long have gender mistrust and inequality been conditioned into our programming (consider all those tender minds brought into the folds of obedient flocks before their intellects have developed sufficiently enough to challenge alleged spiritual doctrine) that they are taken for truth! Arriving en masse at the final phase of the Piscean Age old fictions can no longer pass for absolute truths. Indeed as we separate the wheat from the chaff we experience a disorienting phase of ideological transition.

Let us return for a moment to the point in human evolution when the Age of Aries, that of the angry, jealous God who called for the sacrifice of first-born males was scheduled to give rise to the Age of Pisces thereby inviting Jesus, the gentle fisher of men to teach peace instead. Allotted the benefit of history it becomes clear that the old warring ways were never discredited or discarded. Instead Christ's name was anointed on battles to lend false legitimacy to the old habit of violence. Mars, ruler of the Age of Aries managed to maintain all-out dominion. He could not have succeeded were not mankind amenable to his darkest drives. Originally Mars subsumed the archetypes of the Divine circle into one, demanding worship of **his** image and likeness! And he turned on his beloved Venus. When the bond of true partnership was thus shattered, the world and its citizens entered into a broken wounded state. The mark of divorce was cast upon all living things. It's seen in the wonton abuse of Mother Nature as ecosystems fall asunder. Authority attributable primarily to Mars (the planetary equivalent of a "unitary executive") does not accord with the Creation blueprint set for our world. In fact on the basis of this broken covenant, cruel hierarchies have come to replace the egalitarian circle. The Divine plan sought to inhibit this very thing by allotting to Venus, Mars' counterpart, three powerful positions around the great cosmic dial. There is a place for Mars within the circle. His inclusion is necessary, for Mars represents that point in human consciousness where the self perceives itself as thus. For the purposes of learning in this earthy sphere with free will its cornerstone, cognizance of personal sovereignty is a requirement. However, given the extent that the integrity of the great circle and the relative expression of its players have been co-opted by Mars, a great trespass has occurred. Mars alone cannot speak for all! We will examine Mars further in the opening chapter of part II, for Mars as ruler of Aries awakens all sentient life each spring, and serves as the beginning point on the Zodiac's dial of time. We will go on to explore Venus in her first incarnation embodied as Taurus-Demeter, the great earth mother. An understanding of Venus is not complete without a proper explanation of the three powerful personae she assumes. When diagrammed, these form an Isosceles triangle. This network is purposely framed around Mars! If the celestial circle had been recognized as a holistic template (as opposed to its being undermined), it would have illuminated paths to reconciliation among the twelve quintessential tribes. It works as a mirror of Divine intention. Plus Mars would never have been able to seize such utter and complete dominion over our world. Note the degree to which creative, constructive technologies have given way to weapons development and an obscene international trafficking in arms! When war is planned for profit the monster is let out of the (cosmic) box, or should I say triangle!

Venus presides over Taurus where she actualizes the Earth Mother principle in the persona of Demeter. Her inordinate bounty in the form of precious gems, ore, rivers, and forests is given freely to the children of earth. As Al Gore heroically championed in his environmental documentary, *An Inconvenient Truth*, basic rules of sound stewardship are required of human beings if they expect to continuously partake of the natural world's riches. Instead the vast majority takes too much for granted. Mars misuses his intended power when he turns on Venus to act as destroyer rather than lover and protector. Mars as warrior repeatedly renders arable land into militaristic dead zones. The placental earth is turned into radioactive badlands. As the Zodiac illustrates, Taurus-Demeter, Venus's first portrayal, sits alongside Mars-Aries on the great cosmic dial.

In her second incarnation, Venus appears as Hera, wife of Zeus and champion of marriage. Associated with Libra, the zodiac's 7th house principle, she connotes the status of marital union. In this position, Venus sits directly across from Mars. Polar opposites, the two signs form an axis that represents the interplay of the twin equinoxes, spring and autumn. The pair engages in a seasonal dance that symbolically involves a transfer of power. Intended Divine counterparts, their relationship demonstrates true gender parity. However, manmade religions by attributing Divine will entirely to a "masculine" fabrication of the Infinite have excluded all notions of a holistically balanced cosmic order. Taken as not quite Divine, the female has been left out of the universal equation, and denied her co-equal status. Treated as a possession (formerly as property), we see a related lack of reverence in how **man**kind treats Earth Mother and lays claim to Her sizable treasures. Homage made exclusively to the masculine side of the Deity breaks the first covenant which requires a balanced interplay between the energetic expressions of Yin and Yang. The resulting lack of symmetry has led to massive breakdown for essentially the holy circle has been effectively dismantled. Where the twelve archetypal expressions were devised to people a colorfully diverse world, authoritarian religious institutions instead demanded uniformity upon threat of death! (So-called heretics often championed better ways, but their understanding served as a threat to those who profited from the status quo.) The limits placed on human beliefs and behaviors have effectively sent heavens diverse personae into exile! And the motor of conformity kept on churning, lending to the church-state the false conviction that it owns the right to denigrate entire races of people, starting with the Indigenous. When vast numbers weren't killed or sacrificed to sadistic religious rites, they were abducted into the horror of slavery.

The Zodiac circle provides a basis for an egalitarian, balanced world society. When its wisdom is not honored all sorts of inequality emerge, each prejudice with its own twisted rationale. Women and "minorities" have suffered inordinately in America, yet a similar brutal history has unfolded across the globe. For centuries women (along with minorities) could not vote, own property, or travel freely. Without elaborating via historical examples suffice it to say that when Mars seized dominion the liberty, equality, and full expressive range of women was placed into ultimate jeopardy. Inequality and injustice in addition to sexism and racism, have endured for millennia. All this time established governing bodies have essentially engaged in Mars' rules! Far too many intelligent people take unjust, unequal conditions for the norm, evidence of the way the world works. Notably when Venus assumes her second persona as Hera, she brings the zodiac realm of law and justice to life. Governing this sector of jurisprudence she stands in Divine opposition to Mars. He may champion war, but she champions the cause of diplomacy. When put into practice which approach has proven the more cost-effective, time-tested means for avoiding loss?

In her third and final incarnation, Venus is extended a special status. She is "exalted" in Pisces. It is the sign kingdom that sits on the other side of Aries, its cosmic neighbor. From this last house (12th) on the great cosmic dial Venus illuminates a key metaphysical law depicted by the circle itself. The circle holds no discernible endpoint so it ultimately meets itself. This symbolic property reflects that all things are ultimately connected and come full circle. Akin to the law of karma, it's clear that what you do unto others will eventually return to you. Pisces' special gift is compassion. On the basis of empathy we are able to extend forgiveness. It's equally wise to hold compassion for ourselves, since as a result of our human imperfections we tend to miss the mark. This last sign can be treacherous. It is here that the soul must show it has mastered the lower impulses of the ego. (These take us back to Aries and the egocentric projection of Mars, as governor of the first house). Not only is the 12th house tied to karma, it is termed the zone of "self-undoing." In her final incarnation Venus coaches mankind to learn the "higher love" by acting with concern for the whole, rather than the personal ego alone. How else to transcend naked self-interest, that which works against the progress of the soul?

The powerful mystical experiences that dissolve the ego also accord with the 12th house. Tantric sex falls under this umbrella. Sex can serve as a gateway to enhanced spiritual states. I believe the old church patriarchs instinctively understood the power inherent to deeply sensual acts of bonding. Instead of inviting human beings to gain spiritual empowerment through this natural channel, they rendered sex the great taboo! Historically this planned schism has wreaked damage so pervasive I term it "the great wound." Venus free to fulfill her Divine mandate in the persona of Aphrodite invites Mars, her heavenly consort, to experience the ecstasy of the soul-mate union, which a friend described as a "straight shot to God."

It's interesting that Judeo-Christian theology names **Adam** the first man. The nomenclature runs eerily parallel with the world of physics in that **atoms** constitute the first identifiable particles of matter, of Creation. Given the Biblical admonition: "Let no man tear asunder what God hath joined together," note the sinister repercussions that have occurred since the atom was bombastically split. Not only have grave dangers been visited upon mankind perhaps as a direct result of nuclear fission, this tearing into the very fabric of matter, a dark signature of Mars' insatiable quest for conquest suggests a parallel splitting apart of much more. It's as if the quintessential equation of life itself has been broken since the nuclear bombs burst over Hiroshima and Nagasaki. This lethal tearing into the very fabric of Creation has reverberated in the form of an inordinately high divorce rate and parallel decimation of species. The march to militarism led by the U.S in its role as weapons' merchant to the world now threatens entire ecosystems, inviting a veritable collapse of the web of life! This world was not built to serve Mars alone, nor can Mars by his lonesome make life. The sexism embedded into patriarchal religions and furthered through nationalism has done a disservice to mankind. By downplaying the equal input of women, legacy of the insidious omission of the Divine feminine, humanity has been playing the game of life with half a pack! It's been forced to navigate its shared vessel with only one equivalent oar. Naturally it takes two oars to row upstream, or experience progress. Instead the insistence on only the male perspective causes "history to repeat." For added irony experts observe this "fact" and take it for mankind's inevitable destiny! A far more progressive course would result from the blend of both perspectives; that is logic integrated with feelings. The resultant new hybrid would foster a more enlightened type of wisdom than the one mankind has been thus far limited to. Cultivating the qualities of complementary sentience promises mankind other than recurrent war and conflict.

If Mars' rule does not succeed in bringing on a nuclear holocaust in tribute to himself; then our descendants will look upon our epoch the way we currently view our ancestors' conviction that the earth was flat. Stemming from a sexist mindset the best scientific minds insist our universe resulted from a big bang. It sounds ridiculously akin to the ejaculatory fantasy of a teenage boy, albeit one with an advanced science degree. Evident in this masculine projection is the utter absence of any feminine counterpart. Yet since our gender makeup requires an equal sum taken from both parent/genders, and because the seasons change to grant complementary expressions to Yin and Yang, why would evidence of the union of opposites be entirely left out of the orthodoxies of physics as well as established religion? Such purposeful exclusion blindsides recipients to the higher truth **that our Universe is a love song**, that creation is still creating itself, and it's fueled by something majestic, something akin to cosmic communion! It is crucial that we amend our beliefs to accord with the balance reflected in the great cosmic circle that forms the basis for the dance of time, for movements that course through us and regulate our most intrinsically personal passages. Otherwise a theory like "big bang" will remain in vogue. Used (perhaps subliminally) to defend weaponry, it makes the end product of explosive force something holy. Access to diverse fiery devices turn what otherwise might be thoughtful men into warriors. In homage to Mars flawed individuals temporarily transcend their mortal status by gaining access to the dark godly power of shock and awe. A great many soldiers thereby express their own private renditions of the big bang. And note too that the vast majority of weapons happen to be shaped like readily identifiable phallic extensions! Consider the basic design of bullets, missiles, rockets, submarines, and bombs! In whose image and likeness are these diabolical tools of destruction made? Mars is a destroyer, and that's why the heavenly circle reflects a time-tested, mathematically sound protection plan suitable for reining in this unruly principle, and confining him to an established place and role! It's a lethal fiction to ascribe God's will to Mars' claim to a cosmic exclusivity clause whereby he effectively disables the expressions of the Zodiac's eleven other co-equal archetypes. Mankind's continued homage to Mars is not only deadly; it clearly has led the world to a bona fide dead-end. In every instance wherein a person looks down on another on the basis of sex, religion, race, or nationality fuel is added to Mars' hellfire. We have come to the end of the Piscean age, and the irreconcilable opposition suggested by its symbolic two fish must be transcended. Whether the dueling fish signify nations, religious camps, or the two genders, antipathy has led to impossible levels of madness. Once considered a bona fide Cold War strategy

M.A.D. is a fitting moniker for **mutually assured destruction,** a goal the military's mindset thought worth pursuing! The "logic" behind this deranged strategy is that it would be better for the U.S. to launch an all-out attack that would virtually leave no person living rather than lose a war! Winning is all, the modern armchair warriors proclaim. Few have been to the front lines to recognize that the word loses any remote meaning when senseless devastation fouls the air and deadens the souls of onlookers. Is this goal the one that should claim the lion's share of our nation's tax dollars? Such distorted priorities arise when Mars sways minds and permits no dissenting spiritual voice to challenge his claim to invincibility, not to mention immutable authority.

Following the "As above, so below" inviolate equation, the onset to the third millennium corresponded with the dubious election of a "president" that referred to himself as the unitary executive. Like Mars he took it upon himself to essentially dismantle the careful checks and balances built into the American system of law and governance, and willfully pursued a war against a contrived concept (terrorism) along with its elusive perpetrators. Sending brute force across the globe on a mission to extinguish purported enemies has instead led to an exponential increase in violence. In the name of protecting domestic freedoms his administration has eviscerated civil rights and placed long-established liberties in jeopardy. Many prophecies point to this epoch as a time of a vast and powerful reckoning, a cycle of cleansing. Clearly the world cannot remain on its current ideological course.

In such times of challenge and transition it is beneficial to lift our understanding by considering the inherent truths writ into heaven's circle and coordinated cosmic codes. When we acknowledge the wisdom implicit to this model we realize that the world must now call for an all-out censoring of Mars. While impeachment of the current United States president was taken off the table by Athena persona Nancy Pelosi so that a war of aggression, what The Geneva Conventions term a crime against humanity escapes redress, Bush as the personification of Mars has left the damning data behind. The public record reveals that a war of choice was premeditated with the result catastrophic levels of death and destruction. The God that patriarchy has fashioned against nature along with natural elements of our very selves is the enemy to life. We now live in a world where love is rare, but war is not. How then to get back to the garden, reclaim the circle, and encourage the healed embrace of lovers intended as such from the outset. We must recognize that Creation was not a big bang; it is ever a love song; and we, its progeny are the living fruit of an eternal attraction between co-equal Creative forces. This is why Venus, the principle of love in her myriad forms and counterbalance to Mars has been allotted three ruling sectors, while Mars only one.

Christ, the Divine **son** has been worshipped during the past twenty-two centuries. He arrived to serve as avatar, herald to the Age of Pisces. Now as Aquarius dawns, the time has come for an equivalent acknowledgement of the Divine daughter. Because this entity will strongly influence the nascent Aquarian Age, which answers to the rebel planet Uranus, I chose as its representative a non-traditional persona. Her essence accords with rule breaking, and strikes out boldly in pursuit of new discovery. If Apollo the sun god reflects the Divine son (he may signify Christ), why would his twin sister Artemis not signify the equally Divine daughter? As twin to her Divine brother she is his biological equal and drawn from the same Source. And when allotted dominion over Aquarius, Artemis assumes her throne directly across the Zodiac from Leo-Apollo, acting as his polarity. These twins serve as a striking pair, one destined to govern the Zodiacal axis that will play a key role in mankind's upcoming transition. Is there any question that a radical altering of society's fabric is called for? Already a massive awakening is being summoned as the Divine feminine prepares to assume its role as cosmic counterbalance here on earth. How else can humanity rise and break free of its recidivistic flirtation with endless war and yet another Dark Age?

The principle of polarity is fundamental to the Creation blueprint and demonstrates itself in yet another manner. During the course of the year as noted four sets of lunar cycles activate the sign realms of Venus and Mars, with yet two more directly energizing Leo and Cancer, domains ruled by the sun and moon. Thus **half** of each year's lunar alignments catalyze a dynamic interplay between Yin and Yang. These cycles act as our mirrors. Often they reflect the relative state (balance or its absence) of our closest ties. Who can deny the evidence of night and day? What the astro-logos offers are inconvenient truths to those that would prefer to keep the blinders on, even when the long-established asymmetric rules of engagement have ostensibly driven mankind to the cusp of disaster. Tradition-based rules have been granted homage in service to false orthodoxies. These have then been passed down through many generations. It is time to ask if these unchallenged premises reflect the truth of Creation, or the best that mankind can collectively enact. Only love will heal our wounded Eden, only a return to the intended balance will foster mutual respect, appreciation, and a healthier basis for genuine communion. New behaviors guided by a higher understanding are needed in this phase of global transformation. The *Moon Dance* woman is well prepared to make her unique contribution to an emerging not yet fully awakened world.

And Now May I Introduce The Archetypes Of Time To You! Let the Adventure in expanded Self-discovery Begin!

In the following chapters you will encounter the core projections of the twelve key archetypal expressions that "inhabit" the Zodiac's circle. These personae form the Divine ring of the heavens. By consciously observing your feelings and impressions in relation to time's thematic shifts, your lunar journal will be transformed into a powerful tool. It will guide you to align with the purposes of time. Each persona will be brought to life in a way that makes it distinguishable. Not only will you bear witness to the archetypes of time as they color your own experiences, you will also recognize how these energies impact the persons closest to you. Studying the forces at work privileges you to learn a great deal. Keynoted is a growing awareness of that organic process that accords with time's intrinsic changes of tenor. Truly each of us is a galaxy on the inside! In the next twelve chapters, I invite you to ask these questions:

How much do I recognize myself as Mars, the rugged individualist?

How much do I identify with Demeter, the opulent nurturer?

Is my dominant personality flavor more akin to Mercury, the

gifted communicator? Or perhaps Athena, business woman and insider to power?

Do I fly high on romantic dreams like Apollo?

Or stay close to the earth, learning the herbs that heal as Hestia would instruct?

Am I a staunch believer in equal partnership, kin to Hera?

Or a Persephone questing to understand the mysterious power of sexuality?

Could I be a naked Pan who feels best running freely in the natural world?

Or a born Chronos, ever planning my next strategic move, the clock always ticking?

Perhaps I was cut from the mold of Artemis, a New Age woman ready to rock the world by challenging its previous standards and limited expectations?

Who among us does not identify with the alluring Aphrodite who knows instinctively what sensual congress can mean for the soul, perhaps even for the evolution of the spirit?

Chapter 1

Aries: The Realm Of Mars Awakened
(Recognizing and Taming the Warrior Within)

Aries is the first sign on the Zodiac dial. It is masculine (yang) and correlates with the Biblical Adam, the purported original man first to live on earth. Indeed, Aries likes to be first: the first one to land on the moon, win the race, or obtain the virgin's heart and become the first and presumably only one granted "internal access" to her feminine domain. Linked to the inception of spring, Aries is the sign fortified by that force that summons life's regenerative powers from the eternal source of renewal. Plant life cloaked in winter's semblance of death yields to a rich canopy of newborn greenery. Hibernating animals leave their hollows and return to the warm embrace of the sun. The vast majority of species is compelled to mate in spring; and so begin the rituals of courtship. The songs of birds enrich our mornings. Their often intricate tunes have inspired poets, April fool lovers, and those lucky enough to spend time ambling through parks and green places in pursuit of the joys of spring. Yes, this life force is a great and mighty thing. Wielded positively, its unstoppable passion can build a city, render expressive marvels to fill the greatest of museums, or send bold souls off to distant lands in pursuit of discovery. The **positive** Mars is seen best in the archetypes of lover, creative artist, adventurer, pioneer and discoverer. However Mars becomes a bane to mankind's existence when he steps out of his appointed position in the circle and falls prey to his own lowest impulses, those of rabid destruction. Aries is linked to the first chakra. This invisible vortex is associated with the raw energy sometimes necessary for survival. In early human evolution it was favored since the capacity to meet and conquer immediate threats was mandatory. Mars, along with the first chakra, fuels the human sex drive and animates the basic procreative urge. Even after centuries of antagonistic gender-based programming, the human sex drive remains formidable enough to overcome the chasm set between men and women in their quest for ultimate intimacy. The mating urge remains unstoppable. The fiery passions that Mars embodies both threaten and ensure the continuity of human life.

Mars is also the planetary embodiment of anger. The Ancient Chinese related wisely: "If you can control yourself in a moment of anger, you save a thousand days of sorrow." Great advice for taming this wild force! The road rage driver who invariably crashes will face higher insurance rates for about three years. Quite a literal depiction of those thousand days! Spending a good deal of time on the road one can't help but notice the fury that propels too many motorists. Speed limits are seldom respected. Whether it's navigating dangerous routes in places as remote as the cliffs of Maui to the winding forest roads of Georgia, there is an unmistakable sense that the person(s) behind is all too willing to risk my life along with his own in a speed driven zeal oblivious to anything but the rush itself! In such hurried states persons notice nothing and remain oblivious to the condition of their world. No time is given to stop or feel what exists all around them; or to be present to this alive and sentient world.

In astrological theory the sun, masculine primary life force is **exalted** in Aries. This makes cosmic sense since Aries rouses the spirit of new beginnings perpetually from the timeless ethers as well as the collective consciousness. Although there are considerable destructive powers associated with Mars, it must be stated that every sign and its ruling planetary principle carries both positive and negative applications and expressions. Since every person's birth chart holds a Mars influence, the lessons associated with this planet are not restricted exclusively to those with sun or moon in Aries. As a Moon dancer, you will gradually come into accord with (perhaps even integrate) each story of time. The state of your ego will likely make itself known when Mars is awakened during his reign through Aries.

The Divine intention set for Mars as first principle is to establish each individual's capacity to experience a separate sense of person-hood or individualism. How can the gift of free will express if a person is not operating under her own auspices? The risk here is that the force of individuation may awaken before the countervailing lessons revealed by the other sign principles have been established. The circle model in its entirety provides for intended and necessary counterbalances. These are needed to checkmate the violent propensities that arise from Mars. Each of the twelve Divine principles is a facet of the Zodiac as well as our selves. Since Mars is affiliated with the first sign it awakens the essence of being, and the eventual realization that we are gifted with a Divine spark that endows us with life. Mars signifies the human ego recognizing itself as a separate entity. The first fiery planet inspires athletic competition, the thirst for new discovery, and a firm will, prerequisite to achieving anything on one's own initiative. Its inherent passion can be likened to a double-edged sword, for Mars can just as easily burn down a city as build one. This is why the Biblical scripture: "He who conquers himself is greater than he who conquers a city" makes genuine spiritual sense. An awakened self that does not recognize the rightful boundaries of others becomes dangerous to society. Might only makes right when Mars alone rules. It's been said by expert historians who have pored over the data drawn from seemingly endless wars that "the enlightened warrior best understands the benefits of peace." In other words, the soldier who has experienced battle is unlikely to enter into any willing replay having seen firsthand the unspeakable destruction that war inevitably results in.

Many authorities believe mankind's nature is inherently violent and competitive. The classic novel *Lord of the Flies* assumes this perspective; but fails to account for the social conditioning of the young British boys. Immersed in a society given to aggression, itself the product of a cruel hierarchical structure, these imprints affected the boys long before they became stowaways on a deserted island. Unconsciously the young men recapitulated what they'd already learned. Brutality figured mightily into the mix. Can we therefore use this example as a viable prototype for the alleged "natural order?" Consider the following true event as related on the website: www. commondreams.org. Researchers have noted that baboon societies function on the basis of a strict social hierarchy wherein the dominant males eat first. In the incident cited a Kenyan resort left contaminated food in its outdoor garbage bins which baboons were known to frequently forage. As it turned out the dominant males ate the tainted food and died off. What surprised the observing researchers was that a very different social order resulted when the less dominant males took their places! The new males did not repeat the behaviors of their dominant male peers. Instead roles between males and females became more egalitarian. In other words, Mars need not always rule! Because might has claimed to make right and managed to dictate societal structures for centuries, a great many people erroneously deduce that this arrangement reflects all that could be!

History provides ample evidence to support the theory that human nature is "by nature" inherently violent. One question worth pursuing is: where does the rage that endlessly fuels aggression originate? Apart from tribal clashes that foment ancient vendettas or involve competition over scarce resources, there is also the matter I term "the great wound." Western teachings stem from the religious belief that the first lovers were expelled from Eden and taught that their natural attraction for one another was wrong. A false schism was engineered, and it's held over the centuries under the guise of "original sin." If the sex urge, a strong component of human nature, was implanted to insure the continuity of humanity, then how could it be wrong or sinful? Wilhelm Reich, whose research has been largely discredited by those who benefit from the suppression of his conclusions, offers illuminating insights on this subject. His book, *The Function of Orgasm* dared to examine the dark question few researchers have ever approached. As a German citizen he wished to understand how ordinary citizens could be easily seduced by the martial propaganda of an Adolph Hitler. This subject coincides with this chapter's focus on Mars since Hitler identified strongly with the concept of the Aryan (Mars rules Aries) race. Hitler happened to have been born on the cusp between Aries and Taurus. One could flip through the pages of history and find a great many warriors born under the sign that champions conflict! Saddam Hussein comes to mind. In any case Reich formulated a fascinating theory. He believed human psychology and resultant behaviors stem from an interaction among three levels of consciousness. The first level identified represents the basic naturally uninhibited self. Think Adam and Eve before any apple entered the picture. The next level is essentially manufactured by society in its effort to repress that natural self. The third level, according to Reich, operates as a thin veneer of politeness blanketed over the inevitable tensions generated by the interplay of the former two. While modern society has loosened up considerably (although a resurgence of fundamentalism currently attempts to reverse this trend) human beings have been restricted by countless "minuets of protocol" throughout history. Reich saw the hypocrisy and understood its cost to humanity. He explained further that the three planes of personhood operate much like tectonic plates. When they are forced to abrade the veneer eventually bursts and out comes the sort of violence associated with volcanic eruptions. Reich believed individuals taught that their natural inclinations were wrong were left at war with themselves. The ensuing discomfort turned them against their own basic instincts and the result was their accepting an outside authority figure to make firm decisions for them. Enter the Fuhrer. Was Reich onto something? He, too, was an Aries and understood the power of the sex drive, and how its inversion could warp healthy expressions. Sexual repression, now popularized by the authoritarian Christians in the U.S. is the weapon patriarchal religions use to beat populations into submission. The relevance of this subject to political controls remains mostly a taboo. Parallels between Nazi Germany and current U.S. trends are chilling. The myth of German supremacy and its reverence for the male super-hero was also explored by Leon Uris. In his novel *Armageddon* Uris exposes the dark seduction of the German collective psyche in its near worship of Hitler. Countless citizens managed to look away from Hitler's brutal policies of social engineering as he nearly succeeded in exterminating an entire race.

Astrology sheds light on what fuels state-sponsored violence. The planet Mars is **exalted** in Capricorn, the sign that champions tradition, authority, and conservative values. Capricorn identifies the father as the sole filial authority, and applauds a social basis instrumental to the hierarchical state. Later when we explore the persona of Chronos (who governs the Zodiac's 10th sign-realm) we'll note how the strict father model extends respect to militant authority figures. In sum, Mars supports the pecking order and champions contests that celebrate raw strength and brute force.

Since the human ego and its potential for aggression will always factor into the mortal equation, how can this aspect of ourselves be better utilized? Could persons with an inborn streak of militarism instead be confined to exploding not weapons, but rather elaborate firework displays? Rated by judges from around the world within an artistic context perhaps they'd transcend the need to expel violent ordnance. Such spectacles would invite those who rally for war to instead do their "blast off thing" where victory is no longer defined through a body count. Rather such a status would be earned on the basis of pyrotechnic mastery! Because to stop and think about it, imagine how differently history might have evolved had gunpowder never been invented? Give that premise some thought in relation to Mars, the archetypal inventor and inspiration behind all forms of armaments. He's certainly kept up with modern times. Well-budgeted he's made potent use of vast technological inroads to upgrade his dazzling array of firearms. Much of it stuns the imagination. Yet to support this species of "shock and awe" as seen in the capacity to wipe out entire nation's population pools is morally obscene. When it comes to the myriad ways to deliver death, destruction, and dismemberment, unquestionably Mars rules. Given its military budget, the U.S. pays genuine homage to this god of war.

The warrior archetype may remain a permanent fixture of the human experience, but it's vital to recognize that Mars is not the only viable masculine prototype. Due to Mars' domination of world culture, its image and likeness have sadly proven to be the ones that most directly imprint men. As a college student I lived in London and regularly visited the Royal Galleries. My favorite painter is the Italian Renaissance man, Botticelli. His renditions of Venus and Mars are not only visually compelling, they are also prescient. He chose to paint the great goddess of physical bounty in a way that witnesses the warrior absolutely cowering in her presence. She towers over him. The psychological symbolism suggests men are more comfortable with the unknown variable of secret enemies faced in combat, than in coming to understand the power of love and the spell of vulnerability it casts over them. In Jack London's lesser-known novel, *The Star Rover,* his central character spends time in prison and learns about an inmate left in that most unfortunate restraining device known as "the jacket." To assuage pain this prisoner mastered the art of astral projection and related a poetic vision experienced through his "time travels." Profoundly romantic, it envisions mortal life as the quest of one man (symbolizing everyman) seeking to embrace his beloved, who signifies every woman. From an incarcerated state the inmate attained the gift of enlightenment because he was able to note that human life becomes the intended extension of the universe's own everlasting mating dance, that continuous interchange between Yin and Yang. Whenever this pure force is repressed, violence results. On the other hand when two persons feel enough attraction to take down the walls their egos erect, they are supremely gifted with a communion that involves a oneness of mind, body, and spirit. This connection can lead to high states of ecstasy. "Sex guru" Rajneesh provided significant insight into this dynamic. In *Tantra, Spirituality & Sex* he explains the transition that overtook India once the "Christianization" process set in. Previously sexual rites associated with Tantra had been celebrated. Many people experienced a direct and powerful spirituality through its disciplined sexual practice. Essentially Tantra teaches a methodology to delay climax. Choosing instead to sustain the state of bodies joined opens a virtual conduit that allots access to higher states of consciousness. Prior to Christian beliefs entering India temple art abounded in depictions of the Shivalinga: a graphic symbol portraying genitals united! Once Western groups began touring India's temples people naturally inquired about these oft-depicted shapes, wondering what they represented. Western patriarchal indoctrination showed its pervasive face, as Rajneesh related, when a guide responded, "Hush. This is a private matter!" European Christian values brought shame, and succeeded in eroding the practices of sexuality that link to mystical sentience. The conditioning attached to "original sin" has prevented citizens of Western cultures from grasping the spiritual significance of lovingly expressed sexuality. A collective angst has been cultivated in its place, and it's turned millions against their natural instincts thereby ensuring a ready supply of aggression, the psychic ingredient necessary to fuel conflict (along with every heinous weapon system). Recent American history saw a president impeached for lying about a sexual indiscretion, while a president who's engineered a war of aggression on a fraudulent basis has essentially been given a free pass! Is there a more telling example of the disproportionate status allotted to Mars in our current world order than this?

The state of humanity under the covert dominion of Mars could not be more imperiled. Need more proof that Mars rules? How about a recent initiative on the part of the U.S. military to resume nuclear tests in the Nevada desert utilizing a weapon named "**Divine Strake**"? Mars is an indisputably powerful force, but it's intended to preserve rather than take life away. The gross distortion attendant upon its flagrant misuse must be remedied. Perhaps if each human being learned to personally redirect his own inner rage we would see a reduction in the collective violence expressed in and through our world.

Fundamentalist Muslims and Christians share a similar misconception. Both sects place the undue burden of sexual abstinence on adolescents just when biology asserts a natural awakening of those intended urges. In the Muslim world, women are wrapped in bourkhas and forbidden even innocent social contact with young men. Imagine the schizophrenic state of young evangelical Christians bombarded by a mainstream media that telegraphs a steady stream of sexual imagery while they are instructed to restrain themselves as the tide of hormones ripens precisely at their age? In either cultural milieu the resulting sexual repression fuels the kind of rage that makes for a ready fodder of willing soldiers. Lately the Middle East has heated up as violence has spread like a brushfire. This area, the birthplace of three of the world's entrenched patriarchal religions has become a hotbed of antipathy. Could this result from these religions teaching exclusivity rather than unity? The price of division grows by the day. The fabric of history is stained with inordinate quantities of blood. Mars has expressed in blood senselessly shed in nearly every culture; but it seems the White man takes the prize. It is not that Caucasian males are more prone to violence than men of other cultures. It's that European culture directly embodied the archetype of Mars in its aggressive reach into other lands.

Stemming from the transition of Ages once Pisces rose to replace the ideological references drawn from the Age of Aries, the portrait of the Deity as an angry, vengeful god was never overcome.

Mistaking violence for God's will, the white male plundered the Red race as seen in the decimation of indigenous populations of North and South America. Dutch, French, Spanish and English explorers all felt superior to those they conquered. In the name of the church they demanded "conversions" and tortured those on the receiving end of their "religious" convictions. Another substantial debt is owed to the Yellow race as a result of Vietnam, and the ungodly release of nuclear bombs over Nagasaki and Hiroshima. Likewise, an enormous karmic debt is owed to the Black race for the institution of slavery. Not only did it ravage Africa for many generations, its shadow remains embedded in "the dark continent," and nourishes the continued savagery of tribe-on-tribe brutal conflicts. Currently the debt extends to the brown race as tragically witnessed by the dubious Iraqi debacle. To this ungodly legacy we add the grotesque statistics that point to worldwide matricide beginning with a virtual holocaust conducted against women of power and wisdom during the Middle Ages. Thus Mars owes a phenomenal debt to women. Clearly the expressions of Mars are out of control in the world a great many tribes were destined to cohabit. It's time he was roped back into his appointed position as per the Holy circle that Divine balance might be restored! All suffer as a result of his claim to primacy; that he represents the one true God that nations have fallen to their knees falsely defending!

Where can we find role models of male heroes that make for a healthier society? Years ago Hollywood portrayed the man of character as the hero. Gregory Peck comes to mind as he took on the racist system of justice in the Deep South in the classic: *To Kill a Mockingbird*. He exemplified the gentle strength of goodness coupled with the power of conviction! James Stewart comes to mind in the role of the good citizen who places self-interest aside in order to uphold the greater good in the film classic, *It's A Wonderful Life*. This type of altruism is made conspicuous by its absence in today's media. Many films utilize actors it seems to stylize the latest fashion in guns and weaponry. Such depictions desensitize the nation to its own martial impulses. Is it sane that America has over two billion guns on its streets while two million citizens are currently incarcerated in this "land of the brave?" The vast majority of inmates suffer from alcohol or drug addiction, yet precious little effort or investment is made in drug or alcohol rehabilitation. The penal system along with related components of our society relies upon inordinately punitive measures and tactics. Cruelty tends to beget more cruelty. Where is the compassion? It's found missing in action when Mars rules!

How many war veterans have managed to avoid substance-abuse behaviors? Portions of their psyches maimed from combat remain etched in shadows. Many escape from the conscience(s) they can't live with by utilizing a variety of self-medication strategies. Iraqi war veterans exhibit severe signs of post-traumatic stress disorder, and suicide rates run high. Killing others is not natural, so this response isn't surprising. Even if combat soldiers return sound in body their minds will forever be haunted by acts of barbarianism. I recently did an accounting of past lovers and family members. Almost every male had served in one branch of the military or participated in outright war! We women routinely lay with men who have undergone the ritual camps of Mars and been baptized in unholy blood shed. This remains the norm as long as Mars rules.

Some would say Mars is necessary as defense given our world's history of violence; but the circle model has not been seriously respected or as yet utilized. It provides the blueprint (as well as instructions) for reining in Mars. Otherwise karmic blowback will ensure an endless continuation of war and aggression. The fact that evil and its manifold intentions test human society raises the question how best it can be fought or otherwise countered. Direct battles inevitably lead to new scars, and while the various Masters have taught the power of forgiveness, relatively few persons and societies put this spiritual medicine into practice. The *I Ching*, as oracle, addresses this matter in a manner that is both timeless and contemporary. It concludes that evil cannot be fought by direct means. Mirroring the words of Christ, the teacher of peace, it ingeniously advises that instead of focusing energy on combating evil, it is more effective "To make energetic progress in the good." That's another way of saying, "Turn the other cheek." Consider the evidence: Have America's wars on crime? Poverty? Terrorism? Fat? Illiteracy? ever actually altered any of these conditions for the better? I think not. Rather than get embroiled in struggles that can never be won, The *I Ching* advises that we must invest in alternative strategies and creatively redirect our energies. Metaphysical author Emmet Fox echoes this wisdom by suggesting we build "new mental equivalents." And seer Edgar Cayce concurred by reminding: "Mind is builder." Aries, as sign of the head, relates to the beliefs that guide persons as well as nations. Ideas act as a foundation for how we live and form the basic philosophical structures of societies.

Given that eleven archetypal expressions follow Aries' starting place on the great dial of time, Mars' fundamental projections must coordinate with the other equally Divine zodiac personae. This ideal is yet to be realized in our world. And while Mars is fueled by passion, it becomes a worthwhile attribute only when it's directed at life-affirming acts. When individuals are divorced from natural drives and at war with themselves they are bound to express themselves in detrimental ways. Jean Shinoda Bolen defines Mars as both warrior and lover. I have encountered both archetypes in the same man having lived with an Aries male who periodically broke into fits of Mars' primal rage. Then he would morph into an inordinately tender lover. Cosmic chemistry is a powerful force, and explains why people connect without any evident basis for true or lasting compatibility. I've always wondered if men prone to violence could be conditioned to act differently had they satisfying, sexually nurturing harbors to defuse their abundant angst? I was clearly not the only female considering this option. An ad ran in *Harper's* for some time promoting the book: *The Woman Who Slept With Men to Take the War Out of Them*. Women who venture into intimacy with such men (or with actual warriors) run risks. The news program *60 Minutes* ran a report that exposed the extremely high rates of domestic abuse seen in military families. The crux of this story was the uncomfortable fact that women who reported their spouses' violent behavior to commanding officers saw little redress. Like other "boy's clubs," the military generally assumes a "bubba" attitude. Its covert message is that soldiers given to domestic abuse are just not manly enough to keep their little ladies in line. Sexism remains the unspoken fact of world culture with all too few exceptions. Feminists worked hard to expose that truth and alter its dynamics; however as author Susan Faludi noted in *Backlash*, attacks against equal rights and gender equity have never stopped. Aided and abetted by an ultra-conservative Supreme Court a vicious undertow now takes aim at female reproductive freedom. The rise in religious fundamentalism sees millions returning to patriarchal, authoritarian creeds that make the father the uncontested head of the family. Between the televangelists and a pervasive, well-funded Christian publishing apparatus, recidivistic rightwing initiatives operating under the guise of the church have prompted women to submit to their husbands as if this behavior conforms to God's will! At the time of this writing, Sarah Palin, a newcomer to the political scene but favorite of Evangelicals, is being promoted as a "feminist" leader. Her beliefs are anything but! As real power aggregates into corporate hands and wealth fails to trickle down, Promise Keepers events fill athletic stadiums promising blue-collar men the authority lost in the workplace can be reclaimed in their homes! Religions of this sort function as macho sports with women expected to remain in the bleachers delivering iced tea and popcorn as needed, a whole new take on jock support!

Dr. John Gray made a fortune using simple binary terms to explain the social conditioning mechanisms that effectively link men symbolically to Mars. He pointed out that female behavior is socially conditioned to resonate with Venus. Correct in his assertion that men and women respond to different inwardly directed cues, Gray provided effective explanations to enthusiastic audiences on the distinctions that characterized the sexes, especially in their approaches to relationship challenges. The extent to which these behaviors derive from social conditioning as opposed to biological determinism isn't known. As related earlier, researcher Margaret Mead successfully challenged entrenched sexist assumptions with irrefutable data taken from actual tribes whose social roles departed significantly from those taken for inevitable by modern patriarchal authorities, a/k/a "the experts."

Every sign along with its ruling planet carries a gift. Mars provides the human race with primal fire, raw passion. This powerful force awakens seeds deep within the earth's bosom each spring. It represents half the dance of matter, the masculine "side." And since there can be no life without the magnetic engagement of **both** interactive polarities, it's sheer spiritual suicide for Mars (and its pro-masculine creed of machismo) to exorcize his Divine feminine counterpart from life's quintessential equations! A price is consistently extracted for doing so. Take libido for instance. It acts as a powerful homing device in that it draws men and women together until they work out their previous (past life) karmic debts. I am convinced that the relative positions of Venus and Mars, added to those of Moon and Sun (as found in our birth charts) predestine us to meet those certain souls with whom we harbor contracts from prior incarnations. If logic alone dictated the basis for relationships we would walk away from those ties that compelled us to learn tough, unpleasant, or inconvenient lessons! Instead, following the celestial plan libido operates like glue. Often it "fixes" on a specific party and won't set us free until our intended lessons are learned.

Mars as first cause is analogous to the expression of the first chakra. It emanates a bright red hue. Mystics recognize that white light emerges when all colors are balanced, their varied expressions integrated. Mankind gains nothing by seeking to suppress Mars or the energetic projection of the first primal chakra. The key to transcending the violent imprint of Mars lies in integrating its function with those of the other chakras. Then evolution of the spiritual sort can result. Our world was designed to reflect the expression of many colors, just as music generates from a variety of notes. Mars alone cannot make life. As a matter of fact when Mars rules and demands conformity to his way or the highway, all diversity is expunged. His orientation leads to standardized education, as monoculture replaces nature's diverse forest communities. And that's when war is not being fought or planned! Latent aggression is cultivated through competitive sports where loyalty to one's team becomes a virtual mantra, covert indoctrination. In omnipresent sporting arenas all attention focuses on who's got the ball(s)! A sport like golf may seem serene, even contemplative, while football is inordinately martial in comparison. What they all feature is grown men playing with balls! Modern ballpark spectacles invite the public to feast on displays of raw power in ways that mirror the legendary Roman arena. Plausibly these contests tap into collective memory banks and recapitulate primitive responses, some based on raw blood lust. There's a clear link between competitive sports and homage to the military and its "heroes." Both emphasize fighting for one's team, wearing an identifiable uniform, and worshipping "the oily muscle," as Nietzsche termed it. Today's film industry also relies upon violence, while what passes for rap music glorifies misogyny when it's not advocating blatant violence towards women. These rituals of homage to Mars desensitize a society's members to the ravages of extreme force.

It's been said: "He who lives by the sword dies by the sword." Visionary author Gordon Michael Scallion believes that life, in the form of a thriving and highly advanced civilization, once resided on the planet Mars. In his book *Notes from the Cosmos* he explains what plausibly wiped out the alleged population that once dwelled there. Not unlike today's American military thinkers, Scallion suggests that Mars once supported a leadership that opted to build a space shield for purported security purposes. Highly sophisticated instrumentation was devised and lasted for several generations. However, those who drew up the design plans eventually died, and when new generations advanced beyond their ancestors' culture of fear, they elected to dismantle the shield. Because they did not understand its basic "wiring" their attempt proved catastrophic for the planet. Can any society that lives by fear ever feel safe?

In the *Prelude to Venus and Mars* I explained that Mars is destined to share three species of encounter with his cosmic consort Venus. She is first met as Demeter (Part II, chapter 2), and next represented in her role as Hera (Part II, chapter 7)). Her final embodiment, that of Aphrodite, is where we find Venus **exalted**. In Pisces (Part II, chapter 12) she reigns over the Zodiac's sign of spiritual atonement. Given the dual implication of the two fish, this position also succumbs to escapist behaviors. Could it be that when Mars fails to recognize his spiritual soul-mate and the path of love she offers, that he resorts to substance abuse in an attempt to quell his inner demons, the anger generated from the ghost of what's been lost? Alcohol has been statistically shown to play a prominent role in bar fights, domestic abuse, hate crimes, and highway fatalities. One way or another, Mars is fated to dance with Venus! Each person wrestles with Mars by facing those areas that demand greater self-mastery. This lesson is portrayed Biblically as: "He who conquers himself is greater than he who conquers a city!" Mars awakens the sense of self as primary operating principle. Like a newborn baby this entity is not yet accustomed to the workings of the world, nor has it learned to integrate the diverse archetypal expressions of the circle, those that make for a healthy, balanced life. It's notable that the *I ching* begins with its first kua (a/k/a hexagram) that of supreme Yang. Its powers resonate with the masculine planets Sun and Mars. What follows in the *I ching* as natural progression is seen in its second kua, the expression of supreme Yin which resonates with Moon and Venus. The Zodiac similarly begins with the first masculine principle, Aries, and then moves to the first feminine principle, Venus-ruled Taurus. I find it fascinating that mystical systems originating from unrelated geographical regions and time periods concur! Before we meet Venus in her first incarnation… let's pursue the question:

Do you know Mars? Is there a person in your family or circle of friends that has to be right, and tends to assume the attitude of a bully? Is there a type-A personality who gets angry over trifles? Someone that has to prove he's macho at every turn? Is there a pioneer who has a tendency to move from one adventure onto the next, and seems endowed with an endless supply of personal energy?

Mars In Love

Any who aspire toward conjugal relations with Mars better be prepared to stand up to the heat of raw passion, in addition to equally intense displays of emotion, often issuing from a primitive, aggressive ego-source. Mars pulses with libido, and is given to rages as well as creative surges. This is hardly the lover who would enjoy a sedate night at the opera. He's what you'd call a man's man, and given to wild action rather than prudent, patient contemplation. Given the basic nature of fire signs, don't expect Mars to gracefully hide his light under any bushel. Ditto his heat! It's oddly heartwarming to learn that Mars was Aphrodite's favorite romantic consort. He is so in touch with his body that he makes an adept lover. Surprisingly he strongly identifies with pleasuring his partner. Aimed forever at number one status in the varied races of life, Mars seeks to earn that title in the bedroom as well!

116

Activities that Accord with the season of Mars

Be a pioneer. What does that mean? Are you due for a vacation? Have you ever taken wing on your own? In the film *Harry and Tonto*, an elderly man sets out on a modern vision-quest and arrives at the helpful conclusion: "That the great thing about traveling alone is that you're never alone long." If you don't have the courage to book a flight solo, then get physical. Whether you commit to rigorous yard work or get that old bike tuned up so that it can take you to new places in your neighborhood (or beyond), determine to set your course in the bold direction of personal discovery.

If you recognize that you're harboring animosity, "inquire within" to locate its source. Sometimes if you get going, you can drive the anger (which may represent frustrated personal energy) away. During this phase on the great dial of time honor and embrace the interior explorer, or pioneer; and seek creative ways to tame or channel its fiery impulses. Take the time to recognize what's driving your behavior, especially if it's not taking you to a fulfilling destination. Pay attention to how you drive, as well as what's driving you. When action serves a life-affirming call, it's probably in synch with your greater good.

Chapter 2

Taurus: The Realm Of Demeter Awakened
(Nurturing the Inner Nurturer)

Traditional astrology defines Taurus as the sign realm of the moon's **exaltation.** The moon signifies the supreme Yin force, and it refers directly to the conditions of family life and the mother's role in particular. The moon is allotted special status in Taurus for this strong, steady earth sign signifies the awesome responsibility attendant upon the feminine parental role. Taurus, as fertile earth, represents the fecund soil which nourishes the growth of the plant kingdom. This sign is directly associated with the planting of seeds. When carefully nourished they mature into full harvests. The parent's job by analogy is to nurture the "seed" or offspring. Cultivate the "domestic garden" and human life will thrive. Taurus connotes the realm of the natural world, dominion of the great **Mother Nature.** Just as she provides all living beings with their necessary foodstuffs, it is the mother who delivers first nourishment to her infant in the form of her own breast milk. To fully nourish human life requires more than physical food. Love is the sacred ingredient that supports processes of biological growth. Venus is the planetary conveyor of Divine love; and we encounter her first incarnation as Demeter, the principle of maternal nurture. To the Romans, she was known as Ceres and directly orchestrated nature's harvest cycles. Cereal, a long-established dietary mainstay, derives its name from the root word Ceres. More fascinating is the reputation that has come to define Demeter. According to myth she is most famously noted for her reaction when her beloved daughter Persephone went missing. The pubescent child loved to play outdoors in her mother's abundant gardens. There was no reason for her to suddenly disappear. Nor did it take Demeter's maternal intuition long to figure out who likely played a role in the probable abduction of her daughter. She correctly surmised it to be Pluto (a/k/a Hades). Since Jupiter (Zeus) held official leadership that extended from Olympus to earth, Demeter rightfully made her case to him. Although she counted on his sense of justice, the old god evidenced the same tiresome sexist proclivities that are seen in current world leaders. Both sets blithely dismiss the destructive acts confronted by women on a daily basis. At first Zeus thought he could sit this matter out on the sidelines and avoid stepping on his brother's toes, so he elected to do nothing. Demeter, as a powerful Goddess in her own right, was not without tools or powers of her own. Wisely, she elected to use them. Given command over nature's growth cycles she owned the capacity to shut down the harvests. And that's exactly what she did. This circumstance was none too comfortable for citizens of earth. The people cried out angrily to Zeus, who like most male gods required flattery (if not idolatry). Mortals threatened to turn away from rituals of homage done in Zeus' name. This proved too much for the old god. Demeter's strategy worked. Ultimately Zeus was forced to negotiate. Pure poetic justice (and my favorite non-scientific explanation for the magnificence of the change of seasons) inspired the ingenious compromise Zeus arrived at. Taking into consideration that Persephone had ingested Pluto's pomegranate seeds (metaphorical of the absorption of his sperm) she was compelled to join him for half the year. The remaining time she would be free to return to her mother. The myth explains that Demeter joyously celebrates the annual return of her daughter by ceremoniously drawing all things verdant back to life, and so the harvests miraculously return. When Persephone must once again rejoin Hades, mother Demeter grieves and shuts down the harvests. And so the trees shed their leaves, the animals enter into hibernation, and the natural world assumes the mock death of winter.

Currently climate change is making big news. *The Weather Channel* has become the most exciting thing on television! Could it be chronicling Demeter's Revenge? A great many children are indeed suffering and too much is out of joint. Wars are made and supported by funds extracted from school lunch programs! Seems Demeter has noticed and taken aim at the U.S. Gulf Coast to register her protests in disapproval. Hurricanes Katrina and Ike have recently demonstrated her wrath! People have been taught to consider such abstract connections as nonsensical, pure superstition. Yet the Bible explains in the parable of the Great Flood that nature manifests consequences for substandard human conduct. Scientists may be convinced that myths are fantastical stories that took place (if at all) in ancient times when human intellect was less developed or outright primitive. They are equally confident that time is linear; and that modern mankind is moving on a progressive course towards a distant future. They fail to notice that time circles, as do its themes. Fortunately some researchers have begun to pay attention! Professor James Lovelock authored *The Revenge of Gaia*. He, James Hansen, and Al Gore are a few notables ready to connect the climatic dots!

Supporting the premise that nature reflects mass human consciousness are insights drawn from Guru Yogananda. In his book, *A World in Transition*, opening remarks were presented in his speech delivered at the United Nations in 1949. Yogananda warned that strong earthquakes, floods, volcanic activity, and storms would accelerate unless and until mankind learned to place aside warfare and learn to get along. The Divine covenant between Demeter (Venus = peace) and Mars (war) must be renegotiated, brought into alignment if we expect to enjoy balanced, livable conditions here on earth.

In 1994 astronomers noted excitedly that the planet Jupiter (Zeus) had been hit by numerous rogue asteroids. The discovery team, Schumacker-Levy, lent their name to this particular space event. Across the media so-called experts characterized the action strictly in sports parlance, as if witnessing a galactic ballgame. I had the opportunity to appear on a CBS affiliate in Albuquerque to offer a more mystical explanation, one that interpreted its celestial symbolism. Jupiter is associated with power and authority (on Olympus as well as earth). Thus asteroid hits suggested a clear cosmic sign of ostensibly poor leadership, the equivalent of black marks on the report card of the One in charge. (I drew upon this analogy to create a parody in my unpublished screenplay, *Immortally Yours*. As Zeus' kingdom is shaken he turns in bed to face his wife Hera and asks her assessment of the job he's been doing. She enlightens him by reminding that his concerns have primarily been limited to sports and stock scores, neither taking into consideration the true status of the world he has been Divinely tasked to govern. Furthermore, she points out, he's been delinquent in his recognition of the status of women across the globe.) The point I wish to relate is that by allowing the patriarchal perspective of science to dominate all discussions our understanding of the higher connections between cosmos and earth are lost. Given the anomalous weather conditions generating from global warming, humanity is being forced to reexamine its actions. It may be timely to consider that Demeter's story extends beyond myth. Does it not teach us something vital and fundamental in the way of self-preservation?

In our modern world, Zeus, as symbol of the male ruling elite, is complicit in co-opting the myriad treasures that belong to the great Goddess: the vast and precious assets derived from the natural world. Demeter as representative of Taurus, the second sign on the cosmic dial signifies supreme Yin. She has been empowered to act as counterpart to Mars, supreme Yang and ruler of the first sign kingdom, Aries. Taurus also represents the zodiac's sector of money, real estate, banking, and tangible investments. As authors Paul Hawken, Amory Lovins & L. Hunter Lovins relate in their book, *Natural Capitalism*, when vitally important resources like water aquifers are excessively tapped from nature's storehouses, these precious commodities are taken for free. In other words, Demeter's gifts do not figure on any balance sheets. Transactions that operate solely on the basis of paper wealth become abstractions; there is no realization of actual values, such as the replacement costs potentially involved. People are conditioned to measure a thing's worth based on what it costs, which is to say how the market affixes a price to that item. Absolutely no thought is given to what it costs nature to produce, replace, or repair that item! Indeed a great holocaust against the natural world, which is to say Demeter's kingdom, is unapologetically underway. **Not only do the vast majority of products come from the great Mother, but populations are taught to offer their prayers to God, the father, leaving Her contribution entirely out of the reverential equation**. I believe there is a direct correlation between how women are treated and how the great Mother, source of the vast array of products most take for granted, is denigrated. Were her assets and contributions placed on the proverbial balance sheets that companies use to assess risks, costs, and benefits, how different economic models would look! Hawkins and his colleagues have devised such spreadsheets, and invite economists to consider nature's replacement costs when they calculate their risk-benefit analyses. Humanity is past due for a more enlightened view of what's far too casually trashed or exploited. For instance: when a forest is felled, imagine the costs in terms of time, energy, and resources to replace it. Or consider the horrific denuding of the gorgeous mountains of West Virginia as coal is ceaselessly extracted. Nature's long established covenants between interactive ecosystems are being violently dismantled. Rain patterns no longer fall on lush forests that require nourishment. Rather, they wash homes away. At the time of this writing a landslide of toxic sludge threatens homes and river ways in Tennessee. This crisis is the product of "clean coal" extraction via mountain top removal. Current fiscal models equate the cost of rebuilding after these major losses as a viable basis for extrapolating profit! In other words, when a dangerous toxic spill occurs cleanup costs factor in as a monetary increment! Meanwhile what's truly being lost does not figure into the math! Our present "slash and burn" approach to nature's storehouses is barbaric. Entire ecosystems are being dismantled, and species rendered extinct in the blink of a human generation. What's being stolen or destroyed goes beyond what can be calculated. So severe are the repercussions that a rare and secluded Columbian mountain tribe, the Kogi, came down from their jungle hideaway to plead with "younger brother" to "stop destroying the Mother." This brave action broke a code of centuries of silence. Over the past five hundred years the Kogi have maintained a spiritual heritage. Their tribal rituals link them with the abundant rain cycles that for generations have showered the high jungle terrain. In recent times global warming has begun to impact this exotic region and the rains have ceased to fall. Advanced intuitive gifts cultivated by the Kogi enabled them to understand the root of this climatic rift. They noted that "younger brother's drilling of the Mother" has dangerously altered the climate. And while it's apparent to the vast majority that earth Mother is issuing paroxysms of climatic overload, Wall-mart, the world's largest retailer, recently announced it intends to open 1500 new stores! The "growth" model that the industrial world exports to newly developing nations like India and China only promises to overwhelm yet more ecosystems. Those visionaries that would argue for alternative, renewable energy resources realize that mankind has a small window of opportunity remaining in which to wean itself from fossil fuels, coal, and hardly green nuclear energy. It is clearly time to turn to solar and wind power. The consequences of non-compliance with a more earth-friendly basis for energy production can be viewed in Al Gore's important film documentary, *An Inconvenient Truth*.

A second area where Zeus (along with the ruling patriarchs) co-opts the great Mother's dominion is seen in food production. It would be fitting to adopt a vegetarian diet after reading about the cruel and unnatural ways that pigs, chicken, and cattle are raised on gigantic farms for quick market sales. They are fed filler foods to fatten them up for slaughter; and due to the confined unnatural condition posed by fenced in lives, they must be infused with antibiotics to offset disease. In the agricultural realm, bioengineering techniques now meld what nature never intended to put together. Legalese has been devised to hide the truth of these products from the public. Unlabeled genetically modified food is considered "substantially equivalent" to the real thing. The gap between what the consumer thinks she is buying, not to mention ingesting, and what actually is involved is unconscionable! It hardly provides comfort to know that Monsanto, a company that prospered from the design and deployment of heinous chemical weapons like Agent Orange, is one of the leading biogenetic food designers! That's the moral equivalent of sending one's children to lunch with Jeffrey Dahmer!

And now we come to the greatest heist of Demeter's bounty of all: that which lays claim to her precious seed banks, the genetic labyrinths caringly devised in Her natural laboratories over countless millennia. The inordinately pro-business U. S. Supreme Court ruled that "intellectual copyright" applied to biogenetic companies (effectively giving them ownership of DNA combinations) when **seven** planets gathered in Taurus, Demeter's own sign in May of 2000. (I wrote an extensive analysis of this line-up that appeared in *Dell Horoscope* Magazine. A copy is posted on my website.) Two of the key planets present for the powerful "Taurus congress" were Jupiter and Saturn, the Zodiac's arbiters of law and order. As I will explain later in the book, these two heavyweights reflect the moral foundations of the New and Old Testaments of the *Bible*. The pair meets once every twenty years. Prior to their powerful conjunction in 2000 the last time this dynamic duo united in Demeter's kingdom, Taurus, was 1940 when the Nazis also busily made inroads into genetic engineering. Coincidence? Consider that modern psychology is founded on insights drawn from Taurus native Sigmund Freud. Locked into a sexist worldview he erroneously concluded that women suffered from penis envy. His thesis unimaginatively advocated biological destiny. Modern feminists in contrast have presented compelling evidence to suggest that men suffer from birth envy. After all, matriarchal societies predated our current patriarchal ones; and until men recognized their role in the conception process, it was the female who was glorified as the Divine bearer of life. Instead of sharing in the sacred contract of life once the facts of reproduction were known, Mars turned on Venus. Over the long centuries the patriarchy has utterly managed to devalue the role of women along with the Divine feminine, while devising ways to control birth and all bases for filial lineage. Manmade inroads into agriculture and genetics place Demeter's key resources increasingly at risk, and compromise the long-term sustainability of complex ecosystems.

There are ominous parallels between fundamentalist Christians (along with the Catholic Church) in their obsessive desire to control female sexuality (a/k/a reproductive power) and the German Nazi party. Like their authoritarian Muslim counterparts each exalts the family with the father its unchallenged head, and opposes abortion. Methods of birth control are also restricted when not condemned outright. Such hubris is breathtaking in its support of cultural mores that automatically champion Mars while essentially holding Venus hostage. Add these twisted values to the fact that today the profit motive dangerously drives genetic engineering. Earth Mother spent eons in her natural laboratories advancing a genetic selection process that lovingly drew from the greatest pools of possibility. The diversity in evidence signifies what works! Has any mortal the vision to recognize the degree to which multitudinous species perfectly integrated sustain the web of life through organic systems that have evolved over millennia? Nature is not limited by past performance;

rather like an inspired artist she uses yesterday's creations as a basis for continual innovation. Thus from her organic palette are unexplored options perpetually brought to life. The geneticist in contrast can boast only several years of academic training, does his work for profit, and forcefully compels living cells to line up and form combinations that reflect clone-like redundancy. The manmade model is the genetic equivalent of a shotgun wedding! Once genetically modified seeds are planted in supposedly managed fields, wind and water currents carry them far and wide to root in quite unexpected places. Unintended consequences result as "Franken-seeds" meld with the genuine article. It is neither science fiction nor hyperbole to report that agribusiness sends scouts out to inspect farms to insure that unlicensed farmers are not using (if unwittingly!) the genetically designed seed stocks! In fact when informers find the biotech seed growing in unauthorized farmers' fields, they bring charges against these unfortunate victims on the basis of intellectual copyright infringement! This outrageous breach of justice has even been levied against impoverished farmers in India! One hotshot biotech company that mapped the DNA structure of a particular species of rice cultivated in India over the centuries has laid claim to that product! As a result of the insidious new copyright "law" Indigenous farmers can be sued for violating a foreign company's "free trade" privileges by using seed that originated in their own land! The degree to which profit is trumped over justice invites nature's true capital to be stripped of value, while vital and necessary ecosystems are driven into abject disrepair.

Today's waters extending off continental shelves are so tainted that when viewed from space they resemble the dead zones they've actually become! The tonnage of pesticides, herbicides, insecticides, and industrial effluents poured into nature's sacred waterways is criminal for its negligence. New diagnostic tools have been designed to determine our "body burden," for our interior waterways are accumulating a reciprocal toxic overload. "Body burden" is the determination of which chemicals are harbored in our bloodstreams. Nor does oblivion offer immunity! The truth is that modern citizens have been rendered Guinea Pigs to the chemical industrial complex!

125

Now let us consider another insidious ploy that has led to a wholesale sellout of the natural world along with Demeter's inestimable bounty. Advertising plays upon our senses to establish the image of what is increasingly perceived as "the good life." After McDonald's successfully marketed its "Happy Meals," millions of families began to indulge their children in high-calorie, low nutritional foods. The result? An epidemic of early onset Diabetes, not to mention obesity! The film: *Super Size This!* shed light on this problem, yet McDonald's is not alone in warranting accountability. Due to the fast-pace, high cost of urban (as well as suburban) life, many mothers must work. As a result few have time to lovingly prepare nutritious meals. A great many opt for fast food. Corn syrup has become a pervasive additive found along with trans-fats in many "convenience foods." This is clearly not what earth mother Demeter intended. As a society we're paying a price for faux food filler in the form of public health. I remember observing several friends diagnosed with Chronic Fatigue Syndrome, Epstein Barr, and Candida. Their diets featured denatured foods. These do not adequately nourish the body's intricate systems. American society shows precious little respect for nature or the law of balance.

Many women feel tested by the things they are up against, and indeed stress can compromise their immune systems. Meanwhile the advertising field recruits psychology experts to learn which buzzwords and motivational devices will prove irresistible. This covert strategy lures consumers to dangerous products and habits like smoking. The modern notion of progress accepts domination over nature as a good thing. Precedent is set by the Judeo-Christian conceit that "God gave man **dominion** over the land," and by extension its creatures. A tragically arrogant relationship based on exploitation has been perpetuated as a result. Its hubris stands in marked contrast to the ecologically enlightened attitudes and practices espoused by American Indigenous tribes. Author Dhyani Ywahoo speaks on behalf of the councils of Grandmothers to explain that America's first citizens evaluated their actions by first considering the burden these would impose on future generations. Can you imagine today's mega-corporations considering anything beyond quarterly profits as they go about devouring the earth, shredding the sacred web of life, and backing away from the faintest notion of responsible stewardship? *Public Citizen, Mother Jones* magazine, and reporters Steven Mohkibber and Robert Weissman have tracked the carnage and waste propelled by our culture of Corporate Predators.

Many women rebounding from the various and sundry assaults on their senses now recognize the importance of self-nurture. Some have written books, sponsored classes, or otherwise found ways to share strategies for personal healing. Significant are the ways and means to prepare nourishing food. Conscious young mothers bravely reject bottled formulas and wisely have returned to breastfeeding. Others are courageously accepting natural birth, turning their backs on the medical establishment which generally views childbirth as a disease that warrants orthodox hospital care. The corporate world set its sights on diminishing the value of breastfeeding and managed to utilize advertising to convince naïve new mothers that factory brands trumped nature's richer endowment. This insidious marketing campaign left the dark profit motive free to sabotage the very nature of nurture! Since society has veered towards Mars rules many persons have unquestionably accepted that the "manmade" is the superior product. In such a twisted context the onus increasingly falls upon the individual to learn to take better care of her self. One cannot be a sound source of nourishment to others, if her being is starving for what it requires. At essence every mother is connected to the great Goddess Demeter and holds a responsibility for protecting her offspring. In a world that caters to violence, that sacred calling is also under siege. The false manmade culture presents an artificial view of life that even dictates the desired metrics of the female form! Small wonder that eating disorders proliferate in women. How can Demeter nourish her daughters when the fashion world holds as ideal a ghastly, undernourished image of the female body? I've often wondered how much influence gay male designers have had upon this aberration? While Botticelli's enticing Venus bore small, firm breasts and a wide, round rear end, today's fashion models are as tall and thin-hipped as male basketball stars. The requisite baseball sized breasts suggest a bisexual hybrid that I jokingly refer to as "tits on a stick." (If such an item was sold as a popsicle mold directed at men weaning themselves of alcohol, I wonder how many packages would sell during *Super Bowl*?)

Demeter is the first embodiment of the great Goddess Venus. We will encounter her next as Hera, the wife of Zeus and ruler of the seventh sign kingdom. (It constitutes Libra's natural domain of marriage and union.) Demeter, as the first incarnation of Venus, represents the mother, bearer of life and source of all natural wealth. The vast majority of things we hold in high esteem (oil, copper, gold, gems) stem from the time-banks of her natural kingdom. By extension, Venus-Demeter compels us to value ourselves. Modern women find themselves in a challenging process where they must redefine their concept of feminine worth as a legacy to pass onto their daughters. The "feminist revolution" began the work of altering the paradigm, but it has met nasty resistance in the form of fundamentalist religious delusion. Susan Faludi's important book *Backlash* examined the undertow before it got into full swing. Today the old guard has mounted a new attack by demanding followers to adhere to old, patriarchal ways, means, and mores. These determine to keep women "in their place" as second-class citizens. So long as Mars rules armies will lay things precious to waste. However when Venus enters the mortal equation assuming her role as Divine counterpart, a celebration of the arts follows, and the works designed to lift the human spirit also happen to accrue grand value over time. They become lasting treasures for mankind's enrichment. Museums hold the bounty of Venus while battlefields carry Mars' permanent scars in the form of death, destruction, and disease. Taurus women carry the sentience of Demeter, and may find fulfillment in and through the cultivation of a garden. Surrounded by the plant world and inspired by the great Goddess's evident handiwork all daughters of the Goddess may come to recognize their own inherent creative capabilities. In verdant sanctuaries we are inwardly prompted to rethink the models we have lived by. It is spiritually liberating to detach from the old religious notion that Eve, the feminine, was to blame for mankind's purported fall. To do so is to transcend the not so subliminal message that the female cannot be trusted to follow her own natural instincts. Nor should we any longer allow men to project responsibility for their own weaknesses onto us. (Bible thumpers: since Adam **chose** to eat the damned apple why was Eve blamed? Patriarchy projects many of its own flaws and failings onto the gentler sex in a "Blaming Eve Again Syndrome.")

Mankind has arrived at a juncture where a whole new Eden must be restored upon our earth. Before meaningful action can ensue, a new ideal must be visualized and held firm. It calls for a Divine balance between Venus and Mars. The process of renewal that the natural world requires will by necessity draw upon the regenerative power ensuing from Taurus' polarity, Scorpio. (We will discuss Persephone, archetype of Scorpio, and the intrinsic powers of renewal she bestows in Part II, chapter 8.) Our gift from the realm of Demeter lies in re-establishing our worth as women. It is empowering to come to the realization that we are all Divine daughters, each an embodiment of the great Goddess in an embryonic, evolving form.

Do you know Demeter? Is there a friend, relative, or associate in your circle that Hollywood would naturally cast to play the great Mother, act as the family's personal rock of Gibraltar? Is there someone who always seems to know the right tea to prepare, the perfect meal to offer another as comfort for their mind, body, or spirit? Someone so steady that others rely on her strength and well of nurture for their own well-being and occasional departure from sanity?

Demeter in Love

Taurus needs a partner who accepts her unique contributions to his life. Venus allots to Taurus natives an attractive power that borders on sheer magnetism. That factor, added to the fixed earth nature of the Zodiac's 2nd sign means Taurus is unlikely to pursue an intended lover directly. Instead she's quite capable of drawing love her way. Taurus is by nature sensual, and this quality extends from the art of nurture into the bedroom where this daughter of Demeter takes and receives great pleasure through the erotic arts. Taurus is in touch with her own developed senses and understands how to give a good massage or set a luscious floral bubble bath. Taurus is the master of setting atmosphere, imbuing it with captivating scents and sounds. Lovemaking is cultivated as a slow art, rather than any race to the proverbial horizontal "finish line."

Activities that Accord with this Season
of Venus-Taurus-Demeter

Not only does Demeter's phase of dominion arrive in spring, it happens to be the perfect time to begin a garden of your own. Invent a reason for making contact with the earth for that element is sacred unto Demeter, and central to the cause of feeling inwardly-centered. If that steady grounded feeling is missing then walk the earth barefoot with a conscious intention to meld with the sacred earth under your feet. Often by becoming still in the canopy of a verdant cove or resting under a shady tree can evoke peace or the powerful process of catharsis. If you don't have space for a garden you can still spend time in Demeter's magnificent temples: visit a cathedral forest, lively stream, or seascape waterway. Become one with the natural world and take in the soul remedy poets agree can revive your spirit. If privacy allows, lie down on pine needles or sit with your back against a tree. That's the ideal place to make notations in your journal. Forest companions will stir your inspiration.

In India there are powerful Mantras taught that assist individuals in coming into synch with the four elements. Their specific enunciations are inordinately complex! Elementally speaking, earth signifies the energy of stillness. Biblical Scripture relates, "Be still and know that I am God." Listen to your body; turn down the volume of the world, and tune into the voice of your inner being, your soul. Such a strategy will bring you into contact with the Goddess essence that resides within.

Make note of what you consume, and pay attention to how much waste your choices generate. Bring a reusable cloth bag to the supermarket when you just have a few items to pick up. Why use "disposable" paper or plastic bags? These "convenient" items too frequently end up on reefs or litter beaches where they are taken for jellyfish and eaten. Human detritus thus harms birds and hungry animal scavengers. Perhaps you're ready to cancel a newspaper subscription since news can be easily gotten on-line. The same holds true for catalogues. Make shopping a different kind of adventure by hunting for fashion, furniture, and books at second-hand "recycle" shops. Some of my personal treasures have been found at upscale thrift stores.

Bike or walk when you need not drive. You'll feel better and do your part to lessen the ozone burden on earth mother's lungs, our planet's atmosphere. And by all means get rid of pesticides, herbicides, or any other dangerous chemicals. Do a Google search or shop around at your local health food store to obtain natural alternatives to replace these dangerous industrial products that inevitably end up back in the air, soil, or water table. Do your part to ease Earth Mother Demeter's burdens lest you add to her hot flashes, a/k/a global warming!

Chapter 3

Gemini: The Realm Of Mercury Awakened
Accessing the Inner Messenger

The third cosmic kingdom comes under the rule of Mercury, the winged god known as Hermes to the Romans. He was believed to serve as liaison conveying from Olympian deities those ideas and beliefs required by human beings to facilitate their progress. This infusion of "higher messages" would in turn shape the collective destiny of mankind. Mercury is a Divine messenger. According to the Zodiac the first sign kingdom is relegated to Mars. There the element of fire is enlivened and given bold, vivid expression as Aries. The second kingdom governed by Taurus-Demeter adds the earth element to the Divine circle and brings stability into the mix. Gemini introduces the first of the Zodiac's three air signs. Envision Aries as the quintessential seed, its interior life force awakened as primal **fire**, rousing the expression of Spirit from its vital core. The natural growth process of that seed leads to Taurus where the need to develop a solid root structure asserts. The seed must firmly plant itself into the **earth** to ensure its further growth. As we arrive at Gemini, that symbolic seed sends its first shoots up into the **air** in order to "read" the atmosphere. Its continuing progress is dependent upon responding to environment cues and learning about the surrounding world so it can adapt where necessary. Gemini symbolizes inroads into, and increments of human awareness. Notably its twin counterparts signify the two hemispheres of the human brain. Instrumental to developing the inherent potentials of our brains is education. Speech, writing, reading, and the rudiments of early education are all linked with Gemini's third sign kingdom. Up until relatively recently public education did not exist. In earlier societies viable skills were passed directly from teacher/tradesman to student/apprentice. That mode of direct education also falls under the aegis of Mercury.

132

Let us examine this thing called learning for a moment. When we gaze back in time we realize that literacy was essentially reserved for those of noble birth, or otherwise became the fate of those trained to become scribes within ecclesiastical confines. Before Guttenberg's movable type, hand-written documents ever so patiently rendered formed books. Scholars and scribes generally found employment inside the church hierarchy. And while a few brave scientists worked independently acting as bold iconoclasts, thinkers for the most part either adapted their ideologies to serve the religious status quo, or risked being cast as heretics. The separation of church and state is a relatively new phenomenon. Even today the Bible remains the foundation blueprint of Western law, culture, and mores. Its authoritarian, patriarchal context informs the social sciences, if covertly. Interestingly enough the Bible, primary text of Western civilization, resonates quite naturally with Gemini; after all it consists of two primary texts and these reflect antithetical perspectives. Mirroring the dual nature of Gemini the Bible personifies its own "twin" character! If we examine The Old Testament, its obvious punitive tone resonates with Saturn, the planet of karma and soul-wrenching consequences. The New Testament as antithesis resonates with Jupiter, the planet of faith and miracles. The fact that Western thinking derives from this dual source sets up the premise for a divided collective mindset. Those who suffer from this spiritual dichotomy are wise to pursue a higher understanding, one that transcends polarity by embracing a more holistic vision. Mankind is challenged in this pursuit at this final phase of the Piscean Age, for we've been long programmed and conditioned to see things in black or white terms for far too long.

Religious doctrines relate that Creator extended to human beings the gift of free will. The proper use of this gift requires mental discernment; for how else can one distinguish between so-called good and so-called evil? Mankind's consciousness is projected into an ongoing morality play as these polar aspects of human nature are repeatedly drawn into dramatic collision. The body of literature produced by notable writers down the ages certainly reflects this theme. Indeed this state of dichotomy figures profoundly into the human condition. Everywhere it textures our experience and underscores our basic perceptions. Life is viewed through the prismatic contexts of male or female, black or white, night or day, good or evil, and so on. These marked divisions were exacerbated by the influence cast by The Age of Pisces. Every sign works in cahoots with its opposite. Thus with Virgo drawn into the mix, a focus on categorical referencing sought to make sense and create order out of the mass confusion. The pair (Pisces/Virgo) has directly influenced behavior and perception during the past twenty-two hundred years, the era constituted by the Piscean Age. Our minds have been trained to operate through duality. To an extent the Ancient Greeks paved the way by gathering the masses for grand theatrical productions. The crowd learned to resonate with the twin masks depicting comedy or tragedy. Life tends to weave the two together while deftly spinning a unified thread of destiny.

The *Course in Miracles* explains that our quality of life largely results from our perceptual choices. It explains we may in any given moment choose the path of love or that of fear. Author Joseph Murphy shared a similar view that profoundly influenced my thinking two decades ago. Murphy believed that messages conveyed by the mass media triggered a primitive response level which he characterized as "the race mind." Its prolific relay systems focus on strife, poverty, waste, disease, war, and other debilitating "negatives." His books advocated a training that steadied the mind teaching it to instead focus on higher objectives and healthier contexts lest "the race mind do its thinking for you." Conventional astrology ascribes to Mercury (and by extension Gemini's 3rd house), the qualities of "lower mind." Positioned directly across the Zodiac is Sagittarius, Gemini's polarity, and it represents the kingdom of "higher mind." (A fuller discussion of the powers attributable to the focused mind or power of intention will be found in Part II, chapter nine: Pan-Sagittarius.) Gemini conveys to us what others think. Its penchant for comparison binds the mind to what's ostensibly at play. Sagittarius, in contrast, asks us to formulate a personal philosophy based on inspired understanding, one that emerges from deep inquiry and the expansive education of our minds.

Physiologically a link may be established between Mercury, as messenger, and our central nervous systems. These networks have been designed to deliver data across a complex system of neuropathways. This living grid facilitates perception of the outer world and a means for communicating meaningfully with other sentient beings. Information gathered and processed allows us to reach determinations, a key component of "free will." However, our unconscious minds also record data that we don't recognize; and now that mass media pumps messages 24/7, as cell phones beep and satellites pulse we pick up more signals than we can conceivably process. The messages being taken in place a strain on our nervous systems, and many feel overloaded with information! Not long ago a legal challenge was made against the covert use of subliminal advertising. The amoral nature of covert cues posited under the radar was exposed. Images were engineered to bypass our intellect's capacity to screen them out. Meanwhile countless signals emitted by satellites, radio and television stations, cell phones, and the apparatus of military surveillance enter our minds without invitation. That does not mean these invaders don't impact our cognitive responses. Years ago I entered a client's home and felt something nebulous interfering with the "wavelength" I tap in order to relay intuitive information. It impressed the host when I correctly deduced that a subliminal tape had been left playing! When I type at high speed in order to record an equivalent of automatic dictation, and a plane flies overhead or a garbage truck pauses nearby, the motor sound waves abort my "contact." Conceivably individuals who spend no time communing with their inner spirits might not notice these incursions. The shaman or medium evidences a consciousness that is likely the result of lifetimes previously devoted to focused awareness. Human consciousness, like its biological equivalent, remains in a state of ongoing evolution. Sharper perceptions accrue to those who have worked their senses the way athletes train muscles. Such a legacy is the fruit of lifetimes! Author Jane Roberts channeled *The Seth Material*, and it provides many fascinating insights. For instance a comparison was offered between modern human perception and that attributable to our ancient ancestors. Language, down to its structural basis, plays a significant role in how ideas are cognitively received and conveyed. An important distinction between then and now bears mentioning. Seth explained that consciousness once existed in a state that was not confined to the human body as is the case in our present materialistic epoch. No language equivalent (or words) existed to separate the speaker-observer from the thing being observed! In other words, an individual living in the distant past would not say, "I see a tree." Experiencing his consciousness melded with that of the tree, he would instead relate "I now experience myself as a tree."

Language is powerful. Persuasive speakers have learned to use subtle cues and "buzz words" to win influence. George Lakoff defines a key aspect of this phenomenon with respect to the way issues are "framed" by the mainstream media. Mercury is credited with endowing mankind with the incomparable tool of language. The winged god has reputedly inspired the spoken and written word. Readers have no doubt heard the adage, "The pen is mightier than the sword." Real conflicts have been incited on the basis of slogans that moved minds to violent response. Sadly, propaganda, the dark inverted use of the power of words continues to draw people into calamitous response patterns. The Nazi party learned that "the lie told often enough is perceived as true." Modern advertising makes a killing on that fundamental distortion. One of my favorite films, *Bedazzled,* begins in a workshop where eager employees carefully tear a singular page out of every book, while others busily scratch vinyl record albums. The figure of a modern, sophisticated devil congratulates himself on the advent of at long last, an **eighth** sin: advertising! Consider the relevance of such a "development" to modern times and its influence on the state of our world!

The Ancient Chinese *I Ching* offers timeless wisdom as "food for thought." As related in hexagram 27, we are reminded that we are not merely nourished by the foods we take in, but also by the beliefs that enter our minds. Digested in a different manner, beliefs play a role in generating the quality of life that we experience. During the 1970's, novel inroads aimed at reprogramming the human mind excited promising possibilities. *Silva Mind Control* taught seminar participants to train their words so they would not animate the creative power of negatively-charged thoughts. A friend caught herself falling into cynical mode and quickly corrected her statement by saying, "cancel!" I also met several people who'd gotten involved with EST. It soon became apparent to me that these "mind schools" functioned like brand names, each attracting a specific sort of person. People drawn to the EST training seemed to be extremely self-centered aggressive types. I remember attending a party in Puerto Rico where someone threw a **live** firecracker into the social mix as a prank. When the perpetrator's identity was known (thankfully no one was seriously injured) the response was, "Yeah. He's into EST." These often-expensive programs advertise that a change of mind will evoke a change of life; but the proof shows up later in the pudding. I know one woman whose life has gotten far more difficult to manage because her "program" has her looking endlessly backwards at all the things that have hurt her! Similarly, many people who subscribe to orthodox psychoanalysis remain stuck in the past. *The Bible* says, "Choose ye which master ye shall serve." There are certainly powers attributable to words, including what we believe and which concepts we advocate. As a collective society our values become shaped by the dominant messages delivered. Professor and author Noam Chomsky has done much to raise political consciousness. He has authored numerous books that meticulously trace the degree to which governments (with the help of a complicit omnipresent media) act to "manufacture consent." There is a vast difference between a consensus forged through secrecy, coercion, and obfuscation, and one that arises organically. The latter based on agreement arrived at by persons who reflect diverse interests and positions.

Another facet of consciousness explains the Mercurial nature of our intellects. The human mind has a tendency to talk to itself. Carlos Casteneda's astute shaman-mentor Don Juan referred to this phenomenon as the "interior dialog." Various schools of meditation provide directions to control one's breath. It's a strategy devised to still the mind and tame its otherwise unruly interior thought streams. Don Juan's incisive teachings reached thousands. Among his myriad insights he explained that when individuals experience an actual spiritual epiphany that tends to shatter their prior worldview, all too quickly their minds (via preconditioned thoughts) revert back to previous patterning. The new information is essentially negated. While it's true that most of us have a sincere desire to better our lives, our habits work against this incentive. These habits begin with the mind. In our exceedingly mechanistic era, psychoanalysis is now frequently replaced by pill popping. Many in need find themselves without health insurance or the means to pay for treatment. Self-medicating via illegal substances fills the vacuum when the body of literature promoting the ways and means to self-healing fails to deliver. Quite a few New Age titles address the quintessential "inside job." It would seem that "Earth School 101" extends to human beings the quest for self-mastery, a goal approached inch by inch, lifetime by lifetime. Yet while a great many sincere (if not authentically spiritual) persons busily work on themselves, they now wake to the ominous fact that our democratic society has all but slipped away. Apart from the rare example set by adepts and masters, it is virtually impossible for individuals to sustain healthy inner lives and related lifestyles if the surrounding society is bent on destruction. Both vital aspects must work together holistically. As we build healthier societies, we should support citizens in taking conscious responsibility for life-affirming behavioral choices. On the other hand when the cultural climate supports violence and habits of self-abuse, well-balanced persons hardly constitute the norm. Ideally no one should avoid the work of growing personal consciousness. It's fairly clear that an individual's state of mind factors into their quality of existence. However too many New Age books assert that concentrating on our own "cosmic business" is the only criterion that matters. It's disingenuous to discount the many factors (karmic, astrological, national, universal) that contribute to each person's ultimate experience.

When Carlos Casteneda got the blues, Don Juan prescribed a memorable wisdom as therapeutic alternative: "Seek and see the marvels around you, and you will get tired of dwelling upon yourself so much." I have found this remedy useful. Leaving the buzz of the urban nexus for a peaceful walk or bike-ride in one of nature's blessed sanctuaries does wonders for the inner being. Many people fail to take such breaks. Like rats caught in mazes, they live to work, and their lives take on a machine-like frenzy. In addition, our society has become essentially atomized. Each individual believes all things must be achieved on a personal basis. While statistics relate that wealth has increased (for the top 1% of U.S. citizens) depression runs rampant. It's treated by an assortment of anti-depressant medications. Professor Emeritus Robert E. Lane shed light on the matter by publishing his research findings as: *The Loss of Happiness in Market Democracies*. He concluded that more people value close loving relationships than wealth. And while ours has become a culture where the commercial marketplace (under Mercury's stewardship, for Mercury governs all forms of trade and mercantilism) dominates, it still remains unlikely than one can buy love. Of course that hasn't stopped a dazzling number of Internet sites from setting themselves up as modern matchmakers, nor stopped the traffic in mail-order brides from the Ukraine.

Casting aside the Judeo-Christian mindset, Buddhists believe that all things in our world emanate from a great **mind** stream. (If records are correct, then Buddha was in fact a Gemini, Divine child of Mercury.) I was privileged to spend ten days at a remote exotic Buddhist Monastery just outside of Katmandu, Nepal. The experience of immersion in that small devout world of sincere Buddhist monks was transforming. The session I attended was open to seekers worldwide and introduced Buddhist philosophy and meditation techniques, these designed to still the mind. This encounter brought to mind one of my favorite quotes alleged to have come from the great magician, Merlin: "The best remedy for being sad is to learn something. That's the only thing that never fails. You may grow old and trembling in your anatomies, you may lie awake at night listening to the disorder of your veins; you may miss your only love, and see the world about you devastated by evil lunatics, or know your honor trampled in the sewers of lesser minds. There is only one thing for it then, to learn. Learn why the world wags and what wags it. That's the only thing that the mind can never exhaust, never alienate, never be tortured by, never fear or distrust, and never dream of regretting. Learning is the only thing for you. Look what a lot of things there are to learn."

In addition to Merlin's wise advice, an open mind keeps its bearer nimble, and thus more youthful. The late astrologer Jim Lewis referred to Gemini (Mercury's first zone of dominion) as the "Puer Eternis." Perhaps a fictitious entity, it speaks to our search for eternal youth. Like Peter Pan some wish they'd never have to grow up. In a world where inevitable pain fuels the maturation process, fantasy functions as a probable survival device. Although individuals who dwell in their own "dream worlds" find themselves unceasingly castigated, where would American technology be without the assistance of unbounded imagination? How many novel ideas appeared first in fiction before becoming facts of modern life? Given Mercury's influence over early education, the extent to which right brain faculties have been cordoned off in pursuit of a standardized curriculum model is borderline criminal. When young minds fail to develop qualities of inspiration, intuition, and imagination society as a whole suffers! At present the vast majority is taught to repeat data like parrots trained to perform uniformly. Critical thought is abandoned in pursuit of "teaching" aimed primarily toward test results. Precious, impressionable minds are formatted, just as diverse forest communities are felled and replaced with monoculture! The mind is a terrible thing to waste, as the United Negro College Fund once asserted. The American education model functions like an industry and primarily addresses the **business** of educating children. It's increasingly geared towards "proven results." In contrast the Russian model screens schoolchildren and trains them in areas suitable to their natural aptitudes. Society needs its technicians, beauty consultants, and medical assistants as much as its engineers and professors. Short of instituting a national apprenticeship program, investing in a wise and diversified curriculum would help our national economy. This approach would prepare students for careers in fields ready to utilize their areas of expertise. Forcing youngsters to instead produce the same answers on mandatory exams is a crime against genuine learning, the core passion that true education should champion.

In a natal chart the planet Mercury will be found in one of the twelve zodiac sign-realms. In a sense the Creation blueprint allots twelve quintessential languages (and the resonant perceptual frameworks that accompany each), with an infinite number of variations upon each. Representatives of these twelve thematic perspectives are found in each and every society. Mercurial "flavors" operate like cognitive keys to the human condition since each conveys its own intellectually adapted basis for response. And since Mercury governs travel, here too is another significant realm that relays information in the interest of educating mankind. When people from different cultures and orientations meet a cross-pollination of reference points and ideas ensues. For centuries trade routes have inevitably resulted in interactions that have promoted the growth not only of individuals, but also of entire nations.

During my tenure as Florida Keys television astrologer, I had the privilege of interviewing fascinating people. One, an Episcopal Minister turned shaman visited the Keys to promote his workshop, "The drum is the shaman's horse." A circle of interested seekers assembled to hear his instruction which began with: "Empty your cups." This meant if we arrived with preconceived notions about the encounter soon to follow, there would be no room in our minds to absorb new experiential data. He was right. I attended as a courtesy, but became quickly amazed by the ease with which I traveled on the rhythmic waves the drumming produced. The drum simulates the human heartbeat and has been used by indigenous cultures worldwide. Its powerful sounds sweep over us in a visceral way probably because while we're in the womb our bodies form in accord with our biological mothers' beating hearts.

During college I experienced an altogether different "drumming event" which occurred at a crowded party hosted by Latinos. Suddenly in our midst a young woman began to essentially bounce off the walls. The scene was straight out of *The Exorcist*! Unable to make out what was happening from the buzz of Spanish conversation until the craziness died down, a translator later explained that this woman had been studying trance mediumship. Apparently the drumming unleashed energies potent enough to rouse the spirit that got hold of her! My sensory receptors have opened from the practice of yoga and that makes me quite sensitive to sound. Certain types of rhythmic beats (like those emitted by pervasive boom boxes) cause spiritually sentient souls to recoil.

From time to time we hear about dolphin or whales washing up on shorelines in what appears as a mass suicide. Military technology in the form of low decibel signals (those antithetical to rhythm structures that harmonize with our bodies, in particular with our heartbeats) attacks the sensitive auditory apparatus of these creatures. Attuned to the silent seas they are moved by the slightest vibration in a manner earthbound humans cannot begin to comprehend. Sound waves impact people differently. Unwelcome noise is pervasive in modern America. Agitating sounds enter our homes (and bodies) without invitation and feel like a subtle form of rape. The Bible advises that we respect the Sabbath and honor its symbolic rest beat. This prescription is necessary to all living beings for the purposes of renewal and regeneration. Unfortunately peace and quiet are difficult to come by since the night no longer sleeps. No rest beat is allowed! Small wonder that many persons succumb to psychic exhaustion, while others must rely on sleep medication to acquire any repose at all!

Taking a different track, sound can be potent in yet another way. The understated power that "message is medium" influences the sphere of seduction. I am speaking about that powerful, ineffable quality that emanates from the human voice. It's a fact that a man's voice is the first thing that gets inside of us! The right tone emitted from an appealing male seems to own some kind of passkey to that "cave" earlier mentioned.

Scientists believe that human beings use only ten percent of their brains! Imagine what is stored in the remaining ninety percent? Following the limited scope of logic, I recall a television documentary produced by Ivy League researchers who sought to discredit the out-of-body mystical experiences reported by persons who had undergone near death episodes. This research team found that by stimulating a portion of the brain's lobes, the subjects would describe a visionary passage to the light. Based on this data the team concluded that people don't actually go to the light. Instead what is related is merely a product of brain stimulation. A mystic cued to the wisdom of right brain sentience would interpret the same data quite differently. The very fact that such stimulation produces "a journey to light" suggests the experience has been encoded into the brain, and waits dormant in a computer-like file. When this portion of the brain is directly tweaked the imprinted perceptions readily become reactivated! A lesson on how cellular memory operates was revealed to me in college biology class. Utilizing tiny flatworms (classified as platyhelminth) these creatures were taught to move through a maze in order to obtain food. When cut in half (to reproduce via mitosis) the newborn worms immediately demonstrated the learned behavior! The evidence suggests that discovery becomes encoded and is passed onto new generations at a cellular level. Earlier reference was made to the Seth material. As explained our ancestors were not entirely locked into their embodiment of flesh. They retained a ready capacity to rejoin the light. Could our brains maintain the legacy of this "communion," and when appropriately stimulated recapitulate it? Consider this intriguing analogy: the same portion of our brain that's unused suggests the invisible dimension of the iceberg submerged beneath the ocean surface. We do not hear the whistle that dogs so easily respond to, nor can we see infrared or ultra-violent light. Given the obvious limits of our senses to argue that human beings are thus equipped to answer life's inexorable mysteries is arrogant, if not patently absurd. Author Richard Bach offered, "If you argue for your limitations, you get to keep them." A great many minds approach the inquiry process in search of validation for already arrived upon hypotheses. Those with open minds risk reward since: "Serendipity favors the prepared mind."

When I'm engaged in a creative project fate often plays a role in directing the convergence of events. The evident synchronicity defies probability. For instance, a friend invited me to see the evocative film, *What the Bleep Do We know*. While it raised many intriguing points, in particular how our nervous systems codify experience in a way that compels us to repeat the same behaviors which in turn generate the same redundant outcomes, I felt the film completely avoided the influences of love, fate, karma, grace, astrology, and other subtle forces that exert very real effects. Right after viewing this film another friend called to ask if I'd like to listen to a DVD she'd just received. Having previously introduced me to unique metaphysical film content, I knew she had something important in her possession. (As a Gemini she assumes the persona of Mercury, and passes key information on.) This particular DVD featured the work of Dr. Alberto Villoldo with whom I felt an immediate and intense affinity. Much that he conveyed fell into accord with my own findings; in fact his insights ran parallel with data I was just then relating in this book project! Dr. Villoldo left his orthodox medical practice (specializing in brain research) to study with the Indigenous Incan shaman of Peru! Encountering his material was like meeting

Carlos Casteneda all over again! One key revelation Villoldo drew from the astute methodology of the shaman concerned the way human beings carry past life experience, much like the flat worms mentioned. This built-in propensity explains a great many maladies, dyslexia included. Just as modern computers place files into memory, past life recall is "filed away" in the unused (90%) sectors of our brains. These form an untapped reservoir of "storage space." Suppose the child who suffers from a reading disorder spent his last lifetime in China where texts were read vertically and consisted of complex visual symbols rather than a limited linear alphabet? Each time he focuses present consciousness on attempts to interpret the characters before his eyes, his unconscious flashes backwards. Present data proves competitive with his previous foundation in learning. Many young children experience some form of past-life recall with others naturally intuitive. Yet for the most part when a youngster relates that he's seen a ghost or spirit, the vision is rapidly dismissed by parents and explained away as fantasy. Such perception for some is regarded as taboo, particularly within fundamentalist families. The right brain sphere of sentience is consciously strengthened in societies that honor the practice of shamanism. Children who naturally sense subtler dimensions have likely developed these empathic faculties in previous incarnations. Unfortunately this aptitude is negatively stigmatized by patriarchal left-brain cultures which primarily value logic, reasoning, and cold fact-based analysis.

Don Juan's teachings drew shamanism into discussions in mainstream America. Carlos Casteneda expanded his perceptual field by first learning to remember, and then endeavoring to maintain clear consciousness while in the dream state. Don Juan related that the human mind works a lot like Gemini's twins. While never utilizing astrological parlance, he defined two specific spheres (the dual sides of the brain) of sentience. The tonal was believed to represent ordinary consciousness, that which signified the collective response to consensual reality. Whereas the more magical state exclusively utilized by shaman and sorcerers was termed the nagual. It directly connected consciousness with the diffusive state of dreaming. The experience of reality differs depending upon which perceptual reference system is underway. Seth provided insight into this intrinsic duality as well. He recommended an experiment designed to integrate the seemingly polarized camps of perception. Rather than apportion one's day into eight hours of sleep and the remainder reserved for work and recreation, he advised individuals to wake and sleep at two-hour rotating intervals. This approach would blur the old line between so-called reality (the tonal) and what most term the "fantasy realm" (the nagual).

These examples point out that perception is malleable. There is also the matter of outright deception for minds to wrestle with. Jesus warned his followers to beware the wolf in sheep's clothing. Today's mass media serves its corporate masters and effectively worships Mammon and Mars. The power to control message is a favorite to totalitarian regimes and should never be underrated. America's government was ingeniously devised with three counterbalancing branches. Plus it's generally understood that the **free** press is intended to serve as a 4th estate. Its role is to ensure that the body politic remains well informed. After the triggering event of 911 the press acted sycophantically. Democracy requires the eternal vigilance that only an intelligent, aware citizenry can deliver. No population can fulfill that role when its access to facts is tainted, its consent manufactured on the basis of falsified evidence.

Let's take a look at something that generally passes beneath perception's radar: how the act of naming a thing grants it power. Playwrights recognize that characters come to life through their designated monikers. But a name or title can also mask character as well as conditions. The word may seem all-encompassing and thwart the need for a greater understanding. I recall hearing a bubbly psychologist relate excitedly that now "we have a word for what soldiers endure. It's called post-traumatic stress disorder." Her enthusiasm for the disorder's newly minted label diminished her compassion for the condition itself! As society appoints names to aberrant behaviors these distorted comportments find a place in our lexicon and become somewhat normalized, expected if irrational patterns of response. Metaphysical author Elizabeth Haich addressed this power in her book *Initiation*. She explains that by naming a disease it becomes an established energetic entity. Speaking its name inadvertently calls its being forth! Haich noted that when her young brother became feverish he described a green man coming in hot pursuit. She came to realize that her brother was sensitive enough to see the entity of the disease to which he had fallen victim. People invest time in talking about their illnesses, diseases, wounds, and disorders. Lunching at small, intimate places I am appalled by those who discuss sickness while ingesting their food. Unknowingly this habit reinforces their disorders. By speaking about a compromised condition one unconsciously attaches ownership to it! Nor is it merely accidental that news programs come on during breakfast, lunch, and dinner hours. This timing insures that people will ingest the world's bad news along with their meals. Talk about a recipe for disaster! Negative beliefs are absorbed along with the assimilation of nutrients, a truly toxic combination!

Gemini's twins remind us that comedy can serve as apt medicine for treating tragedy. Laughter proves therapeutic! Indulge as needed! Until the modern world comes to honor feminine sentience, a focus solely on left-brain solutions guarantees continued imbalance, and shortsighted asymmetric approaches to the problems that ail us. One by one we can embrace the counterbalancing gifts inherent to right brain starting with the development of intuition. Anyone can learn to listen for inner cues. In time the voice of innate wisdom is easily recognized. Turn off your television and allow the seduction of silence to lead your mind to new places. Author David Korten predicts a *Great Turning* to be inevitable. Such progress requires new perceptions. Civilizations cannot afford to be navigated by logic alone, the mind proves limited without due credence granted to the all-encompassing heart. Since human beings take on bodies for the purposes of learning we are encouraged to continually grow our awareness. That requires modifying belief systems that have served us in the past. A number of sources insist that the mind fixed on positive intentions can change one's life for the better. Still there is the law of karma to reckon with. Metaphysically speaking, the jury is still out. However it can't hurt to lean towards constructive thinking, particularly if one's personal goals and pursuits align with the greater good.

A Word On Retrograde Mercury cycles

Devotees of astrology recognize that Mercury can adroitly assume the cloak of trickster. One way he's capable of wreaking mischief is by entering a dubious retrograde cycle which occurs every four-months. During these three-week passages it is risky to purchase autos, electronic appliances, computers, or even pens! It's equally inopportune to book a trip, unless you have no problem with lost luggage, changes of plan, or annoying delays. During these retrograde phases expect an increase in nuisance calls or wrong numbers, confused agreements, late checks, or bank teller machines going down unexpectedly. Avoid signing legal documents or entering into binding long-term agreements. Since Mercury engages the perceptions of both twins, retrograde cycles compel us to look at things, including our own lives and current events, from a different perspective. That could be a good thing if you tend to operate within rigid parameters and regularly adapt to fixed protocols. Mercury facilitates adaptability and prompts us all to explore new options. As Scripture indicates, "There is a time for every purpose under heaven." During Mercury retrograde cycles, cultivate flexibility, and consider that the capacity to practice contingency plans just might constitute a fine art!

Do you know Mercury? Have you a friend, relative, or associate who is constantly on the go, given to ambidextrous multi-tasking? Is there someone perpetually speaking into their cell-phone, responding to emails, making the big sale, or otherwise getting their point across even if it entails more than one simultaneously conveyed perspective? Is this individual more fun than a barrel of monkeys, and sometimes just as mischievous? S/he acquaints you with the latest bistro, novel film, or hip discount boutique that just opened, or is nestled into a secreted alcove you never noticed before.

Mercury in Love

You'd think with the interior dialog Gemini was born to

negotiate that external communication would be a distraction; yet the Mercury born needs a twin-partner with whom to vigorously volley ideas. That is, someone both twins can mentally relate to. Gemini is playful and given to teasing. They are turned on by mental challenges, and therefore require partners who can match wits with them. Given their outlook, dualistic by design, projection becomes inevitable. From the Gemini perspective it may seem that a partner runs hot and cold. In actuality, Gemini's significant other(s) responds to the contradictory, dichotomous signals coming at them! Only the most enlightened Gemini will own that understanding. The Zodiac features two other dual signs (Pisces and Sagittarius), so if Gemini gravitates towards intimacy with one of those, it will lift projection to a whole new level. The result? A relationship that relays signals like a sophisticated quadraphonic wrap-around sound system!

Physically nimble, Gemini natives move with ease, demonstrate flexibility, and can prove adept gymnasts even in bed. For real and lasting compatibility their best mate must speak their language; and in all probability it must be uttered in more than one dialect. Should too much get lost in translation, humor will come in handy as an antidote!

Activities that Accord with the Season of Mercury

The winged Mercury governs streets, commercial venues, and roadways. One way to appreciate Gemini's dominion phase is by visiting a lively street market. If possible walk, bike, or use alternative transportation to get there. Establish intimacy with place! And if you find yourself in the mood to explore your immediate world in a manner never previously experienced, then patronize an out of the way café for your morning java. Afterwards meander down colorful streets, browse used bookstores or intriguing thrift shops, and claim your great bargain of the day.

Gemini rules the hands, so you might elect to enroll in a course that assists your developing a new skill. Consider calligraphy, weaving, painting, strumming an instrument, or updating your computer skills.

As the Zodiac zone that governs short trips, Gemini's hour of power favors taking wing on a spontaneous outing, picnic in the park, or journey to a neighboring town you've never taken the time to thus far explore.

Mind games, crossword puzzles, and board games come under Mercury's purview. Wear your thinking cap and put someone else's strategy to the test!

Take the kiddies to the local library to instill in them a love of reading.

Study a foreign language, join a book club or current events discussion group; read someone else's published diaries, and by all means, savor the process of devising your own journal entries.

Chapter 4

Cancer: The Realm Of Athena Awakened
Transcending The Family "Program" and Past Conditioning

Although the moon is a majestic luminary, she casts no natural light of her own. Instead she reflects the sun's radiance. Mystics believe that Luna serves as a conduit. She projects to earth the varied vibrations collected from the other planets of our solar system. I have chosen the archetype of Athena to represent the fourth Zodiac realm for several reasons. Her persona as drawn from myth is a fascinating one. Foremost, Athena denies that she originated from a mother, and instead asserts that she stemmed from the head of her father, Zeus! Now this is the perfect metaphor for the type of female who identifies with established bodies of patriarchal power and seeks personal empowerment through them. In other words such women offer allegiance to the status quo and thereby obtain power, prestige, and privilege by identifying with the boys' clubs. The Athena female retains an emotional distance and barely recognizes the degree to which her complicity with unjust systems impairs the lives of less fortunate (or empowered) women. Like the crab that resides within its shell, Cancer is known to build up a wall that can render her emotionally indifferent to the detrimental impact of policies implemented by the corporate state. These certainly exact a toll upon the vast majority of women. Jupiter, the planetary embodiment of Zeus, happens to be **exalted** in Cancer, the sign of families and bloodlines. Bill Moyers once facetiously stated that if you want to succeed in life, your best odds come from choosing your parents wisely. While the American dream purports to offer opportunity to every citizen, increasingly do powers extending from wealth determine the direction and outcome of citizens' lives. Jupiter is the planet of prosperity. Its affinity with Cancer suggests the relationship between personal destiny and the fiscal status of one's family of origin. Many Cancers in their quest for security marry into influential families; that is if they don't already come from one.

Having symbolically emerged from Zeus' head, Athena takes shape as the feminine projection of patriarchal thinking. Her sense of self is inextricably tied to male authority and its belief structures. In exclusively identifying with Zeus, as father, Athena demonstrates homage to a masculine lineage rooted in practices that are sexist, racist, and class-biased. Even when the Athena woman achieves on her own by attaining an academic degree in science, law, or psychology, the theories underlying these scholastic pursuits derive from and remain defined by men. Athena's devotion to tradition restrains the social progress of society, and assures that minorities will remain held back and/or fiscally restrained. Beliefs held sacrosanct within families are passed down from generation to generation and too often taken for true or inevitable. If Athena is not overtly deferential to her own father, or engaged in acquiring the laurels of academia, she will likely show allegiance to a specific male figure of power through whom her life will take on meaning, her ambitions evolve. Situated so close to Zeus' head (reflective of the belief structures of the patriarchy) Athena is cut off from feelings of compassion, caring, and true consideration. According to myth, Athena is the deity that champions warriors. She is a very powerful symbol for America given that our nation's birth date of July 4 consigns to her celestial rule! Little wonder that on today's increasingly militaristic global stage women like Condi Rice, Nancy Pelosi, Sarah Palin, and Hillary Clinton tout a macho stance that's more appropriate to male warriors! These are daughters of Athena! Seldom do they challenge the validity or deluded moral basis for war, our current Middle East War included. This quartet's members distinguish themselves only in terms of how to manage the bombastic debacle. History offers a number of women who have strongly portrayed the Athena archetype: Golda Meir, Madeline Albright, and Margaret Thatcher come to mind. As so-called civilization extends rights to women, frequently it becomes the Athena woman who is first welcomed into the male bastions of power. It makes sense that Athena would meet the criteria of the selection process. Ideologically she poses no threat. She wins approval because those hiring have no interest in ultimately altering the status quo. There is a silver lining in this cloud since clearly the Athena woman is no fool. When she's promoted other women make note of it; so she indirectly acts as role model to other females who entertain genuine ambitions. Athena is unlikely to advocate policies that lessen sexism in society, however she inadvertently paves a path to the "top" for women. Too concerned with her own security to rock the boat, Athena's status acts like a beacon to attract women with more liberal and liberating agendas. When Cancer native Colin Powell, at one time a favorite of the conservative right, spoke against Affirmative Action, the same programs that built his own career ladder, he identified unconsciously with his "inner Athena." (These archetypes impact and influence both genders.)

In the previous chapter we encountered the persona of Mercury, guardian of media and communication. Athena expands upon this venue by introducing marketing and its often insidious devices. The merchants of culture recognize it's frequently the female (housewife) who decides upon major purchases for the home; and the home is Athena's zone of dominion. The products families are conditioned to buy speak loudly for what a culture values. And products are exceedingly important to a society that has come under increasing if not covert corporate rule. This is where the analogy between Athena (Cancer) and her opposing sign Capricorn (Chronos) must be explained. What Athena markets ultimately serves the corporate state. Both signs, Cancer and Capricorn, function as a complementary pair and work in tandem to maintain the tradition-based status quo. Its axiomatic results are taken for inevitable; that society will always find itself structured like a ladder composed of class-based economic tiers. As a writer who has been published in a number of major magazines, I am yet to meet an editor or publisher who is not a Cancer or Capricorn! These are the sign kingdoms directly invested in tradition and the preservation of the status quo. In our "Communication Age" a great deal of power ensues from owning major media. Editors and publishers serve as gatekeepers to modern culture. They profoundly influence mores, attitudes and consumer-driven behaviors. When *Ms. Magazine* started up it was initially supported by grants and donations and thus able to bypass advertisers and their influence over content. Gloria Steinem penned a still significant essay that brilliantly exposed the ways and means deployed by advertisers to influence editorial content. Current magazines use the glossy allure of fashion to render women prisoners of their less than perfect bodies. The emaciated look is in. No wonder we see displayed across an ocean of colorful pages paper-thin models. Nor is it by accident that American women wrestle with deep insecurities when confronted with their actual body shapes. Very real tragedies stem from the unrealistic images young girls are expected to meet. Bulimia and eating disorders have become a silent epidemic. Athena's sign (Cancer) represents the stomach, and by extension signifies what we eat and how we nourish our bodies. The speed of modern life (added to media's hypnotic insistence that we must own every new technological gadget in order to experience bliss while struggling to meet the rising living expenses) leaves precious little time for things like healthy meal preparation. Enter the fast food utopia that America has fashioned to fill the tummies of its citizens with dubious quantities of faux filler. How many of us are being genuinely nourished? Due to the absence of quality nutrition, citizens' blood sugar levels rise and fall like parabolas. The emotional roller coaster that results is often misdiagnosed, and the "condition" treated for something it is not. As is often the case with the medical paradigm in its current corporate incarnation, symptoms may be negated while cause is left unchanged. A dietary deficit can readily lead to hypoglycemia and its effects simulate depression. A great many people currently self-medicate using alcohol, sugar, street drugs, or anti-depressants, partly because they have no idea of the connection that exists between what they eat and how they feel! Experiencing internal pain people naturally seek ways to alleviate it. Athena answers as the great friend of advertisers (who profit from sales instead of exposing the unsavory truth about their frequently unwholesome products) that she is! It's doubtful that Oprah Winfrey recognizes herself as a projection of Athena, but her popular television program claims to help individuals change their lives. Yet too often she assumes the role of unapologetic advocate for conspicuous consumption. The craving for more stuff drives the engine of consumerism; but mother earth is left gasping from the ecological overload a steady stream of manufactured wants creates.

The voice of spiritual awareness is not one which solely allots hosannas to God the father while failing to show due respect for the state of the Divine Mother. Her precept would likely echo the American Indigenous credo: "Live simply that others may simply live." Oprah's favored guest, Dr. Phil readily acts as one of media's ubiquitous "programmers." In emotional rants levied against the way desperate people cope with lives they barely can manage, he offers no compassion. Neither does he extend the slightest allowance for those factors that play into individual life equations, some a direct result of the narrow national policies that pit the individual against a great many unfair things.

As John Dean masterfully explains in his book, *Conservatives Without Conscience,* American society is witnessing a dangerous resurgence of the authoritarian personality type. Such persons are narrowly committed to a singular set of norms, a moralistic "one size fits all." Their very belief structures undermine the tenets of a naturally occurring diverse, democratic society. Dr. Phil personifies this mindset as football coach crossed with stern Southern Baptist Minister. Utterly convinced there is **one** right standard (or path) for all, he acts as enemy to the very essence of individualism. The Divine gift of free will only produces genuine learning if persons are permitted to make use of it! Universal laws are in place to rope in trespasses without Dr. Phil narrowing the range of behaviors (twelve sets) that human beings are destined to follow.

America (as an entity) is identified with Athena since its own birthday July 4 marks the nation a "Cancer entity;" and one that is soon to experience the opposition of Pluto along with its likely karmic blowback. Having fallen to militarism, the U.S. has essentially energized "the martial feminine," which is a grotesque distortion. From Capricorn (2009-2024) Pluto will teach not merely Americans, but humanity exactly what happens when too much of a nation's treasure is placed in homage to the military-industrial complex. Meanwhile working people are losing benefits, inclusive of health care, while wealth is being engineered to aggregate upwards. Social programs are everywhere being cut as prolonged commitment to an illegal war robs the nation's storehouses of investments intended for far worthier projects. Instead of focusing on these travesties the media echoes the voices of "the programmers" whose impassioned speeches direct all responsibility toward generally powerless individuals, those caught in spirals of deepening despair. Too many leaders demonstrate a dereliction of duty when it comes to authentic accountability. They have sold out the public's interests in their grotesque misuse of authority. When well-paying jobs are shipped overseas to boost corporate profits without regard for the communities left devastated, individuals thus impacted are not appropriate targets to pin blame or accountability upon. (At the time of this writing citizens are being asked to foot the bill for Wall Street's playing fast and loose with pension funds and retirement savings. Dangerous deregulation has allowed its gamblers to lose trillions on the artificial instrument known as "derivatives" along with overrated hedge funds! A fiscal tsunami now circles the globe to destabilize numerous economies.)

Angst is the natural response to the many tests ordinary citizens face, especially when leaders entrusted to preserve the commonwealth have effectively sold them out. Human beings are essentially wired to avoid pain; yet our culture accepts a woeful array of products and behaviors that offend sound sensibilities while undermining health. People are taught not to feel, to turn away from evidence revealed by the state of their inner lives, and instead focus externally on a race to acquire material goods. Media encourages a deluded pursuit of happiness. Rather than address the causes of pervasive societal dysfunction, it's easier to mechanically shut down the emotive mechanisms. Hence we have millions ingesting anti-depressant drugs, staggering numbers of obese persons, and a covert number of alcoholics. These maladaptive behaviors are at best attempts to fill the empty void that results from living in a state alienated from genuine, instinctive feelings. Americans share a collective incapacity to identify with authentic emotions; after all the workplace won't allow for such "indulgences." And when people lose the capacity to accurately assess self-satisfaction because they run perpetually "on empty," they make reliable shoppers! The Athena "model of success" requires their numbers! When pseudo-needs are vigorously marketed, few find the time or inclination to observe what's taking place on the inside, which is to say within their souls. For a lot of people it takes all they've got to keep up with the financial logistics of modern life.

Although America touts itself a nation that holds reverence for family values, the workplace is cruel towards working mothers. Athena ensures that obscene sums are made available to the military while only scant funds are allotted to Head Start or subsidized daycare programs. Women who must take care of aging relatives while still earning their livelihoods face impossible choices, a debilitating factor that's equally true for single moms. Adding insult to injury right wing pundits disingenuously volley jaded questions around that suggest women's work constitutes a luxury option rather than a necessity. In today's uneven economy Athena supports the business model, and its highest priority is getting the job done with monetary profit its bottom line. Hers is a de-feminized sentience. Sizable financial rewards are extended to those women who can close off their emotions and assume positions within the patriarchal paradigm, the model that Zeus built. Woe unto the rest!

Traditional astrology assigns to Cancer the symbol of the crab. To this tenacious creature the shell becomes a biological extension of its home. A Cancer woman of means once told me: "If you get a good address, the world will give you credit for the rest." In our Cancer nation, people of secure means are increasingly migrating to small, gated communities. Taking the quest for security to the max, the public stands by as funds are hemorrhaged into a new "Homeland Security State" that's quite fond of surveillance directed at peaceful citizens. Although the country was founded on the brave ideal of freedom, today's public seems all too willing to forego liberty in pursuit of a national state of scrutiny. (The threat of terrorism drummed up to coincide with Saturn, the planetary embodiment of fear, crossing our nation's sign/Cancer from 2003-2005.) If "you are what you eat," then perhaps a society becomes what it invests in. Demonstrating homage to Athena, The U.S. currently holds the dubious honor of being the number one arms merchant to the world! A well-respected *New York Times* columnist once stated, "There can be no McDonalds without McDonnel- Douglas." In other words international commerce (a/k/a trade deals) relies upon military support; that is when key fiscal negotiations are not forged at bayonet point! The inviolate spiritual lesson: "The ill-begotten goods will have to be given back" applies! No nation is above the law of karma.

Cancer, the established sign of the moon and her tidal forces suggests a strong psychological parallel with the undertow exerted by memory. Americans are enchanted with the allure of their historical past and mindlessly indulge in nostalgia. Anyone who's ever camped out or walked through wild countryside at night senses the power of the radiant moon. If a tiny computer chip can hold incomprehensible amounts of data, imagine what Luna retains having kept watch over humanity across the ages? Her light yokes us to ancient bonds, perhaps to our ancestral lineage. If we momentarily embrace stillness under her rays we can sense those silent timeless connections. On an individual basis the moon acts to codify habits or patterns of response. Thus while we imagine that we are reacting to events in the present, we may in fact be reacting to past impressions or the psychic echo of unhealed wounds. In the Ancient Tarot the Moon card reflects the abstract world of the subconscious. In that realm unprocessed impressions ebb and flow across the elusive terrain of our inner lives and act like invisible tides. Nonetheless it is believed by Western culture that our conscious minds exclusively control and direct our destinies. Thought and logic belong to the air element. Its cognitive parameters are insufficient for penetrating the mysterious depths of the water element, the basis for our feelings. Memory bonds us to the chain of life and speaks through a language of biological continuity. Consider the baby developing within the watery womb. Her physiological development unfolds in accord with the continuous sound of her mother's beating heart. If the fetus is a female, her eggs will develop while she's still inside her mother! Thus a pregnant woman holds the future seeds of her grandchildren, as they, too, become conditioned to the drumbeat of her heart! Human life takes shape in this watery world.

Birth is the first instance where the art of letting go becomes mandatory. Cancer, sign of the crab, comes equipped with tenacious pinchers, and Cancer natives find letting go an exceedingly difficult thing to do. A healthy acceptance of the law of change or what the Buddhists term impermanence allows us to cherish those precious experiences that cannot last forever. To cling too tightly chokes the life out of a great many bonds before their natural denouements arrive. On individual and collective levels people tend to romanticize the past to better live with what's absent from their lives in the present. Nations seem to take this approach when it comes to defining their national identities. Observe the way U.S. students are exposed to American history. Fact and fiction are braided together to form a largely false tapestry. The notion that Columbus discovered America leaves out the troubling truth that there were already established Indigenous tribes with viable cultures of their own previously living here. The historical account is rendered by and through the perspective of the dominant culture; in America that happens to consist of White Anglo Saxon Protestant males. People speak of the "good old days" in our land, but every era has countenanced grave injustices. James Carroll, eloquent columnist for *The Boston Globe* explained that our nation is engaged in a continuous process of evolution. It's caught up in a struggle between entrenched interests and the ideals upon which this experiment in self-governance arose. Carroll's assessment perfectly defines the focal tension depicted by the United State's "birth chart." Its sun sign is Cancer (thus supportive of the past status quo and families of established means), while its moon sign is Aquarius, champion of liberty and dedicated to egalitarian ideals. As Carroll described in a column written one July 4 to commemorate the nation's birthday: "America by definition is unfinished, because it forever falls short of itself. Born as a challenge to authority the structures of its public order evolve within a framework that continually transforms conflict into the energy for change." He correctly identified the nation's basic dichotomy and how its adherence to the past bucks up against its larger aspirations. America has been wrestling with these demons since its inception. Violence was used to seize lands from the Indigenous; slavery was institutionalized; and for a brief time even witch-hunts were conducted in Salem, Mass. During World War II the nation saw the unfortunate internment of Japanese citizens, and even now struggles to enact legislation that would curtail "illegal aliens" from crossing our southern border. The irreconcilable "relationship" between America's natal sun and moon positions is reflected in the gap between its just democratic aspirations and the protection of vested elites who place their personal security above the welfare of others.

In the previous three chapters we learned that Aries came to life as **fire's** first expression, rousing the quintessential spark of life, seed-like, to reach next for secure roots. Taurus then emerges as **earth's** first expression. The rooted seed progresses as it reaches above the surface to discover (and make contact with) the atmosphere. Gemini, **air's** first expression is roused. Next in the seed's evolutionary journey it acquires enough data about its environment to warrant a direct sentience. Feelings are born as Cancer comes to life introducing **water's** first expression, and completing the base of the four quintessential elements. It is through water that basic empathy arises. Ideally this sphere of sentience allots to human beings the capacity to identify with their brethren. Because Cancer is the first of the three water signs the capacity to relate on the basis of shared feelings has not yet matured. This may explain why Cancer people can appear sympathetic, but seldom will go out on a limb to place their personal security at risk. Their comforting words can seem like empty lip service. Athena works wonders with public relations however since she can deftly manipulate others' emotions. While appearing to care she is unlikely to support initiatives that threaten the status quo. Having denied her mother, Athena owns no direct empathetic link to women's needs, rights, or perspectives. Her tendency to identify with the "man's world" and its established protocols is nearly organic. This fact of her character makes her the favorite hired by conservative organizations when they are forced to "accept minorities." The Athena woman poses no risk to the old order. It's clear that she is no friend to feminism, yet ironically she may further its cause. That's because once she takes a position at father Zeus' corporate table, she opens the door for other women with more progressive views to enter and eventually assume their seats. Athena functions as something of a paradox. On one hand her very presence (by gender standards) teaches the patriarchy to respect the voice of the feminine. Yet she is not interested in advancing the true status of women. That aspiration is better served by Artemis, Hestia and Hera!

Since the sign of Cancer, Athena's domain, represents the family structure, it's worth noting what Professor George Lakoff offers on the subject. He's published evocative interpretations of contextual "frames" of language. Based on his research findings Lakoff noted a keen analogy between individuals' political dispositions and the structures of their families of origin. Individuals raised in strict homes dominated by a strong father figure gravitate towards conservative politics. This authoritarian top-down model generally demands that offspring structure their lives to suit the narrowed values of their conservative parents. The persons raised in such households (lest they own indomitably rebellious spirits) tend to identify with conservative causes, or the Republican Party. The alternative family model he related as that of the nurturing parent. Within these more open family systems children are encouraged to pursue broad perspectives and express themselves creatively. They are trusted to find their own truth on the basis of exploration, education, and inquiry. Such families tend to produce more progressive thinkers.

I remember coming upon a study that claimed Republicans tend to be happier than Democrats. The definition of happiness is subject to challenge. Suppose a person's concept of happiness only takes into account her status in the world; then it's easy to own personal satisfaction. The expansive consciousness that takes into account the larger social fabric might not find itself especially happy in today's world. Athena is comfortable enough adjusting to her own cozy shell. She can close off the conditions of others and focus on personal fulfillment, although she will pay a price in the form of short-circuiting her own spiritual need to grow empathy for the whole of mankind.

Edgar Cayce explained that one of the greatest of life's achievements was to build a happy home. In Tennessee William's famous play, *Night of the Iguana*, he offers a poignant scene between a spinster who takes care of her Grandfather, and a cynical priest disowned from the religious flock due to his alcoholic tempests. In answer to probing questions the dutiful woman responds, "Home exists between two people when they can rest together, when they build a nest in each other's hearts." That sounds good, although many of us would also request (as did Virginia Wolfe) a "room of one's own." Privacy alternating with quality time spent with others is probably the sanest prescription for inner balance. Still as populations seek security and increasingly pursue goals of material acquisition, how do the inevitable bouts of climate change figure into the calculus of personal and collective security?

Athena's cleaving to her father Zeus presents a challenge to the traditional role assumed by the mother in family life. Author and medical expert Dr. Christine Northrop pursued the question, "what happens when the mother goes missing?" She noted that women who lose their mothers early in life tend to identify with the "great Mother" in a mystical sense. Some crave the attention they never got by seeking celebrity status. In telling interviews aired on *The Actor's Studio* it's clear that a high percentage of Hollywood's luminous stars come from broken homes. And while it's often the father who leaves, the asymmetric family paradigm seems to evoke in many talented persons the urge to be widely seen and noticed.

The actual denial of one's mother is an altogether different matter, and carries with it a probable rejection of feminine feelings. The Athena female may show no interest in natural childbirth. She will probably prefer to be medicated; her baby delivered without any conscious discomfort or unnecessary inconvenience. Women who opt for unnatural births (modern hospital procedure) have a higher incidence of post partem depression. Is childbirth intended to function as a key Initiation process, a gateway to enhanced feelings of connection added to a heightened understanding? Can a society willing to medicate away primal emotions understand what this forfeiture might mean? It is the same with grief. We were not designed to be robotic creatures stuffing, repressing, or denying our emotions. Adepts have explained that earth is a unique planetary environ, one specifically designed for the experimental expression of a wide array of sentiments. Feelings function as the colors through which we design the canvas of our lives. Nor are the **hues of time** haphazard. The moon conducts the music of spheres into a series of reliable rhythm structures. These guide us back to the core of ourselves. To turn off the mechanism by which we identify feelings is to render our interior lives a spiritual wasteland. Our moods wax and wane in accord with the moon. These link us to the larger celestial cycles. As living creatures we tap into a great cosmic sea, and through our alignment with the moon we own the potential to develop empathy for others' feelings and experiences. Martin Luther King said, "We are caught in an inescapable network of mutuality, tied in a single garment of destiny." How profound and true; yet the full realization of this revelatory statement cannot be known or appreciated if the individual opts for chemical numbing.

A discussion on Athena is not complete without mentioning men and the moon! Cancer men feel her tidal fluxes profoundly. They wrestle with fierce emotions that other men manage to avoid or contain. One wonders if men endeavored to land on the moon to symbolically reclaim their long disowned feelings? Perhaps crossing this spatial threshold represents a small step in the recollection of the Divine feminine, an attempt at healing mankind's fissured template by making direct contact with Luna. Whether the mother is denied or embraced, her persona impacts the destiny and emotional development of her offspring. On an anatomical level Cancer is believed to "rule" the breast and stomach. Note these zones directly relate to the newborn's first nutrition. Plus the breast happens to constitute the body part erotically prized in our Cancer nation. More breast augmentations occur in America than anywhere else in the world. I recall a *60 Minutes* segment where cynic Andy Rooney pointed out that breast reductions were conversely the rage in Brazil, an "ass" nation. Breast milk was designed by Mother Nature to provide primary nurture for newborns; however Athena helped change that. Supporting man-made encroachments over things natural, Athena (by virtue of her connections with the business world and its advertisers) directed women to trade their inherent nutritious formula for the modern, convenient, if artificial equivalent. This "development" opened the door to a world full of faux food fillers. Once the substitution of bottled infant formula came to replace breast milk, the Divine intention of the great Mother Demeter became corrupted. The nourishment associated with the Mother, the feminine principle of origin, is what Athena denies. Poetic justice would amount to seeing Hugh Hefner's ridiculous face placed between two bare breasted women with a caption beneath reading: "Got Milk?"

We might also note the correspondence between this sign's

nomenclature and the dread disease cancer, now occurring in epic proportions. The plethora of industrial chemicals awash in our air, soil, food, and water table no doubt plays a contributing role in the breakdown of human immune systems. Add heavy metals absorbed through deodorants near key glands, and one recognizes a deadly mix of factors. These toxic exposures are exacerbating cellular breakdown. Industrial solvents are being absorbed into our bodies, and this cannot be healthy. Some believe the rejection of breastfeeding sends out its own biological cue that compromises healthy breast function. There are also attitudinal and psychological causative factors. Astute author Louise Hay elaborates on the connection between our issues and our tissues in: *You Can Heal Your Life*. I personally worked this issue by recognizing the relationship between a hardening of my breasts and an emotionally trying set of events. Entering into meditation I asked for guidance and was provided insight into the condition. I was shown that the breast as symbol of nurture represents the way women go about doing for others while often forgetting to take care of themselves. During this phase I was earning income, doing all the housework, preparing meals, driving the children to school, shopping, and keeping my mate satisfied. I realized the degree to which my life was totally centered on everyone but me, and resentment was building up. When I understood what fueled the condition, and moderated my diet by cutting back on caffeine, my breasts returned to normal. This was not the first time I witnessed healing by changing my behavior and consciously tuning into the mind-body link. Had I opted for traditional medicine I likely would have faced expensive tests and been prescribed drugs. I am not advocating the "self-help approach" for everyone. Some diseases serve a karmic purpose. This topic will be explored when we meet Hestia in chapter 6 of part II. What it's hard to argue against is that it's a sound personal investment to choose a wise, balanced diet and adopt lifestyle practices that support wellness. This is a lesson of relevance to every sign or archetypal path. Allowing our feelings, as opposed to denying or distorting them can often prove cathartic. *Moon Dance* was devised to assist you in that process.

Athena's sacred mandate is to instill in travelers on her path the realization that all are members of one quintessential family, that of mankind. How we treat one another is of utter importance to the evolution of our souls. This approach also supports the long-term prospects for mankind's survivability.

Do you know Athena? Have you a friend, relative, or associate who likes to play by the rules and tends to put business first? Is she quick to mask her sentiments, known to act in ways that protect personal security? Is there someone in your circle who is a "Daddy's girl," or has for much of her life been under the wing of a mature, powerful male mentor? Is there an individual who shies away from spending time in the great outdoors where she might get dirty or bitten by insects? Someone who prefers to be at home contained in the relative safety of her private castle?

Athena in Love

Since Athena is cast direct from the family mold, any romantic basis for a relationship takes a back seat to what her close relatives consider important or worthy in a mate. Not one especially resilient after a broken heart, she'd rather err on the side of caution and choose someone whose lifestyle will provide her with the comforts she requires. Still karmic necessity manages to play a role in the mate selection process experienced by all signs. Most people are imprinted by their family system's dynamics and as a result unconsciously draw mates who recapitulate familiar patterns. The realization of this "replay" is often obscured until it's too late! By the time Athena recognizes she's managed to attract a mate whose dysfunctional family programming matches her own; she's locked in! The birth chart pattern (as established between sun and moon) draws resonant components to life that take shape as the type of partner we attract. Intimate ties emerge from our charts and reflect not always desirable qualities. If Athena's love life produces drama it's usually the result of a push-pull driven by her own internal tensions. A focus on security leads to reciprocal fears of abandonment. This may cause her crab claws to clutch too tightly and thus choke the bond of its natural expressions. Ultimately, as concluded from the myth of Oedipus, one cannot run from her fate. It always manages to find us. Nor can anyone deny the birth mother in the hope of avoiding the lessons attendant upon life experienced through the feminine gender. Athena may unconsciously seek a father figure; someone that she imagines can provide her with strength and stability. But so long as she runs from herself and a fearless inventory of her feelings, no one can fill the void that ensues. What she ultimately seeks is the part of her psyche that she has disowned and must reclaim.

Activities that Accord with the Season of Athena

Terry Cole Whittaker some years ago conducted a charismatic television ministry out of California. One key insight she related is relevant to our discussion of Athena: "If you want to change your life, then clean out your closets." America is probably the only nation in the world where people own so much stuff they actually rent storage spaces to contain what doesn't fit inside their already hefty homes! When we give things away we make space for new opportunities and encounters to enter our lives. It's practically a spiritual law!

Given Cancer's rule of the home domain, projects aimed at improving the domestic ambiance are favored in the season of Athena. Plant flowers, paint your living room, alter the arrangement of furniture to reflect the best flow of energy that Feng Shui can deliver. Cull old photo albums to better organize your personal treasure. Consider commissioning a family portrait; or allot time to researching your family tree.

Invite relatives old and new over for a barbecue. Make a mid-year resolution to eat pure, organic (as opposed to processed) foods. Cultivate a backyard or windowsill garden!

To bond with your offspring, consider a family trip. Do your homework and first check *The Weather Channel* since Demeter's been feisty of late in expressing a feminine prerogative to change her mind. In her case that translates to climate instability!

Get in touch with friends you haven't connected with in some time. Rent old movies or DVDS and trek down memory's nostalgic path.

Write down events that still trouble you, and then toss the paper into a brass bowl or vessel that can withstand fire. Set a match to it and burn the words as you consciously bless and release all those you believe to have trespassed against you. If you do this ritual with sincerity you may find that you feel much lighter (or even emotionally liberated) as a result.

Chapter 5

Leo: The Realm Of Apollo Awakened
Summoning the Courage to Know the Heart

Traditional astrology casts upon Leo rule by the sun. Poetic license led me to choose the archetype of Apollo to best personify the Zodiac's fifth kingdom. The Romans allotted the name Helios to the mythical god destined each morning to draw the sun across the sky. Imagine the sheer passion that drives his chariot, the rush experienced in ever reaching for the great sun, forever seeking proximity to **the light**? The fifth kingdom summons the fire element from the ethers for its second incarnation. The ebullient sun with its intensely radiant glow has for cultures been worshipped as The Divinity or Divine Source. Since Leo natives directly identify with this stellar body they naturally gravitate towards the limelight. Observers tend to describe Leos they know as show-offs. How can any "child of the sun" hide her inherent light under a bushel? Apollo's sunny nature exudes a ready supply of charisma. And given that the bright solar sphere sits at the center of things, a parallel orientation becomes Leo's reference point. This may explain why the zodiac's lion is accused of being self-centered. The Tarot depicts the feline nature in the form of an angelic woman holding open the jaws of the grand, ferocious lion. What does the image imply? Perhaps that the higher self (our innate spiritual essence) must hold the reins to direct the "animal passions," not vice versa. In other words you either ride your erotic drives or they ride you. The king of the jungle survives on the basis of his raw courage. Leo, representing the Zodiac's realm of the heart, owns a capacity to know love to the fullest. As poet Kahlil Gibran shares in his eloquent work, *The Prophet*: "When love beckons you, follow him, though his ways are hard and steep." Continuing, "But if in your fear you would seek only love's peace and love's pleasure, then it is better for you that you cover your nakedness and pass out of love's threshing-floor, into the seasonless world where you shall laugh, but not all of your laughter, and weep, but not all of your tears." These profound words describe the experience of what it is to love, and it requires great fortitude in a world too often given to anything but love. In gifted moments romantic love imparts an ecstasy not unlike the feeling of ascending on invisible wings toward heaven. There, like Icarus one runs the risk of flying too close to the sun. All too rapidly its heat can melt our wings and leave us to an inevitable fall. Gravity invariably invokes its own "reality check." Shakespeare's incisive observations on human nature prove timeless. Regarding quixotic passion he noted often it was "consumed by that which it was nourished by." What then of Apollo's basic urge to fly? Is that fantasy inborn to all persons, or an imprint specific to Apollo? Leo native Amelia Earhart followed the urge by becoming the first American female pilot to cross the North Atlantic. Imagine the feeling of owning the upper atmosphere in her simulated journey toward the sun?

The first four signs introduced the quintessential elements. Now as we enter the fifth cosmic kingdom, we see a pattern begin to emerge. Fire will once again be followed by earth, air follows next and finally water, until the sequence repeats for the third and final time. Aries first embodied the power of fire as it stirred the life force into a symbolic awakening. In Leo this firepower moves from the head to the heart and fuels the all-consuming experience and expression of love. Author H.L. Chaloner explains in *The Wheel of Rebirth* that romantic love is a necessary step in the soul's evolution. Ultimately each individual comes to the spiritual point where they must reach beyond romantic love's embrace to gain a wider experience and application of Divine love, or love for the whole of mankind. *The Course in Miracles* begins its instruction by stating: "This is a course about love, which goes beyond what **can be** taught." This rather ironic introduction mirrors the truth that "logic limits love." Yet even *The Course in Miracles* makes its best logical arguments to prompt readers to choose love over fear when they find themselves confronted by life's many inequities. Another powerful insight into love is taken from Charles Fillmore's *Forty Days of Lent*. He links the ninth day of Lent with Love and states eloquently, "No condition is a barrier to love, only the incentive to love more." While poet Gibran advises: "Think not that you can direct love's course." It's rather that love will direct yours if love finds you worthy! Gibran explains further that romantic love will shake you to your roots. Thus it hardly proves a recipe for the faint-hearted. Jesus also imparted the centrality of love's importance by stating, "And the greatest of these is love."

Apollo as the Divine circle's keeper of the light retains the love of Creator should mankind ever forget its Source. Conveyed in art, literature, music, and theater has any topic received more inspired tributes, interpretations, or renderings than conjugal love, or its spiritual counterpart: love of the Divine? Much of the world's ancient art focused on depictions of deities that predated Christianity. The rise of Christianity was supported by a sizable investment in art projects primarily commissioned by the church. Call it an effective PR campaign that anticipated modern times. During the Renaissance, art moved from a focus on exclusively religious themes to one that embraced more human subjects. A flowering of expression took place on canvases as subjects of pure whimsy, still life compositions, portraiture, pastoral scenery, and landscapes all came to life. A visit to New York's Metropolitan Museum of Art, the Royal Galleries in London, or The Louvre in France provides the viewer with a comprehensive visual chronology of the evolution of aesthetic themes. Leo's rule of the fifth house, the Zodiac domain of the arts, links this sign with all forms of creative expression. When something marvelous is born through our human efforts we essentially imitate Creator having taken on a capacity to create. I often wonder if the extension of free will expressed in a dazzling display of human invention and innovation might not impart back something vital to Creator? Is our world a cosmic co-creative experiment? Does all of Creation grow on account of the sum of its participants' expressions, particularly the inspired ones? Cynics may cleave to alternative views. In the compelling film series, *The Matrix*, all possible human responses are already programmed into the "system." I prefer to think that humans fully utilizing their artistic, imaginative endowments can at times surprise Creator (as a parent learns unexpected things from her offspring)! After all ours is a universe still engaged in the infinite art of recreating itself; and we humans are midwives to some incomprehensibly beautiful and inordinately complex processes, developments, and outcomes.

Genuine love prompts a commitment of the heart. Singer Phil Collins related a common fear in his popular tune *Foolish Heart*: "You've been wrong before, don't be wrong anymore." How should the romantic soul who's already known heartbreak respond to the hip adage, "Follow your heart?" Can we truly discern our heart's message distinct from that of libido? At times both appear to work pretty closely together. Of course there are many types of love, but the English language offers only a single word to reflect them all. The ancients had a range of words to capture different concepts and experiences of love. There was Eros for romantic, sensual longing, Agape, for holding a thing in high spiritual regard, Philos for friendship, or dispassionate love, with Thelem reflective of the desire to fulfill a lofty ideal. Love also takes shape as a magical synergy that joins the artist with the gestation of her work, the parent with her child, and the lover with her beloved. Leo's 5th house invites and inspires stage productions, too. The magic of theater invokes a realm that truly mimics Creator. The experiences of love and art both glorify the human spirit and at times can make people feel undeniably divine. When romantic love is new each pair enters into bliss, a world designed it would seem exclusively for two. Soon everything outside their private bubble invades the all-too temporal Nirvana. Compelling as the invitation to get lost in another may be, the high generally proves fleeting. Ultimately there is neither guaranteed transport nor long-term occupancy available at any rarified oasis. Romantic love's parabolic journey is a ubiquitous theme woven into a wide array of myths and stories, both ancient and contemporary. Think Hollywood's tragic romances. When human affairs go awry, when fate descends to darken our brightest moments of happiness isn't it our reflex to cast our eyes upward in an effort to determine the source of the shadow? And who knows, perhaps light emanating from an ecstatically alive and loving human heart might very well challenge the radiance emitted by Olympian deities. As a number of myths relate, these entities seem given to exacting revenge, or otherwise putting mortals in their places! The heavenly bliss that leads lucky lovers to conjugal communion may evoke "something upstairs" that purposely sends harsh lessons intended to trick, challenge, or ultimately separate them. Modern literature extrapolates on this theme in hundreds of ways, and generally fashions romantic love to end in tragedy. How often do heroes and heroines of famous love stories escape that fate? *Romeo and Juliet* provides the evident example. Reborn as *West Side Story*, both tales portray conditions of a surrounding world directly set in opposition to the lovers. Confronted by hostile circumstances to remain together is to risk death, while splitting apart results in a mortal blow to the heart. It happens that Saturn, the planetary arbiter of karma and those life lessons designed for its implementation (via soul-wrenching lessons) is considered the "enemy" of the sun. Therefore Chronos, keeper of the dread hourglass and symbol of Saturn's influence upon the mundane plane, reminds us that all good things like love come to an end. Saturn-Chronos influences our fates by determining the time allotted to them. By enforcing the temporal nature of all things mortal he casts a grave shadow. Inevitably the count of time asserts that love's hour cannot last. Yet reaching beyond mortality author Dick Sutphen conducted evocative past life regression seminars. These powerful experiments in consciousness yielded intriguing evidence to suggest that romantic love indeed extends beyond the grave! Many have noted the unmistakable sense that a tantalizing "stranger" felt stunningly familiar from the onset. How do we explain such moments when individuals suddenly connect? (Thorough astrological analysis can reveal the whys and wherefores as demonstrated by the interface between both individuals' planets, there correlations between cosmic chords can be analyzed on the basis of themes energized by the "shared fusion zones.") Whether love is immortal or otherwise, Shakespeare imparted timeless advice: "This thou perceiveth that makes thy love more strong, to love that well which thou must leave ere long."

Leo's fifth house kingdom also governs the affairs of children. Jesus taught "Be ye as children to enter the kingdom of God." While many take the kingdom of God for a tangible place, more likely it refers to the "state of heart" that experiences the world through the fabric of love in which it was woven. To be a child is to maintain one's sense of innocence. That is not possible if one retains the psychic baggage accrued across the years from hard or disappointing experience. Egyptian mythology offers a parallel: once the human body dies it will be inspected by spiritual guardians who bear it witness. To determine the future course of the deceased soul, they gently weigh his heart on a scale where it must balance against a feather. To be young at heart is to willingly release the resentment gotten from broken dreams and betrayed confidences, "souvenirs" collected over a lifetime's journey. Such a practice keeps the heart light and youthful. Perhaps the extent to which we offer the alchemy of forgiveness to those who have trespassed against us determines the "specific gravity" of our hearts, whether they can balance against any feathers? Children of Apollo, whatever their ages, remain playful. Many are natural teachers because they readily identify with children. Plus they tend to morph into classroom hams! Leo's artistic fifth house wedded to Apollo's rush toward the light suggests limelight. Leos expect to be the pivots of attention. With the sun their internal navigator it's the cosmic equivalent of being born to "central" casting! Apollo is privileged to ride upon his glorious chariot. The wide panoramic view afforded expands his outlook. Some Leos become quite philosophical as a result. What Apollo observes from his revolving solar station is the movement of the other planets ascribed to their specific orbs. Witnessing the behaviors of the full Zodiac cast by virtue of his central position, he recognizes how each character is portrayed. All operate in accord with a great plan. Still Apollo is particularly keen to the dynamic dramas he's privy to! Perhaps this explains why the Apollo-born distinguish themselves in Hollywood, a significant number winning acclaim in the direction of motion pictures: Alfred Hitchcock, Roman Polansky, Madonna, Sean Penn, Robert Dinero, and Apollo golden boy himself, Robert Redford. These stars have gravitated to the film world to leave their indelible imprints behind as legacy. Hardly surprising that Leo Redford named his movie enterprise for aspiring young artists, The Sundance Festival! Taking the commandment of *Genesis* literally in the form of: "Let there be light," Apollo answers with a resonant creative response that consists of: "Lights! Camera! Action"! Just like magic movies come to life for vast audiences, and Hollywood's luminaries become anointed "stars." Their glamorous lives are vicariously lived by those who might otherwise succumb to quiet desperation.

Many people are fascinated by the daily vicissitudes met by the Hollywood glitterati. Their personal stories take on mass appeal and are zealously marketed to the public. The guerilla tactics of a paparazzi press deliver Hollywood's legends beyond the stage as the camera's scrutinizing eye follows. These icons can at whim create cultural standards that millions will readily follow. One such image is that of the "Latin lover." Leo natives Lucille Ball, Melanie Griffith, and Ben Afleck represent but a few that fell under its allure. Whatever tests the hopeful heart encounters (whether the product of personal failings or those sent by the gods) is the choice **to love** ever wrong? Is the motivation to extend love ever wasted? Perhaps the answer to these existential questions is best revealed through the life-to-life continuum. Just as the birth chart represents where the individual soul left off in terms of progress drawn from former incarnations, intimate bonds suggest a parallel plan of continuity. Readers may wish to pursue this subject. I recommend Dick Sutphen's: *You Were Born Again to be Together*, and *Past Lives, Future Loves*.

As one born with both the sun and moon in Leo, it's been my experience that the sign of the lion encounters especially challenging karmic conditions with respect to conjugal love. (I hope to elaborate on the four types of Initiation a human heart can encounter in its efforts to know love to the fullest. This assessment will be the subject of a future work.)

Leo has long been considered the sign of royalty and thus by extension represents kings and queens. Currently Leo's polarity, Aquarius prepares for its much-anticipated cycle of dominion for the age of dynasties is about to give way to that of the truly democratic state. The progressive social order expected to result will hold as sacrosanct the dignity of every human being. Mankind is advancing beyond allegiance to a centralized power. The reign of Divine right of Kings has passed; and the challenge before every individual is that of awakening to the realization that all are holy. The true Aquarian Age leader will not act to glorify self, but rather to improve the conditions of those s/he is destined to serve. At the onset of the Piscean Age Jesus was accepted as the son/sun of God. Modern mankind has now arrived at the juncture where it must summon equal reverence for the Divine daughter, his feminine counterpart. It just so happens that Apollo is a twin. And soon his sister Artemis shall emerge into the cosmic limelight. In many ways she signifies the Dawning Age of Aquarius. Visionary writers are seldom aware of the force behind the prognostic intimations they feel compelled to share. Their pens act as conduits tapped into higher sources. Mystics believe that guardians exist to assist mankind in its evolution. These silent partners work with souls capable of demonstrating the spiritual understanding necessary for the conveyance of advanced prophetic messages. Plausibly George Lucas served as such a vessel as demonstrated in his writing the *Star Wars* trilogy. In the figure of Luke we find a glowing Apollo, while his twin sister Leah is equally endowed with potent powers. It is through their alliance that the death star championed by Darth Vader is defeated. This story may well signify the central myth for our times. Future students of literature may study it the way my generation analyzed *The Iliad* and *The Odyssey*. These twins drawn from Lucas' vivid imagination symbolize a balance between the Divine masculine (son) and Divine feminine (daughter). When the two act in concert, they are capable of defeating Mars, the usurper of the holy circle, and ongoing threat to our planet's prospects for peace. It is by Divine design that Apollo's (Leo) kingdom sits directly opposite that of Artemis (Aquarius) on the great cosmic dial. Currently as the Aquarian Age is summoned from the dreamtime (giving rise to something akin to a collective nightmare at this closing phase of the Piscean Age) the relationship between heaven's twins must be recognized and then reconciled. How else might their massive creative endowments inspire future generations with new paradigms of purpose, passion, and possibility? When both sides of Divinity join together, balance, wholeness, and grace thrive. Indeed this is the likeliest prescription for mending what hath been torn asunder. The world of exclusivity, false privilege, and divisiveness is passing away to be replaced by one where the unique contributions of all citizens will be welcomed. To usher in this promising new cycle Apollo and Artemis must join forces and work in concert. (We will learn more about Artemis' attributes in chapter 11, Part II.)

Since Apollo essentially identifies with the light, his disowned shadow is inevitably projected. According to Carl Jung "the shadow" represents the shaded portions of the human psyche that individuals refuse to own. Disassociated this darkness, collectivized as evil, is targeted at specific persons who unwillingly serve as "scapegoat populations." These groups bear the castigation of devalued worth on the basis of entirely false pretenses. Targets of horrific acts the fate of these unfortunate souls proves that civilization has not earned that (civilized) status. "Whatsoever is done unto the least of these" negates any notion of spiritual progress. When societies repress their darkest impulses the results become war, culturally accepted forms of violence, serial killers, and cruel, corrupt rulers. Apollo as being of light is repelled by such behaviors for "light beholdeth the darkness and understood it not." Since opposites often attract, Apollo may find himself seduced by the type of person who acts without due regard for personal accountability or the faintest consideration of others. According to myth, Apollo always managed to fall in love with an unavailable if attractive consort. He also tended to reject the available ones who wanted him most. Every sign has liabilities to cope with, but Leo is most identified with living from the heart, a tough prospect in a world where a great many are committed to other priorities. The sunny lion struggles with periods of inner darkness especially when romantic love doesn't conform to his preferred script. Regardless, the heart remains Apollo's compass. It is precious and tender. Therefore travesties of the dense mundane world compel him to periodically distance himself. At these junctures he must seek a direct infusion of light. As keeper of the light, the one destined to perpetually draw the radiant disk across the sky, he cannot afford to become entirely **of** this world. To do so would compromise his connection with the Source, basis for his own intrinsic radiance. It poses a near mythic task to reckon the mysteries of the human heart inside a shopping center world. Should conjugal love fail, Apollo must find the strength to replenish himself by returning to love's Divine Source. For many this spiritual course may become a long and earnest pursuit. Since we enter this world through the channel of imperfect parents wounded by their own past histories and karmic scenarios many of us recoil against the very love that would cast out our darkness, guide us towards the light of healing. Fortunately for Apollo, born to the realm of the lion, he too may possess a magical feline quality that allots the capacity to access nine metaphorical lives. Some people readily bounce back from a broken heart, while others remain immobilized. Apollo suffers in the experience of mortal love, but finds the replenishment to start anew because he opts to love again. This gift emanates from the Divine Source of luminosity planted within him, a resource that never falters.

There are those who due to pride would rather turn their hearts to stone than ever risk loving again. Their inner beings become private tombs immune to the vibrant rhythms echoing from the beat of their hearts. There is a parallel expressed by the weather. Regardless of the apparent density of cloud cover, the sun's expressive rays are always shining. This metaphorically explains love's hidden miraculous power to heal. The return to wholeness may require patience, a commodity found in short supply in our instant gratification culture. Where there is an absence of love we might consider what it costs a society to become instant? What price is paid in the collateral of relationships that like buds too quickly grabbed never gain the chance to bloom into the flowers they might have become. There is a peculiar aberration found in some unfortunate Apollo types who demonstrate a twisted attraction to love's innocence, or should I say innocents. Instead of treasuring the heart of the child on a symbolic plane, the distorted Apollo pursues romantic love by seeking out under-age children. Jon-Bennet Ramsey was a Leo born for the stage, but her life was cut short by an abductor. Roman Polanski (a Leo) was once cited for sexual indiscretions with an under-age minor. Vladimir Nabakov, the novelist fascinated with *Lollita*, created a character in fiction through which to pursue this taboo.

The human heart, biological throne to Apollo, is associated with the fourth chakra. It is situated at the center of our seven innate invisible energy vortexes (albeit visible to high clairvoyants). Each accords with one of the human body's major organ systems. The first three chakras reflect those drives that come under the auspices of free will. These include the physical appetites of the body, the energetic expression of our emotions, and the deductive reasoning drawn from the "lower" mind. The heart situated at the center conducts both the upper three chakras--which facilitate higher awareness and heightened spiritual empathy, along with the three lower ones. Based on its position central to **all** seven chakras, love is foremost recognized and responded to when the individual has found and can retain a balance among the first three chakras. The reward for such an alignment centers consciousness in the heart. Allow me to explain: envision the first three chakras as three sides of a perfect equilateral triangle. The triangular form depicts harmony. Its equal sides point to balanced expression among the respective zones of body, mind and emotions. Clairvoyants explain that the hardest of the "invisible bodies" to master is the one correlated with the emotions. If an individual fails to demonstrate self-discipline with regard to her body she will likely manifest illness or excessive weight gain. Shame may place a covert veil over intimacy. The individual who fails to nourish his mind in pursuit of new learning retards his own growth and likely thwarts his partner's, too. Nor does the person without due command of her emotions create other than conflict and chaos wherever she endeavors to share a nest. When key aspects of our personal lives are out of balance it is impossible to remain centered in the heart. We're too busy wrestling with our own internal "demons." It's been said that one must love herself in order to love another. Self-love requires that we master, or at least bring into harmony, the drives and ruling motivations associated with the first three chakras. When this "triangle" is brought into unison, consciousness can remain centered in the heart. This level of personal mastery once established invites the higher states of awareness to naturally filter down. The heart remains the chief conduit; but it only conducts the energies associated with the higher chakras when the entire being has come into alignment. This protection is for our own good. One who experiences the transcendental state of at-onement, glimpsing the relatedness of all things previously perceived as existing outside the self, is compelled thereafter to choose to act from altruistic motives. Don Juan referred to such activity as "a payment to the spirit of mankind." He lamented the fact that its universal account remained under-funded. Ours would be a very different world if every child was conceived and raised in love. Instead, we remain tethered to the historical chains of karma until cycles of redundancy are transcended. One strategy to that ends is shown in being kind to one another. The late William Sloane coffin offered, "We must be merciful to one another since we live at each other's mercy." It's a shame that popular books like *Women Who Love Too Much* and *Smart Women, Foolish Choices* describe the path of unconditional giving from the heart as a flawed course of action. No mention is made to recondition the men who under thrall to Mars send thousands of women to hospital emergency rooms every year. The patriarchal bias inherited from religious rhetoric still sees fit to cast all blame upon "Eve" for the unbalanced actions taken by "Adam." The world needs love indeed! Given today's context, one wonders how behavioral psychologists might interpret the unselfish works of Mother Theresa, Gandhi, and Jesus? Behavior that doesn't readily put self-interest first is seen as dysfunctional. And even by taking a self-protective stance pain cannot be avoided in this life. It's inevitable. The vast majority will likely know heartbreak all too well. The forgiving heart can heal and learn to open again. Few Leos would trade the experience of loving for never having loved at all. However it's apparent that our issues over time filter into our tissues. This disconcerting fact helps explain the prevalence of heart disease in modern America. The overly rich, high-fat diet that has become the norm for too many plays a role; but so, too, do the "energetic patterns" that individuals harbor as a result of "failed" relationships. Unprocessed psychic debris gets stuck in the heart. The Apollo nature's levity can only ascend if life is based on freely loving. The daily somnambulistic waltz into job slots that squelch creativity proves deadly to our spirits, although efficient if the societal goal is conformity. The heart, key to the state of the inner being, knows when it's being cheated! To Apollo, a dead-end career niche is tantamount to wearing chains. After all he was endowed with wings to fly! The rise of the corporate state has narrowed professional opportunities considerably. And while a few brave souls succeed in defining their own career paths, the vast majority feels left behind. Author Marcia Sinetar champions, *Do What you Love, the Money Will Follow*. This strategic initiative can lead to success, but it requires about as much faith as learning to fly. Tithing, an established religious principle advocates that one can secure a blessing by donating ten percent of their profits to a spiritual institution or humanitarian cause. Apollo by instinct generously offers his gift of light to the world. Living in accord with our inner calling places us in synch with a generous flow pattern. The universe, which author Gregg Braden describes as a responsive field, tends to reciprocate by providing us with what is needed in return. I operate with this understanding, and it's taken me on amazing adventures. Arguably it takes courage to abandon a secure paycheck in pursuit of a potentially fickle society's response to your concept, talent, or product. Perhaps a time will come in human evolution where the vast majority will be employed in work that is both cherished and meaningful. Work that comes from the heart and is loved! We have a long way to go before arriving there! Currently a whole lot of people labor in routine dead-end jobs that foster lives of quiet desperation. Hearts pay a price for this collective sense of heavy gravity. In meeting the demands of the material world personal core desires are often betrayed. High levels of heart disease reflect the protracted angst that results from this trade-off. Many individuals adapt to demanding jobs with the hope they'll one day save enough money to break free and pursue their real career passions. What percentage actually arrives at that goal? Heart health would fare better in a society that didn't so readily bow to Mammon and keep Apollo earthbound. His winged spirit is required to reinvent a social order that emerges from love. When one's lifework comes from the heart, it is impossible to hold a meaningless job. Ultimately all human beings are progeny of the Great Spirit. Apollo knows that if one wholly identifies with the light, there can be no sustained darkness. Mankind's historical record challenges this notion because those powers that seek to obstruct the Light also wish to minimize its representation on the earth plane. To accept the path directed from the source of inner illumination requires bravery. The sun god's affinity with the lion supports Apollo's quest: to live true to his heart. Others may opt for lives of external comfort, but Apollo must place higher ideals first. No external authority can substitute for the source of transcendental wisdom that issues from Apollo's innermost guide, his own luminous heart.

Our inner Apollo prompts us to make love a sacrament by acknowledging that a spark of the sacred dwells in each one of us. And often it is in sharing, living, being love that we are transformed. That may be the greatest esoteric secret of all!

Do you know Apollo? Who is the most charismatic member of your family circle, someone that naturally plays the role of entertainer and loves (to the point of needing) to be the center of attention? S/he is lively and animated when in the company of children, and perhaps too frequently assumes the cloak of braggadocio in endless boasts of romantic conquests when not rallying enthusiasm for successful projects that resemble high-stakes gambling.

Apollo in Love

Leo-Apollo is said to fall in love with love. Lucky perhaps is the one targeted by the radiant beam cast from Apollo's innate source of fire. Leo does his best to place his beloved on a pedestal and where possible treat her to the largesse of the kingdom. The lion is a showoff. Hollywood is celestially governed by Apollo's fifth house domain. Naturally Leo unconsciously seeks after the limelight and prefers an attractive partner to show off to the world. There are those Leos who may instead prefer someone low key who will not compete for the spotlight. For this impossibly romantic sign, sex is best when it takes on an aura of magic. No sign lives for love, pursues erotic adventure for the sheer rush of passion more than this one!

Activities that Accord with the Season of Apollo

Although hardly in vogue these days, you could break with convention and throw a bona fide costume ball. Rather than ask guests to "come as they are," I'd suggest the more imaginative invitation that they instead "come as they were." In other words challenge friends to dress in a manner that relives the possible persona they experienced in a previous lifetime. (Don't we all harbor intimations of who we might have been?)

Apollo's hour on the stage invites you to join a summer theatre, enroll in a painting or sculpture class, volunteer as nude model at an art school, or become a camp counselor. Express yourself daringly!

Follow Julia Cameron's advice from *The Artist's Way*. To court

180

creative inspiration it's best to periodically break away from your ordinary routines. That's right; even if it means playing hooky and taking off somewhere you've never been before. Court the muse of spontaneous creative combustion, and rekindle your inner fire by breaking out of your own redundant pattern. The mouse in the maze may find the cheese, but there's certainly more to life than dairy products!

If you haven't dated in some time, join a matchmaking service! Court Cupid's legendary arrows. Or write a poem or eloquent love letter.

Visit a Humane Society and adopt a cat, or sponsor a child in a 3rd world nation. Take a chance on following the most generous impulses that issue from your heart!

Chapter 6

Virgo: The Realm Of Hestia Awakened
Mending the Inner Healer

In the Zodiac's sixth Divine realm, we encounter Hestia, goddess of the hearth as well as the temple. Jean Shinoda Bolen defines her as one of the Virgin Goddesses. As such her identity is fulfilled without the assistance, participation, or validation of any male person. She is naturally empowered from her own inner source, and represents the second "incarnation" of the earth element. Tied to nature, Hestia is endowed with an ancient, if uncanny knowledge of healing herbs and natural medicines. In traditional astrology Virgo connotes the virgin. She signifies the sign-realm directly associated with health and diet. Just as Cancer rules the stomach, and Leo the heart, Virgo represents the body's complex intestinal network. A marvelous organic plumbing apparatus, its workings are mirrored by the mechanical operation of our own kitchen sinks. There we readily note what happens when the pipes get clogged. Edgar Cayce identified "poor eliminations" as the central cause responsible for a wide array of diseases. Those born with key planets in Virgo-Hestia's zone of dominion often face health karma. It facilitates major mandatory lessons that eventuate in the coming to terms with one's career path, or ethos of service. The adage: "Physician, heal thyself" tends to apply. Through efforts taken to overcome their own challenges the daughters of Hestia frequently become conduits for others' therapeutic processes.

Modern media conditions most individuals to expect life to deliver them endless pleasures. They seldom face their intended spiritual lessons until forced to do so. There's nothing like an illness to cause a rethinking of one's lifestyle and previous priorities. Indeed a health challenge suggests the time has come for renewed contact with the inner self, that holy sanctum within. Not surprisingly in many indigenous cultures fasting plays a role in the healing process.

By this means the body is given a respite from the usual expenditures of energy required for processing and digesting food. Fasting may include a willful entry into a mode of silence or solitude. Mystics believe that our cells are programmed to heal themselves. This inherent mechanism becomes disabled when the body succumbs to Cancer or AIDS. Edgar Cayce was asked about the prospect of curing the dread disease in readings recorded during the 1940s and accurately predicted that it would be a long time before that medical hurdle was overcome. This is why it makes sense to honor the adage: "Prevention is worth pounds of cure."The growing holistic health field supports that initiative. Earlier in the text I offered the contention that "Mars rules." Its "force first" approach influences the way medicine is practiced in the United States. Conventional methodologies orient towards cutting out "offensive" material, or otherwise poisoning it via chemotherapy or radiation. Holistic medicine in contrast assists the body in its effort to heal itself. The body requires vital fuel to succeed in that mission; and that's where herbs, vitamins, minerals, and whole foods come into play. These items generate from Hestia's natural field of expertise.

Years ago while living in the Bible belt I was invited to go horseback riding with a nurse who worked at Shands Hospital (it's an adjunct to The University of Florida). Out on the expanse of Payne's Prairie with a notable chill in the air I asked if the virtual worship of the Gator football team played any role in the practice of medicine. She replied it was the **only** thing surgeons discussed while performing operations. They enthusiastically shared scores and plays when not bragging about the team they were flying off next to see. Repeating my question: "So you're saying that football does influence the practice of medicine?" She replied, "I don't see how it could not."When logic's cold left-brain approach dominates medicine intuitive feelings are short-circuited. I believe that both "sides of sentience" taken in balance provide for inspired approaches and the best applications of therapeutic modalities.

Currently forty-five million Americans carry no medical insurance; so increasingly the responsibility for sound body maintenance falls on our selves. Medical doctors are not required to study nutrition; but gurus of holistic traditions recognize the importance of vital foods when it comes to sustaining or regaining sound health. The Hestia woman is by Divine design a natural healer. Diane Stein contends that *All Women Are Healers* in her book by that title. Listening for our body's cues guides us to the foods we genuinely need. Orthodox medicine and its male priests arrived on the scene rather late. The original healers were women (or shaman of both genders). Their knowledge of herbs and therapeutic practices was passed down through oral traditions that spanned centuries. This heritage was decimated during the Middle Ages when several million women were slaughtered based on the allegation they practiced witchcraft. The church would not countenance true power accruing in or expressing from females. Wise women have long functioned as midwives; that is until modern medicine pushed birth into hospitals where it's generally been treated as a diseased condition. Male doctors have co-opted delivery and sought to rob it of its gentle lineage by censoring female practicing midwives. The MDeity continues to devalue, when not placing into doubt the contributions of intuitive, holistic health practitioners. It controls access to remedies while belligerently upholding a left-brain mechanistic approach to all forms of therapy. Modern hospital birth often reflects brutal insensitivity. Mother and baby are quickly separated just after the newborn emerges to bright lights and is given a slap on the butt. Welcome to earth under Mars rules! Dr. Robert Mendelsohn explained that just before the turn of the twentieth century numerous birthing women would mysteriously die during childbirth. Only later was it learned that doctors routinely passed from room to room while treating patients suffering from contagious, communicable diseases without even bothering to wash their hands! The doctors became effective carriers of infection and unknowingly introduced these dangerous microorganisms into women's wombs while delivering babies! Due to doctors' arrogance the condition became so prevalent it was given a name, "hospital bed disease." Dr. Mendelsohn exposes a great many disconcerting facts about the medical profession in his books: *Confessions of a Medical Heretic* and *Mal(e) Practice*. He makes the case that doctors operate like a priesthood right down to their use of arcane (drug) formulas. Accustomed to wielding authority, members of the MDeity do not like being questioned, especially by women.

There's the tacit assumption the doctor knows best, and women can't expect to be experts about their own bodies. Meanwhile American hospitals are rated 37th in the world; and the fourth leading cause of death in the United States stems directly from botched up medical "care." This includes malpractice, surgeries gone awry, and drug reactions based on unexpected contra-indications resulting from patients ingesting three or more drug "cocktails!" (The effects of big pharma's products are seldom studied in combination.) Educating myself I made the conscious choice to experience home-birth. I read everything I could find on natural childbirth to prepare. Suzanne Arm's *The Immaculate Deception*, along with *Spiritual Midwifery*, written by The Gaskins (who perform homebirths on "The Farm" in Tennessee) added to literature published by La Leche guided my path.

Although the medical field makes the claim it's extended life spans, a great many factors have contributed to that phenomenon. One is sanitation; that is the indisputable benefit of indoor plumbing. To imagine the way people lived before the medical field emerged is to envision an epoch where compassion still mattered. Today the medical field operates like an industry. It serves foremost the profit motive and therefore directly undermines the Hippocratic Oath! As Michael Moore's recent film documentary, *Sicko* portrays, the caring element has largely gone missing from modern healthcare due largely to the intercession of the insurance industry. Because money matters more than human beings' quality of life, it's lucrative, not to mention cost-effective to treat effects rather than eradicate cause. A good example is early onset Diabetes. This recent health crisis emerged as prodigious quantities of sugar and/or corn syrup were routinely added to ordinary foods like breakfast cereal! Instead of eliminating the cause behind the sugar-overload, people have instead been treated with drugs. They are not taught to remedy their dietary fare! Medical school is expensive, and drug companies spend millions in search of cures. (They probably spend that much on advertising products.) To recoup these costs, big pharma has turned doctors into glorified drug merchants. When individuals are kept on medical maintenance programs (i.e. drugs for life), guaranteed profit is generated. The treatment of cancer has become a big business in the United States. Although it's a virtual certainty that exposure to hundreds of toxic chemicals plays a role in the burgeoning Cancer epidemic, rarely is any link suggested between the profligate use of pesticide, herbicide, insecticide, food additives, coloring agents, preservatives, and the foods we ingest, along with the water we drink, or air that we breathe. These unnatural chemicals are continuously assimilated by our bodies, and often stored in fatty tissue like the breast. A new test for "body burden" identifies well over one hundred industrial solvents now found in our bodies! Better living through chemistry? Or has modern mankind (women particularly) been rendered a vast Guinea Pig experiment! A plausible explanation for breast cancer could involve the use of underarm deodorants. These heavy chemicals are applied to a region close to both our lymph nodes and our breasts. The absorption of metallic particles could trigger a reaction in our tissues. Has anyone studied this possible link? Instead sentimental pink bears are sold while a disingenuous atmosphere of smoke and mirrors engulfs the numerous treatment centers. It's not politically correct to discuss the obvious analogy between toxic exposures and astronomically rising Cancer rates.

Hestia, as representative of the sign of Virgo, champions cleanliness as well as purification rituals. This universal therapeutic strategy promotes clearing the body of debris and toxic substances. It calls for relinquishing dangerous, self-destructive lifestyle habits like smoking, and curbing excess sugar and caffeine intake. Years ago I lectured for *The Whole Life Expo* (Fort Lauderdale, Florida) and was fortunate enough to hear the research results of enlightened oncologists. They vigorously studied the medical models other countries utilized in their treatment of Cancer. The team concluded that America's reliance on chemotherapy seldom eradicated Cancer. At best it would add about eight years to the individual's lifespan. The Cancer almost always returned. In contrast, at the Huffland Clinic in Germany, a more holistic approach directed toward healing the whole self: body, mind, and emotions (spirit) was utilized and Cancer actually disappeared! Another dynamic speaker I encountered was author Sherrill Sellman whose book *Hormone Heresy* clearly explains how the pharmaceutical industry has managed to frame every stage of a woman's life into a pathological condition. Drugs have been contrived for menstruation and cramps; other drugs have been designed for birth control, with still more used to speed or slow down labor. Childbirth is often facilitated on the basis of the busy physician's schedule, bearing scant resemblance to any notion of a "natural delivery" for countless young mothers. Later drugs are offered for fertility, and yet more drugs for menopause! It's a travesty. Patriarchal medicine has co-opted nature and turned normal processes into virtual diseases! Much that is taken for disease can be remedied by and through diet or lifestyle changes. The medical model prefers that citizens remain tethered to one of their many "managed" treatment programs!

Earlier in *Moon Dance* I related that mankind has arrived at the "changing of the guard," or final phase of the Piscean Age. The sign that stands opposite Pisces and represents its natural polarity is Virgo. Astrologer Alan Oken wisely deduced that each age borrows qualities from its polarity. Thus the Piscean Age that gave the world Jesus, the **fish**er of men, also holds reverent regard for his **Virgin** Mother, Mary. She reflects a state of purity and perfection. Offered as Divine proof one can transcend "original sin," the holy virgin allegedly never succumbed to the temptations of the flesh, i.e. human sexuality. She overcame what the church demands be avoided at all mortal costs, except within the confines of marriage where it's granted a conditional pardon. If Mary conceived during an Immaculate Conception, by implication all conceptions to follow were unclean, neither blessed by heaven. The church has long lobbied that sex outside of marriage is a sin powerful enough to damn the human soul for all eternity. What bunk! It's evident that twisted beliefs about sexuality have distorted far too many Catholic Priests. Lawsuits stemming from child abuse are notorious. Countless women have been robbed of a capacity for sexual pleasure because their minds have been trained upon dutiful distortions and a conditioned habit of sensual repression. With warped notions drilled into them repetitively some can't easily transition from "good" girl (i.e. celibate) to responsive sensually forthcoming marital partner. Sex researchers understand that for women the climax is a complex process. It results from much more than anatomical stimulation by penis, tongue, or hand. Women respond best when their emotions are powerfully engaged. A man can have a sexual response to a doorknob! By in large if a woman experiences a loving bond with a man, particularly a sensitive, erotic one, she won't require any feminine version of "Viagra." (Nor does smoking a "man's cigarette" to compete for lung cancer prove "she's come a long way, baby.") Since the advent of patriarchy women have fought repeated battles for control over their own bodies. The feminist movement largely emerged as a call for reproductive freedom. Women took justifiable issue when abortion debates were handed over to men and nuns! Are they the arguable experts when it comes to *Our Bodies, Our Selves*? Nor is this debate yet satisfied. It's remarkable that modern America still pits the question of a woman's right to choose against the fundamentalist religious views of an ignorant segment of the citizenry. Purporting to constitute the moral majority, as the bumper sticker attests, it is neither!

Hestia as virgin Goddess may choose to decline sexuality altogether. Because this persona works best within the culture of female monastic life (the roots of which predated Christianity) she may prefer female sexual partners. Lesbianism is not consigned to any specific sun or moon sign since it results from varied factors; however, Virgo does make a good cosmic case for it. The sign of the virgin does not resonate with penetration to the degree other zodiac signs do. Virgo can live a celibate life, a fact suggested by its link to the Tarot card depiction of the Hermit, i.e. one who resides in solitude. Many prefer to live alone. The typical Virgo is a perfectionist who requires neatness, cleanliness, and order in her midst. Not only sun, but moon or Mars found in Virgo can render the individual incredibly compulsive. I have observed friends and family members with these signatures. They remind me of ants as they scurry busily about putting everything back in its place. These behaviors are both efficient and automatic. It's as if they can't stop themselves. I don't suppose such persons could surrender to truly wild, spontaneous sex if there were dirty dishes sitting in their sinks! Control-based standards hardly allow others to relax when sharing homes with those compelled to unceasingly meet standards of perfection. There is a method to Creation's madness in that every principle on the great cosmic dial serves a necessary purpose. Virgo's penchant for sterile conditions is perfectly conducive to laboratory experiments or medical environs. There are moderate Virgos, and a few who function in absolute chaos. Those who embrace traits opposed to their natural inclinations portray a condition known as the "reaction formation." Since every birth chart brings a variety of archetypal voices to life, Hestia's presence may be overridden by other personae, as in counterbalancing planetary placements. For the most part the monk poses as an apt signature for Virgo, the sign that suggests the honorable St. Francis of Assisi known for his kindness to animals. Virgo also resonates with Shakespeare's Friar Lawrence who brainstormed the apothecary mixture that rendered Juliet virtually dead so that Romeo could revive her in the mortuary and ideally elope with his star-crossed lover. Friar Lawrence reminds:

> "For naught so vile on earth doth live
> But to the earth some special good doth give.
> Nor aught so good, but strain'd from that fair use,
> Revolts from true birth, stumbling on abuse."

Every modern pharmacist should memorize that quote. From the astrological perspective Hestia governs the zodiac's sixth house which pertains to health matters, herbs, and even pets. Ancient priestesses recognized that their animal companions imparted special powers. This connection was portrayed with wit and charm in the film classic *Bell, Book and Candle*. Kim Novak as modern witch sends her cat to the apartment of the man she is tempted to enchant. This wonderful film concludes there is no magic greater than love, the oldest spell of all! Alice Walker speaks compellingly about the special bond that exists between a woman and her pet in *The Temple of My Familiar*. Although scientists too often denigrate the intelligence of our four-legged companions, these unconditionally loving beings convey numerous messages nonverbally. And it's a fact that widows and widowers fare better if they share their homes with an animal companion. Americans annually spend billions of dollars on their pets! Yet a great many creatures still end up in shelters. The Buddhist belief in reincarnation sees **all** life as equivalent participants in a vast, endless mind stream. It differentiates itself into the countless living forms we observe. To the Buddhist, a fly can reincarnate as a person and vice versa. They believe it is auspicious to find one's self in human form, and very unwise to waste the opportunity constituted by this "precious human lifetime." Therefore while embodied as a human being the Buddhists advise diligent work in the form of good deeds as a strategy to work off past karma. Conscious altruism put into action efficiently burns karma and guarantees an advantageous future lifetime. This understanding sets the foundation for the Buddhist order and its monks. The path of service is consistent with the Zodiac's 6th house, realm of Virgo-Hestia. And because Buddhists recognize the sacredness of all sentient living creatures, they particularly lament the foul treatment of animals worldwide. In the United States, one grave injustice to animals is seen in cosmetic tests done on rabbits and small mammals. University and private labs do horrific things to animals retained as prisoners. Such heartless protocols are justified as necessary measures for testing the efficacy of new drug treatments. And whereas animals in the past were raised on farms to graze freely, that is now a rarity. Increasingly large "industrial farms" treat chickens, hogs, and cattle like factory parts crammed into impossibly small spaces. These unfortunate creatures are often force-fed to fatten them for quick market sales. Most are shot with antibiotics to ensure they won't become sick from the cruel, unnatural conditions they are raised in. Not only do we humans become what we eat, the same holds true for animals. Mad Cow disease was in part derived from cows fed the remains of other cows! This is a travesty. (To learn more about the benefits of a vegetarian diet, I recommend: *What's Wrong with Eating Meat*, by Vistera Parham.)

It's also worth noting that acts of purification have figured into religious and spiritual practices throughout the world. To the Hindu, incense is burned before the images of the deities one offers prayers to. The Catholic Church uses similar rites with an intention to clear the atmosphere. It would prove inordinately beneficial if mankind focused on similarities amongst religious practices rather than areas of disagreement. Author Gerald Jampolsky asked wisely in his book *Love is Letting Go of Fear*, "Do you want to be right, or happy?" The premise applies to Virgo given its attachment to the ideal of perfection often accompanied by a need to be right. By reflex Virgo tends to project her inborn critical acumen at everything and everyone. Hestia is Divinely mandated to alter imperfection, to bring that which is dis-eased into a state of healing. However her incisive critiques are not always painless or easy to implement!

The *Course in Miracles* asks the question, "How does the teacher of God know when healing has been delivered?" The answer as given is that the result is not for the giver to determine. This *Course* goes on to offer, "All illness will disappear at the instant it is no longer necessary to the sufferer." Perhaps that holds true if the afflicted individual has perfect faith. However as an astrologer who has seen chart indications of health karma play out true to cosmic form, I have to wonder? Miracles are said to represent a speeding up of natural processes. Certainly many things once thought to be impossible are not. Countless books on self-improvement promise renewed health through lifestyle changes. Some sources attest to the therapeutic power drawn from focusing the mind on positive intentions and improved outcomes. Still texts on reincarnation link disease with personal karma. A predisposition for medical problems may become exacerbated as a result of inherited family genetics, lifestyle choices, or exposure to toxic products. The karmic factor helps explain why one individual utilizing dietary changes heals while another does not. I regard the body as a temple, and believe we each are given stewardship of our "instrument." It makes sense to act responsibly by making life-affirming choices. Competing images designed to work against this goal include the countless toxic temptations the marketplace dresses up using glamour, promises of sex appeal, or power. When something as pernicious as cigarettes can be sold to millions, the power of advertising becomes clear. Readers may recall the legal cases brought against big tobacco companies when they boosted lethal nicotine levels and blatantly lied about it. They were well aware of the addictive properties of their product when their boards of directors chose profits over persons' health. I met a Virgo woman so hooked on cigarettes her face had been disfigured by a cancer that eroded her nasal passages. She was forced to wear a prosthesis over one eye, and yet she still smoked! A guru leading a meditation seminar was approached by a sincere student who asked,

"How can I quit smoking?" The sage replied, "Love yourself more." Quite plausibly whatever pain we harbor (emotional, physical, mental, or spiritual) constitutes a call for healing. As Louise Hay points out in her illuminating book, *You Can Heal Your Life*, personal long-standing issues eventually impact our tissues. Medicine tends to treat symptoms while too often neglecting cause. Problems tend to recur and generally assume the physiological paths of least resistance.

Genuine health is based on a homeostatic balance, the harmonic integration of our physical, mental, and emotional bodies. According to Carlos Casteneda's teacher, Don Juan, the human body is actually a "luminous egg." It is not as physically dense as we have been conditioned to see or believe it to be. Following from this context, Edgar Cayce's clairvoyance enabled him to view the human aura. Each of our body's major organs emits an energetic force that imbues the aura with specific color. The result is a field of light projected around the human form. It is analogous to the layers of atmosphere that surround our planet. (Modern industrial effluents have managed to damage this precious ethereal web too.) Cayce was able to recognize degenerative ailments on the basis of discoloration to the aura. He understood that dark blotches indicated impairment to specific organ functions. Once a major disease is established in the body, it is expensive and inordinately difficult to treat. However, if instead it's recognized at its onset less invasive options can be utilized. While I sojourned in Singapore I met a number of persons dedicated to the study of Pranic healing. This methodology, what conventional Western medical practitioners would refer to as an alternative treatment focuses on the body's energetic field instead of a direct manipulation of physical tissue. Intuitive adepts are able to see the **light field** that surrounds the human body. Its subtle indications can be "read" by seers who may then direct healers towards appropriate areas at risk. Across the world spiritually astute healers make reference to the light field that radiates from the human body. Furthermore they understand that its discolored regions point to the deterioration of specific organs. This enlightened methodology is yet to be put into practice by Western medical practitioners.

Edgar Cayce's trance readings often referred to Ancient Atlantis.

There too we find therapeutic technologies that directly made use of light frequencies. Our ancient counterparts harnessed the light condensed into gemstone crystals. The subtle emanation of their rays was directed into the body for the purpose of delivering remedies. This understanding found its way to India where astrologers have traditionally advised wealthy patrons to wear specific gemstones to ward off dangerous planetary cycles. Perhaps there is something to this strategy!

Mainstream Western medicine considers these approaches unscientific and primitive, the work of mere superstition. Entirely engrossed in materiality, Western medicine has lost all sense of primary spiritual cause. Between immunizations and the never-ending effort to sterilize environs against bacteria that are themselves programmed to endlessly adapt, a fight against nature leads to the creation of ever-new foes. Just as the rainstorm arrives to cleanse the land, holistic health experts believe that certain childhood diseases provide a similar cathartic release. To suppress non-threatening infirmities may foster the development of worse illnesses. Plus the use of antibiotics has rendered certain strains of virus resistant. A similar strategy applied to the eradication of insect pests I witnessed firsthand years ago. Residing in Puerto Rico I watched in horror as old trucks sprayed Malathion through residential neighborhoods just as families sat down for dinner. I began a letter campaign of protest directed at the mosquito "control" program being conducted by the University of Puerto Rico. One of its proponents answered my letters in a debate published by *The San Juan Star*. He offered statistics to make his case; yet his numbers revealed the obvious: that implementation of this dangerous spraying program saw mosquito populations drop on average 50%. The issue he failed to address was what happened to the surviving 50%? The program facilitators repeatedly increased the dosage of Malathion only to see the same percentages recur! In other words, the mosquitoes were being artificially forced to adapt more quickly, thereby speeding up the natural selection process! A wiser more natural approach was utilized on a neighboring Caribbean island. There residents were asked to diligently clear their yards of old pots, tires, watering pans, tanks, and anything that could hold stagnant water. By reducing the source of mosquito proliferation an improved situation resulted. As a rule, it's generally more cost-effective to work with Mother Nature than against her, lest one seek to know firsthand the impact of Gaia's Revenge (as orchestrated through her ubiquitous elemental systems).

The Buddhists embrace principles sacred to Hestia for they not only understand but also live by the ethos of service. It makes sense that when you act in a manner that makes this world a better place for others, you inadvertently improve your own karma for this lifetime or one yet to come. And service can be a wonderful thing. It's good for recipient as well as donors. Unfortunately patriarchal society has relied upon the unpaid labor (vast pools of diverse services) of women for centuries. This unacknowledged revenue stream stems from religious orders where women opted for, or otherwise found themselves destined for lives of lowly servitude. The legacy of the nun as fostered by the Catholic Church comes to mind.

Traditional astrology assigns to Virgo rule by the winged Mercury. Gemini is its cosmic cousin since both signs are governed by Mercury, the planetary champion of teaching, learning, speaking, writing, and crafts executed with the hands. When we give anything a name, it becomes its own entity. Shakespeare rhetorically asked, "What's in a name? A rose by any other name would smell as sweet." A consummate wordsmith he consciously chose the names to suit those characters he would immortalize in his grand dramatic works. Mercutio from *Romeo and Juliet* demonstrated a Gemini-like character in his ready use of wit as demonstrated through devilish word play. J.K. Rowlings made a fortune on her imaginative *Harry Potter* series, and part of the recipe for that success is to be found in her ingenious use of names for characters and places as sprinkled throughout her evocative storylines. Concluding our discussion linking Hestia to Mercury we note a Virgo-like influence over modern education. Its entire academic apparatus operates through a separation of disciplines. Specialized arenas of study define the modern educational model. According to this established system one person may become accredited in science while another masters mathematics. Certainly there is merit to educating minds with respect to the particulars. However, too keen a focus on specificity can and does undermine the awareness of the Gestalt. The student is led to cultivate expertise in a certain field while demonstrating ignorance towards the fundaments of a more holistic education. The medical field is notorious for missing the forest for the trees. In one of my favorite films, *My Dinner With Andre*, the narrator's mother is hospitalized. Andre explains that he intuitively recognized the seriousness of her condition, and was preparing himself for his mother's inevitable demise when the medical doctor, a specialist, kept telling him she would be fine. The doctor focused on the body part he was trained to treat and failed to recognize the true state of the entire human being before him. As a result of the Doctor's cheery prognosis Andre was left to experience something tantamount to a semi-schizophrenic state. His own perceptions told him one thing, while the doctor, the presumed expert, suggested something else entirely.

There are many approaches to healing. Given the stress of modern life added to the range of chemical agents armed against us, it's likely that many of us will find ourselves compelled to explore "the paths less traveled by" in pursuit of personal healing. One thing I've learned on my journey is that you must let the healer in. A good massage therapist can enter your body's energetic field as intimately as a Tantric lover. Once "inside" s/he can facilitate a release of toxic material stored not only in tissue mass, but also within the light field that surrounds the body. Visualization is helpful, as one is advised to see her body already operating under optimal conditions. Metaphysical author Emmet Fox describes this as "building a new mental equivalent." In this case it's one based on sound health. Individuals should guard against reckless use of language. For there is often an unconscious tendency demonstrated unwittingly when people refer to an illness using the possessive pronoun. To say aloud "my cancer" is to take ownership of a life-threatening condition! This verbiage sets into motion an inadvertent hold on a compromised (diseased) state of being.

Hestia imprints human beings with the useful realization that service to others is sacred; and that we are all ultimately here, in bodies, to heal each other.

Do you know Hestia? Is there someone in your circle of friends, family, or associates who knows the latest herbs? Her savvy extends to teas and natural remedies. She seems to know what to offer to mitigate a variety of symptoms. Is there someone you turn to when your plants need watering, your pet needs a walk, or you're going out of town and need someone to collect your mail? Someone who has a good grasp of duty, details, and discipline? Hint: She's the most efficient individual you know, and her home is as neat as a pin!

Hestia in Love

Hestia is a meticulous, fastidious sort who may perceive lovemaking as a duty. She recognizes that it's a creative way to mend or heal a strained tie as well. Due to her dedication to the ideal of service, her lover's needs are dutifully accommodated in both the kitchen and bedroom. Virgo needs to feel that s/he is right, and thus requires a mate neutral enough to deflect adversarial sparks that could otherwise ignite conflict. Of course Virgo can always choose a mate who embraces a resonant belief system. If both tend to look at the world through the same prism, the basis for critique or critical debate is defused. The daughters of Hestia demonstrate love by administering thoughtful care to their partner's body, mind, and sometimes soul.

Activities that Accord with the Season of Hestia

Okay. You know you love lists; and there can never be too much order when it comes to satisfying the typical Hestia-girl. In her private world, large or small, everything must be consigned to its proper place! And Hestia's daughters do tend to load the stuff on since earth signs identify with tangible items, "possessions r'us" style. Hestia's phase of dominion is the appropriate season to put your recipe file in order, organize your bookcase, or clear out closets and drawers. Good Will, Hospice, or Salvation Army could probably make use of what you're not using.

Pick up a novel cookbook and avail yourself of the ways and

means to prepare exotic healthy vegetarian recipes or ethnic dishes. Stock up on herbal teas and while you're at it, sample real Chai from India!

If you don't know how to execute a specific skill and are willing to learn, get a guidebook for directions. Maybe you can refinish a cherished piece of old furniture? Invite friends over for a painting party, and if you're really courageous offer them fine wine and gourmet pizza and turn the occasion into a minor home remodeling enterprise!

Prune your plants.

Take an inventory of your cleaning supplies and get rid of toxic chemicals. There are effective natural alternatives that don't wash down your sink to return to the water table leaving some poor frog or amphibian with two sets of genitals.

Consider using a subliminal self-help tape to assist you in releasing a self-defeating habit like smoking.

Design a prayer altar.

Indulge in a facial, pedicure, or manicure. Visit a day spa so that therapeutic cleansing rituals will leave you feeling much like a Goddess.

Clear your intestines of old debris with a colonic.

Buy fresh flowers to reenergize your domestic atmosphere since these provide a potent dose of recharge direct from nature.

Make an informal pilgrimage to one of Florida's springs and bathe in refreshing, purifying prehistoric waters. The Fountain of Youth is yet to be discovered!

Chapter 7

Libra: The Realm Of Hera Awakened
Attaining the Ideal of Balance

In the seventh Zodiac realm naturally associated with marriage and partnership we meet Hera, who was known as Juno to the Ancient Greeks. Queen of Olympus she was married to the all-powerful Zeus (a/k/a Jupiter). However according to myth he was also believed to have been her brother! Hera represents Venus' second incarnation. We encountered her first in the persona of Demeter (Part II, chapter 2). As representative of Libra Hera holds dominion over the seventh Zodiac house. This sector sits directly opposite to Mars' throne as situated in Aries, the first house. The interplay between the first and seventh houses sets the template for all close partnership arrangements. This dynamic interplay reflects the truth inherent to the adage, "opposites attract." What exists in polarity either proves antagonistic or synergistic. Much depends on the state of the egos (parties) involved. As the symbol for Yin and Yang reveals, one circle is enclosed perpetually within the other. In this way both combine to form a complete whole. When two individuals recognize their inherent attraction and work effectively as a team, it's a beautiful thing. However, as Edgar Cayce cited family life (and therefore the attractions that lead to filial unions) tends to act as the hotbed of karma. Close relationships often trigger exceedingly tough lessons in human growth. Apparently that factor was not much different on Olympus. Hera, champion of marital union, had her share of crises to cope with. Zeus, ever the philanderer, disguised his appearance (as perhaps only a god can) in order to share intimate moments with compelling maidens on earth. His brazen infidelities were sometimes cruel and often embarrassing. For mortals (and apparently immortals as well) few wounds prove more painful than marital infidelity. Faithfulness, the ideal of Hera's existence (and staple of her identity) was repeatedly violated by the callous "extracurricular" activities of her spouse. Hera's fate is given to upholding the power and sanctity of the institution of marriage. As one of the timeless principles on the cosmic dial, her Divine oath of allegiance to her partner is potent and means everything. Yet typical to the reasoning of those taught patriarchal value systems, Hera is chastised for her **responses** to Zeus' behavior. The "Blame Eve again syndrome" castigates Hera while taking a "boys will be boys" attitude of leniency towards her spouse. Down the centuries Hera has borne the rather dark reputation for casting spells designed to punish Zeus' partners-in-lust while his considerable trespasses are laughed off! Since the sexual revolution, infidelity is no longer reserved for men alone. In Shere Hite's book, *Women and Love*, she reveals her research findings: three quarters of married men **and** women admit to having (or having had) an extra-marital affair. What bearing does this have on the covenant of marriage? Is fidelity merely quaint? The state of and definition for marriage are profoundly altering in our world. Committed gays demand legal marital rights but this goal is impeded by fundamentalist political factions. Wherever one looks clearly the institution of marriage is undergoing growing pains.

Hera's personality is equated with Libra's balance scales. The sign of justice projects onto the state of marital union the expectation that each partner's rights, privileges, and responsibilities will be equally respected. That is the only way the scales can balance! How could women appreciate that intended status when up until relatively recently they were considered the property of men? Even today in fundamentalist regions women own few rights. A decade ago female professionals residing in Afghanistan pursued careers and enjoyed many freedoms practiced by their sisters of Western cultures; but all that violently changed when the repressive Taliban seized power. Women are now kept under virtual house arrest, forced to wear bourkhas, and generally denied access to public life. The pain they endure on a daily basis is unimaginable. Hera's rages have been falsely construed as a kind of madness. Yet madness is the natural response to injustice that long goes unchallenged! As Susan Faludi pointed out in her book *Backlash*, the definitions for mental illness (rendered in desk reference volumes used by professionals in both the legal and psychiatric field) are devised exclusively by men. As cited earlier in this book, the usurpation of the circle by Mars has led to modern social hierarchies built upon sexist notions. Present power structures extend from uncontested Judeo-Christian precepts that recognize "god" as a white male equivalent. Across the world Caucasian men have used this godly presumption to wield power over others, especially women and people of color. This behavior has led to redundant wars and certainly lacks any basis in Divine justice. Libra, as the realm of fairness, equality, law, and partnership sets up a direct and permanent challenge to the authority asserted by Mars in his claim to absolute power. Acting as polarity, Libra embodies the principle of justice and seeks to curb the fiery god's abuse of authority along with his insistence that humans pay homage to his war-oriented image and likeness. A nation's level of spiritual evolution is demonstrated in how it treats women and people of color. Until civilization supports true equality structural imbalances will continue as the "norm" and erode peaceful attempts at communal life. When any privileged group makes a claim to exceptionalism, it treats others as second-class citizens or worse. Long-standing hierarchies that divide society into haves and have-nots are the result of beliefs that do not recognize all citizens as equal. Established elites are loathe to accept challenges to their reigns of power. Because heaven's lesson plan is foretold on the basis of predictable planetary movements, indications suggest the old status quo is in for quite a shift. To briefly summarize the nature of upcoming cycles, Libra constitutes one of the four cardinal signs. It is mandated to uphold social justice. During the seven-year span of 2010-2017, planetary heavyweights will occupy all four cardinal signs and form a cosmic cross with Libra pivoted at one of its arms. Signs that by design champion competing interests clash. Around the globe critical battles will ensue over human rights, equality before the law, and economic justice. The challenges obstructing mankind's ideals will prove formidable. Political infrastructure is already in place that challenges privacy, free speech, and the right to peacefully assemble. In America right wing judges have been appointed to regularly side with big business interests (profit/mammon) over labor. Prominent judges think little of granting carte blanche to polluters who compromise citizens' rights to safe food and drinking water. Increasingly high courts are granting government agencies the right to spy on citizens; and during the Republican National Convention there were even pre-emptive arrests made! What happens to a society when the means for redress are blocked at every turn or legislated away?

Hera is the Zodiac's chief advocate for matrimony while also a supporter of fair play. Placing these two components together, it becomes clear that the Divine marital ideal is best served by and through equitable partnerships. Having followed the lead of "Mars rules,"American society champions the individual's personal freedom at the expense of relationships. The sacred notion that "two become one" has been undermined. Sexism's imprint plays a part in crippling the prospect of true union, which is to say a coming together that approximates the helpmate ideal, the state of two persons committing to each other's growth. Gender parity remains a radical notion due to centuries of patriarchal programming aided and abetted by fundamentalist traditions. As mankind approaches that point on the great cosmic dial where the Divine daughter, Artemis, is summoned to usher in the much-anticipated Aquarian Age, the genders must come into positive alignment. This process of aligning Yin and Yang forces will gradually be enacted on a global scale. The cosmic clockworks have been calibrated to prepare for this realignment phase. In fact every one of the five outer planets (their orbits range from twelve to two-hundred-forty-eight years) has transited Libra in the past fifty years. Each has played a key role by essentially infusing Hera's realm with vital evolutionary force. The outermost planets remain in signs for anywhere from seven to twenty years, and thus embed specific lessons into entire generation pools. Uranus, the maverick planet (directly associated with Artemis/Aquarius) crossed Libra from 1968 until 1975. Individuals born during that seven-year phase are apt to rebel against previous norms and explore (if not downright engineer) more egalitarian partnerships. Pluto, the planet of massive overhaul established through profound endings that eventuate in cathartic new beginnings crossed Libra from 1971 until 1983. This planetary ambassador of profound transformation marked individuals born during that phase with a need to pave new relationship paths based on mutual empowerment. Such persons will find themselves compelled to design more equitable roles for each gender to play in the world we share. Neptune, the planet of inner dreams and fantasies crossed Libra from 1942-1956. It roused the ideal of romantic love based on the quest to find and secure the one true soul-mate (even if trial and error led its bearers to a number of potential contenders).

There is nothing arbitrary about the plan that animates our solar system's cosmic clockworks. Transits of the outer planets represent scheduled visitations, cycles timed for didactic purposes. The movement of these bodies articulates a dynamic progression that gives rise to a progressive set of themes. Ultimately these prompt human growth. New understanding emerges which essentially evolves the entire human equation. Astrology allows us to anticipate those cycles intended for specific increments of conjugal learning. Where my generation held Pluto in Leo, my daughters are both marked by Pluto in Libra. In Hera's kingdom Pluto's promise of rebirth calls for gender equity in all love-based bonds. Born after the feminist revolution, after my generation laid the groundwork, these daughters are privileged to experience more enlightened partnership than was possible to my peer group. It's as if the earlier generation boldly headed west in Conostoga wagons so their descendants could enjoyably reside in already colonized villages.

Balanced roles based on genuine mutual support (a good definition for true partnership) are something new in the way of mankind's experience. Plausibly matriarchal societies predated our patriarchal civilization and directly empowered women. But the current worldview has held dominion for centuries and prefers to keep people in the dark with respect to alternative models. It presents what currently exists as the only viable way for a society to organize and operate. The Mars-rules model puts the pressure on individuals to better their lives. And there is certainly nothing wrong with persons holding high standards and competing with their own personal bests to "become all that they can be." But this is only half the equation, one side of the great cosmic coin. Conscious persons who commit to healthy lifestyles will find their efforts undermined if the society they inhabit does nothing to curb the trespasses of others. An individual may train the mind to think positively and still not notice a stray bullet heading her way given there are two billion guns on American streets today! Personal peace is exceedingly difficult to cultivate if the surrounding society invests in violence and supports notions of vengeance. Since Libra is the sign representative of justice it speaks to our criminal justice system. One aspect worth examining is what our society considers legal. Under Mars rules it's not surprising that gun ownership is championed as practically a birthright. Alcohol, tobacco, fast foods, guns, and violent pornography are all lethal products, as are cars when driven under the influence of "road rage." Yet these elements are considered lawful unquestioned components of modern American life. The angry, aggressive society does not place a high premium on peace-loving healthy citizens. Everywhere experts abound touting the ways and means to "personal security," "personal growth," "individual investment plans," " personal accountability," and of course "personal success." Note that everything is **self**-centered. What does this species of sentience cost in the way of relationships? What is missing is a "marriage of minds." During the present age phase transition the navigational wheel must be taken away from Mars, that means the collective's focus on the ego-driven self. Otherwise if Mars remains the determinant of mankind's direction, our earth vessel will assume the course of a calamitous war added to ultimate resource depletion. What are missing from our shared reference contexts are those values associated with Venus. She is the natural partner, intended co-pilot, and Divine counter-balance to Mars. The pair was Divinely devised to work as complements. Without equal representation afforded to Venus as well as Mars the great balance skews off course. Evidence of this dis-equilibrium is seen in the compromised state of too many integral ecosystems. Patriarchal "authorities" have broken the vital contract that human beings share with nature. To remedy the situation societies must invest in Venus. In other words instead of hemorrhaging assets in support of wars, grants and subsidies must be directed at programs that teach peace, tolerance, and social justice. One need not look far to realize that works of beauty accrue value over time. That can hardly be said of Mars who through war has ravaged great cities and laid civilizations to waste. A healthy society requires input from both Venus and Mars on a proportional basis. In an enlightened civilization males would not be continuously prepped for war via vigorous sports programs, nor taught to identify with Mars and his brutal rites of passage. Instead young men would be encouraged to embrace their inner anima, the voice of Venus. That would advance the cause of inspiring males to really learn to love. The converse process is underway given that many women now readily identify with their inner animus, or Mars. This is seen as women take on independent positions in society, even in the military. Some emulate men by devoting their lives to competitive sports and that all-important macho goal of who gets the ball(s)! As gender roles evolve through the current challenging transitional phase many worthy women are finding it almost impossible to find men of their own ilk. Few males seem truly open to equal balanced partnerships in spite of lip service to the contrary. They remain products of past conditioning. Just as wealthy individuals tend to vote for policies that benefit their personal fortunes, many men prefer to retain the privileges allotted to their gender and see no reason to alter the status quo that has served their needs down the centuries. Altruism is not an attribute prized by Mars or the Mars-driven society. Another insidious obstacle to gender equality is found in fundamentalist religions. References to ancient so-called holy books are used as rationale for denying autonomy to females, especially when it comes to reproductive freedom of choice. False religious precepts belie the greater truth: that the essence of Creator is found in each individual regardless of gender. Any belief system that endorses the holiness of one half of humanity (male) while casting the other half (female) into iniquity is blasphemous. Programmed over centuries the Mars premise allotting personal advantage only to certain "chosen groups" defies logic and insults justice. However a great many people identify with and unconsciously endorse this lopsided status quo. Therefore it becomes exceedingly difficult to promote a just society when the "law of the jungle" dominates in support of the notion that might makes right, a deft economic inversion of social Darwinism. While personal initiative is generally a good thing, no matter how great the individual's personal efforts, society must come half way. It ought to welcome the skills and gifts that each has to offer. This is not possible when conventions adhere to "Mars rules" and divert the lion's share of collective resources towards the military-industrial complex, the prison-industrial complex, or the growing hospital-pharmaceutical complex. The present American economic model (which author Naomi Klein defines as "Disaster Capitalism") focuses on causing rather than alleviating harm. Casting our cognitive nets to the other side, it makes better sense to redirect our efforts toward nurturing the creative aptitudes of citizens rather than breaking them down only to later mend them. Since each person is in part a creation of society, that society benefits by supporting the best (rather than the beast) in its citizens. Contrary to what popular pundits say, life is not just an inside job; it also requires the work of mutuality, shared efforts aimed at building communities that value items and behaviors of innate worth.

The medical and psychiatric fields treat individuals for a wide range of maladies while the socio-economic factors that cause or exacerbate these conditions remain unexamined. Venus-Hera has been appointed the Divine task of building and sustaining social orders that are based upon equity, fair principles, and a respect for just law. As a universal principle, she cannot rest until these ideals are incorporated into communities around the globe. Even today women remain largely left out of circles of power, distanced from those that own the capacity to set policy. As previously explained, it's frequently the Athena female granted such influence; but her intrinsic nature provides no challenge to orthodox power and its established policies. She may symbolically bring women to the table; yet her respect for the status quo impedes progress and often actually helps to hold women (as well as people of color, or those lacking financial status) back. Athena's sign-domain, Cancer, directly challenges Libra and its social justice ideals.

Hera, as the second incarnation of Venus holds another powerful tool at her disposal, that of beauty. While Plato waxed lyrical about the relationship between beauty and truth, nature had other devices in mind when she devised her aesthetic ideals! Take the Venus flytrap: it allures its prey to their final destination. Women endowed with highly attractive features often have their pick of men. Usually such women "marry upwards." I recall a client who was a beauty queen (and a Libra) and won major contests. She came for a reading to ask my advice. Although sexually captivated by a young man of modest means, her ambitious parents insisted she marry a wealthy older man. Libra may be governed by Venus, goddess of love, yet in her 2nd incarnation she expresses through the cool and detached air element. Air is associated with communications and the realm of the mind. It tends to favor commerce and the wit to negotiate the best deal. Libra also happens to expressly resonate with logic, and it's been said that logic limits love. The woman in question chose status over romantic love and paid a price for it. Wisdom most likely exists at the midpoint between feelings and logic. As a society conditioned by left-brain logic, we must make greater room for expressions of the heart.

On the subject of beauty, Hollywood has learned to capitalize on its powerful allure. The culture of celebrity invites audiences who suffer from quiet desperation to escape their own lives by vicariously identifying with the glitterati brought to life on the big screen. Beautiful women, preferably naked, generally act as sidekicks to men whose power is demonstrated in the lethal use of force. These gorgeous creatures acting like cheerleaders pump up macho men who often readily portray the most barbaric elements of human nature. Glamour is also extended to "sex up" a host of bad habits. The big screen makes smoking, killing, and excessive alcohol consumption all look good. Many people mimic what they see there. It's as if Narcissus reborn can take pride in his modern image reflected across film's magical reflective surface. How the rest of us collectively see ourselves depicted by this influential medium manifests in the form of an insidious feedback loop that impacts the entire society. Increasingly do individuals copy what they have seen. A tolerance for violence in film, rap "music," and television translates directly into a martial cultural fabric. Consider what is defined as art these days? Recently *The Academy Awards* winner of best song went to a vile tribute to pimps! This misogynistic selection should have seen every American woman boycott the movie industry! When a network called "Arts and Entertainment" features the likes of *Dog, the Bounty Hunter*, our culture begins to resemble a sewer. The media focuses on high tech bodies, propped up artificial breasts, and a thinness that distorts the very notion of beauty. Sadly, popular glossy magazines hold women to a concept of the feminine ideal that few can meet. To be fashionable is to conform; and when too much of one's energy is devoted to their outer image, what precious little time is left to develop the more lasting qualities of character? Image is grossly over-rated today. The marketplace holds the power to falsely trap the ego in never-ending quests to obtain enviable objects. These fall out of fashion every year. Thus built-in obsolescence is flaunted while prudent conservation becomes the uncool taboo. Women (and currently metro-males) are driven to alter their bodies in pursuit of the fashionable image du jour. Ironically in nature's kingdoms it is the male who must wear the colorful plumage and display what he's got to win a desirable mate's attention! Would high heels be fashionable if men had to wear them? Check out this quote taken from actual English Law, circa 1720:

"All women of whatever age, rank, profession or degree whether virgin, maid or widow that shall impose upon, seduce and betray into matrimony any of his majesty's subjects by scents, paints, cosmetic washes, artificial teeth, false hair, iron stays, hooks, high heeled shoes, or bolstered hips, shall incur the penalty of law now in force against witchcraft and like misdemeanors, and that marriage, upon conviction, shall stand null and void."

Since Hera's stature derives from marriage to a powerful male figure, the "Hera woman" expresses in our world as the female who unites with a captain of industry, entertainment mogul, or political big shot. She reminds me of Hillary Clinton. Note Hilary's stoic capacity to reserve rage when cast into Hera's virtual mold. Even when faced with humiliation when it was made public that her powerful Zeus-like spouse's shape shifting brought him into sexual congress with other women she maintained her composure. Hilary is hardly the only public figure to deal with the ugly fact that men of privilege frequently seek the sensual company of mistresses or "comfort women." Cultures worldwide evidence this trend; but as illustrated in *Men Can Moon Dance, too*, this behavior is less a de facto expression of human nature than the product of long-term sexist conditioning. It has limited the natural expressions of both genders, women most notably. Is then fidelity a bond apt to be broken? Is marriage to one individual a viable norm for the entirety of life?

Those lucky enough to have united with true helpmates, which is to say persons capable of deep caring who share a parallel trajectory of growth, may indeed spend their entire lifetimes together. And while many quest after hopeful soul-mates, these bonds often present karmic tests of the fiercest sort. Venturing into this realm is not for the faint-hearted! Bonds insistent enough to haunt our souls often lead us toward formidable lessons. With any bond less magnetic, parties would simply walk away at the first sign of heavy testing. Even when confronted with best-case scenarios the mating dance is seldom easy. Good relationships take real work! Having explored diverse spiritual sources in my own search for understanding, a particular encounter with a trance medium stands out. His entire anima shifted as a voice with a distinct accent spoke quite knowledgably about my life. This encounter genuinely moved me. The discarnate trans-dimensional being explained that the original marriage vow, "Till death do us part" was intended for an era where individuals generally lived for about forty years. Since modern persons live the equivalent of several "till death do us parts" due to lengthened life spans, his recommendation was not to take the notion of "one true love" too seriously. The spiritual channels I've met believe we each have a number of soul-mates. A few further elaborate that there is only one true twin flame. Some people are gifted with spending their entire lifetime with the same compatible partner. This scenario was not unusual to my father's generation; yet it's rare to my own. Regardless of the time span allotted to any significant union, the law of karma holds true. We must make efforts to do unto others as we would have them do unto us. If men fully understood and respected this universal law they would not be able to casually dismiss their often-careless treatment of women, the "second sex." Ignorance of the law provides a poor defense. A great many males unwittingly set into motion the conditions they themselves will meet in future incarnations taken as women!

During Hera's month of dominion the full moon will invariably fall in the opposing sign of Aries, where Mars is roused. As the polarized signs of self-awareness and partnership are simultaneously activated, aware individuals are prompted to pay closer attention to the state of their unions. Tolerance is a good thing to practice in conjunction with honoring the spiritual advice: "Judge not, that ye not be judged." Hera's cool head and penchant for logic endows her with natural intellectual aptitudes. She is suited to careers in the fields of law, counseling, public relations, math, science, and architecture. Even so, one way or another partnership tends to mark the destiny of the Hera-born woman. It's been wisely stated that we can't love another until we love ourselves. Hera instructs that the first and primary relationship is with the self, for contrary to popular opinion no one on the outside can truly make us happy. A Libran male friend who expresses his inborn connection to Venus by sharing awe-inspiring photographic images imparted special wisdom to his second wife (my best friend). By enthusiastically encouraging her to pursue her own path to excellence he gently helped her recognize that he could not make her feel whole. On the plus side he was always supportive of those activities that led her to feel complete in herself. As a result the pair has been able to design one of the most satisfying unions I've had the opportunity to witness. Two halves do not a whole partnership make. Each must bring the fullness of self (an encounter based on the arduous journey to self-awareness) to the proverbial table. Self-acceptance leads to peace within. Hera prompts us to hold and honor that centered place within. From that consciousness a satisfying union can generate.

Do you know Hera? Is one of your friends always committed to a righteous cause, involved in writing letters to congressmen to see unjust matters brought to justice? Is someone close to you active in a non-profit organization, or otherwise married to a powerful attorney, lawmaker, or captain of industry? Is she always fashionably dressed and neatly coiffed? Is an associate the director of a gallery or house of fashion?

Hera in Love

Hopefully daughters of Hera will not meet the unfortunate incidence of infidelity head-on. However, this challenge certainly marks the fate of Hera. Forgiveness is holy, but becoming an enabler to another's destructive behaviors undermines any woman, and directly violates Libra's expectation of fairness and mutual respect. I have observed Libra women in "arrangements" where their unions remained legally intact, but both partners lived separate lives. Hera is born with the priceless asset of good looks, and she is apt to use this endowment advantageously. Sadly, a marriage that looks successful to the world may lack the substantive element needed to hold it together. Many Librans know the pain of divorce firsthand; but they are quick learners and usually find in their second or third marriages, a truer basis for lasting compatibility.

Activities that Accord with the Season of Hera:

Libra represents the sign where balance can be established between both of the brain's hemispheres. Halfway around the Zodiac dial a bridge between feelings and intellect manifests. This state of balance is prized by Hera. The practice of Yoga celebrates equipoise. Its careful postures bring the mind and body into alignment. Gentle exercise constitutes a healthy, loving embrace of the self. Yoga also calms the mind and results in clear, often profound thinking. World-renowned authority on comparative religions, Houston Smith said "Days just go better when I begin them with yoga." Tai Chi is another discipline that brings the mind, body, and emotions into equilibrium. Energy alignments that begin in the body improve the workings of the subtler bodies. These in turn harmonize the spirit to balance moods.

During Hera's phase of dominion, visit an art museum, gallery, or florist shop. Try your hand at flower arranging, needlepoint, or fashion design.

Allow a chiropractor to give your spine a healthy, regenerative tune-up.

Buy yourself a gem or piece of jewelry. Splurge on a new outfit. Your senses are sharpened so it's natural to more keenly note pattern, design, texture, and fit.

Join a dating service if you've been out of the social loop too long.

Get your hair styled and indulge the muse of beauty. Pay a visit to the opera and invite the power of song into your soul.

Dance. Share in a vigil for world peace.

Imbibe in fine chocolate. It's practically a sacrament when the moon passes through Hera's domain.

If your weight is off-balance, begin a nutritious program aimed at reducing excess calories along with fatty food consumption. It will prove a gift to your self, and self-image.

Chapter 8

Scorpio: The Realm Of Persephone Awakened
Evoking Transformation: The Quintessential Inside Job

We met Persephone earlier in *Moon Dance* when the discussion centered on her mother, the great Goddess Demeter. To refresh the reader's memory, Persephone, as the daughter of the keeper of all verdant gardens naturally loved to play outside. One day the pubescent female went missing. Since a woman's intuition often proves a reliable and timeless homing device, Mother Demeter correctly surmised that Persephone had indeed been abducted by Pluto, the dark god of the underworld. According to the astrological lexicon Pluto is the **recognized** ruler of the sign of Scorpio. However, as a feminine (Yin) sign Scorpio's essence deserves complementary representation by a Goddess. And since its stellar realm is positioned directly across the zodiac from Taurus, home of Demeter, the thematic principles associated with these two signs remain perpetually interlocked. Just as Athena's connection with Zeus symbolizes the father-daughter bond, Demeter's relationship to Persephone articulates the mother-daughter bond.

Orthodox astrology consigns to Scorpio the zone ruling the dead. More glibly stated it's the sign of sex, death, and taxes: the great inevitabilities! According to myth, Pluto (a/k/a Hades) governs the underworld. Here the spirits of deceased souls must navigate their way across the River Styx to what mysteries await them in the afterlife. As a result of her own abduction and the subsequent covenant drawn up by Zeus to satisfy all injured parties, Persephone's fate demands that she make repeated passages between the world of darkness and that constituted by a return to light. This pattern is consistent with Scorpio's inherent themes of rebirth, regeneration, healing, and transformation. Persons born under this eighth sign will at one point or another assume the journey of the phoenix. They must find the strength and courage to throw off the past, leave darkness where it belongs, and return to the light. In other words they must summon the strength to start over and begin life anew. Tied to the realm of death and rebirth, endings that lead to new beginnings, Scorpio's inherent power of transition is fueled by the alchemy of forgiveness. Just as the scorpion carries lethal poison in a tail ready to strike at any time, there is a reflex inborn to Scorpio natives prompting them to act out of vengeance when they face real or imagined threats. Overcoming the urge to attack is a key karmic lesson associated with this sign. Subjects destined to follow the lesson plan of the zodiac's eighth kingdom are complex. On higher planes Scorpio functions as something of a launch pad enabling the soul to make great progress if it learns to shed the past, release others from their "trespasses," and bravely embrace mystery in the shape of whatever is yet to come. Picture the number eight: one circle sits succinct to itself yet it forms an interlocking feedback loop that connects perpetually with another circle. Together these twin circles connote the symbol of infinity as it visually depicts the mysterious nature of life's continuum. From the vantage point of a singular lifetime we cannot envision those circles yet to come! The knowledge of karma proves useful in providing a plausible basis for extending forgiveness. For as mortals born to witness events on the earth plane, we don't always live long enough to see justice served. A radical trust is required to believe in a process left unseen. The life-to-life continuum demonstrates where we harvest in the present those activities rendered in the past. As *Moon Dance* asserts, this legacy is written into each birth chart. Acting as a spiritual blueprint each spiritual map defines that lifetime's unfolding plan and purpose. The birth chart also depicts those lessons that will inevitably test us profoundly. Because mankind has found itself ensconced in recurrent cycles of violence down the centuries, the vast majority is unable to escape the legacy of aggression. Often it will erupt in close relationships. This helps to explain why it is that for many people life itself becomes a **journey of recovery**. We may prefer to believe that our wounds generate from imperfect parents and their flawed capacity to express unconditional love; but when the history of our world is taken into account, it is shortsighted to expect spiritual grace from those who have also suffered the redundant sins of their own fathers and mothers. From the standpoint of reincarnation it's logical to conclude that we've all contributed in varying ways to the violence now pervasive in our world. Only a massive call to put down arms and join hands can heal our wounded planet. Every Master teacher has taught the power of forgiveness; it presents the only way to expunge the long legacy of trespasses both extended and received. This approach is the sanest strategy for insuring the promise of life to future generations given the irony of all ironies: that the so-called Holy land, birthplace of the three foremost patriarchal religions has currently become the hotbed of inflamed hatreds. Where better to put the holistic power of atonement to work to heal what has been broken in the way of humanity's fundamental oneness? Such an incentive aimed at wide-scale catharsis has already proven to be effective. Ingeniously put into practice by the architects of The Councils on Truth and Reconciliation that convened in South Africa, this model demonstrates the ways and means for overcoming entrenched enmity, even that which has been firmly established. Once the dread racist Apartheid system came to an end Black families who had been on the receiving end of harsh, even murderous treatment likely felt the reflex to "get back at" their former oppressors. Yet something miraculous happens when retaliation is replaced by healing. To sit across the table from the person(s) that violated you and speak to their soul, sharing what you experienced raises their humanity. Genuine catharsis thus results. Racism continues to insidiously thrive within the United States, particularly in Bible belt states. Perhaps the presidential victory of Mr. Obama will change things. Meanwhile we're yet to see the sons of the old klans-men sit down and look into the eyes of those their family members harmed and thereby recognize their shared humanity. In Spike Lee's brilliant film, *Malcolm X*, a depiction of the Black leader's moment of realization is brought to life when after years of traditional religious training he comes to realize that Jesus could never have been a fair-skinned man. The co-optation of "God's" image and likeness by the Christian church framed the deity in a form that falsely allotted to Caucasians a sense of Divine ownership. Millions have never pierced this fiction to understand the enormity of the "false witness" they've been given.

Persephone, as archetype for Scorpio, suggests several key components of human sexuality. According to myth she was not only abducted, but also raped. When Zeus cast a verdict favorable to his brother (the abductor) Pluto, Demeter mourned the loss of her daughter by closing down the harvests. Zeus was forced into making his determination. Because it was learned that while in the underworld Persephone ingested pomegranate seeds (these metaphorically referring to sperm), she inadvertently took a portion of Pluto's essence into herself. Ultimately this intimate act sealed her fate, and bound her thereafter to the mysterious dark god of the underworld. Thus Zeus decided Persephone would spend half the year with Pluto, and return to her mother for the remainder of the year. How apt in that Scorpio is linked with silence and mystery. We can scarce imagine what happens in the underworld, the zone where Persephone is consigned to spend a sizable portion of her existence. What is it like to reside in a place of darkness? Modern science may explain earth's seasonal changes as a result of the recurrent tilt of the planet's axis; yet I find myself drawn to myth, to a more poetic explanation for the shift from vivid spring to autumn's crimson orgiastic dance of death. On elemental levels we are all linked to the powerful interlocking transformations that chart our life courses. Given the labors of the great Demeter, it makes sense that she'd utilize winter's cloak and canopy of stillness to obtain her own much deserved rest. I imagine that many multi-tasking women can identify with the sheer poetic justice of Demeter stopping the harvests to regroup, and conversely celebrating in abundant greenery when her beloved Persephone returns from Pluto's realm. These profoundly rhythmic elemental dances are a thing of beauty, perhaps more so prior to the advent of aberrant climate change, a/k/a global warming. And given the tempests of war, climatic upheaval, and fiscal uncertainty in a world governed by the least conscionable, how does a mother properly protect her child? How does she insure that her daughters not become fodder for rapists? That her sons refrain from joining the ranks of legalized killers in the military, or Goddess forbid become sexual predators in this permissive era? Modern U.S media is awash in sexual imagery. Pornography is purportedly the most profitable thing "sold" on the worldwide web. The smut industry simulates harmful acts perpetrated against women as a disturbing basis for erotic release. Interviews with serial killers reveal that porn plays a major role in what incites their acts of rape and predatory violence. Tragically children are being sexualized from a tender age. All around them pulse overt sensual innuendos, while popular chants refer to women as whores in widely applauded "rap music." Added to this atmosphere are the ubiquitous lingerie advertisements that render women objects despite the battles long fought by feminists working diligently to retire this stereotypic notion. Innocence has been collectively abducted by the entertainment world as it has become a modern embodiment of Pluto-Hades. Meanwhile from a biological perspective, hormones used prodigiously to speed the growth of cattle end up in children's bodies. These unnatural chemical agents have given rise to premature puberty in American youngsters. Girls begin to menstruate and develop breasts at a younger age. They witness sex-pots like Britney Spears "shaking her thing" in public spectacles, while the tide of peer pressure compels them to explore sexual relations before they've developed mature enough emotions or reasoning powers to temper the force of biology's blind naked instinct. Adding insult to feminine injury far too much media portrays violence to women as banal everyday fare. It's frequently the naughty girl, or sexually liberated femme who comes to a bloody conclusion in the film's storyline. This fate mirrors the judgment call of the Christian church, if in slightly disguised form. Nor has sexual liberation led to any promised land. So long as men believe they retain a superior gender status, many will take full advantage of those women who have freed themselves of traditional constraints in pursuit of their own sensuality. Intimacy thus renders females vulnerable to males in numerous ways. The most obvious one is pregnancy. When a young girl's quest for love meets betrayal, that wound will call out for healing. The process of personal recovery often takes years. Time is painfully exacted as one gradually learns to forgive. In the final analysis any poison we harbor, including painful, lingering emotions or eroded feelings of self-worth, creates a toxic environment for its bearer.

Persephone's cycle of dominion encompasses the celebration of Halloween. It's believed by mystics that the veil between the dead and the living becomes especially thin and permeable during this season. Hence a holiday in homage to the not quite so dead spirits among us! Television host John Edwards built a following by contacting, in fact allegedly speaking with deceased relatives of his live audience while on the air. Who doesn't want proof that life goes on? That the bond of love endures beyond the passage of the mortal body? The natural world reflects the higher truth of life's continuum in a perpetual circle of season changes. Human beings, stubborn and earthbound, lose sight of the evidence presented to them by nature's manifest examples. Most have been taught to disregard connections among things both proximate and distant. The limited stance of the ego presumes to know all that is. This presents a problem for children born in the season of Scorpio since they often possess psychic gifts. Some from a tender age prove sensitive to the presence of discarnate persons, whether deceased relatives or guardian spirits. The definition for the word occult is "for those with eyes to see." It's not that the occult world is secreted, but rather a particular perceptual acuity is necessary for penetrating its otherwise invisible dimensions. There are people born truly receptive, while there also are many pretenders. A rash of books purport to offer the advice of angels and guides. Most hoodwink the gullible as too many allege to channel archangels. I have explored sessions with numerous self-proclaimed mediums only to find a handful genuinely authentic. It begs the question, just what or whom do these counterfeit conduits bring through? Actress Shirley Maclaine shared her quest for enlightenment in several popular books that looked beyond traditional explanations for life's unsolved questions. She expanded the concept of personhood to one that extends beyond the boundary of the physical body. In spite of these sources the truth, what exists on the "other side" essentially remains a mystery. Those interested in pursuing the subject of past lives may wish to read the following: *Many Lives, Many Masters* by Dr. Brian Weiss; *You Were Born Again to Be Together* and *Past Lives, Future Loves* by Dick Sutphen; the scholarly, *Other Lives, Other Selves* by Dr. Roger Woolger; Jane Robert's *The Seth Material*; and the staple, *Edgar Cayce's Story of Karma and Reincarnation*. To strongly identify with Persephone is to experience a passionate need to know more about your own soul's legacy. Hypnotic regression therapy can also draw intriguing data from the well of the subconscious. There the record of past lifetimes may often be recovered. Many present-day phobias and predilections originate from former lifetime experiences. These peculiarities can cue us into past life activity and previous conditioning. In Richard Bach's *Illusions*, a renegade pilot helps a young woman overcome her fear of flying by identifying where the phobia first originated. A fuller understanding of the journey of the soul enriches our present life experience by providing answers that can be found nowhere else. It also immeasurably assists our capacity for forgiveness. *The Bible* infers that "Justice belongs to the lord." Although many people struggle with their unwillingness to forgive perceived trespasses of others, the spiritual truth is that such action does not offer the "perpetrator" a free pass. Rather it is a gift to the individual harboring the poison in that it liberates her from the effects of carrying so much toxic baggage around! While the scorpion is not harmed by his own lethal cargo, the human being who retains old poison indeed is. As added caveat, the scorpion's association with the zodiac's 8th sign proves prophetic in an unexpected way. Scorpions have been known to survive nuclear bomb tests in the Southwest desert! How apt that they represent the sign of immortality! They are perfect symbols to represent the journey of the human soul as it takes on continuous embodiments!

Given the dictate of the law of karma: "Whatsoever you do unto the least of these, you do unto me," what thus becomes the fate of the Plutonian rapist abductor? We know that rape victims and persons who have been violently assaulted require time (and often therapy) to heal on all levels, but what of their attackers? Consider the interior life of a serial killer or rapist. One need not sympathize to peer into their hearts of darkness. We can scarce imagine what it must be like to dwell in perpetual shadow-lands, not that anyone escapes the legacy of his own karmic account. Mythology's influence is also witnessed in the terminology used for criminals. Often they are referred to as underworld or underground characters. This designation is especially associated with organized crime. Slick criminals may bypass the law of the land, but the universal law of cause and effect cannot be overridden. Any who direct action against their sisters and brothers becomes a wounded spirit. The ensuing identification with the underworld suggests a reluctance to bring personal actions and motives into the reconciling light of truth. It is doubtful that there can be healing without allowing what was harbored in shadows to risk illumination. To dehumanize another person is quite truly to wound a portion of one's soul. The violator is left with a sense of separation from the greater whole, consigned to a zone of emptiness. According to the published chronicles of Edgar Cayce, Gordon Michael Scallion (*Notes from the Cosmos*), and H.L. Chaloner (*Wheel of Destiny*), health disorders in the present may stem back to earlier incarnations, even those experienced during the era of Atlantis! Suffering rendered unto others returns to the self! This is why I question whether science will ever conquer all diseases. It seems that as soon as they "wipe out" one problem two new disorders surface. Given today's media culture one has to wonder if disease is not being marketed to satisfy the profit lust of the pharmaceutical industry? The pain processed in our bodies may be a significant way that old karma, the sum of wounds leveraged against others, returns to us.

America as a nation is given to extreme expressions of violence. Those impacted by acts of aggression generally require therapeutic assistance. Mercy is appropriate, as is the realization that violence always begets violence. In the U.S. an entire floor of the F.B.I is devoted to serial killers, two million citizens are incarcerated, and a rape occurs every hour. Rape is also a pervasive war crime which raises the question: why do men vent so much rage against women? And why do "nice guys" find violence directed at women in media sexually appealing? These acts and related images are pervasive and featured in a wide assortment of "entertainment" venues. The answer takes us back to the great wound earlier described as a chasm set between the genders. By defining sexual communion as an alleged sin the church orchestrated a misconception that induced a plethora of aberrant behaviors ever after. Consider the Catholic Church's decision to defend hundreds of priests against charges of pediophilia. Pluto-Hades doesn't just abduct girls it would seem!

Sexual communion wields the power of transformation. Women who do not naturally experience orgasm are not only victims of a religious programming that demands their unconscious forfeiture of natural pleasure, something deeply metaphysical is also lost. If we spiritually examine the fabric of shared destiny then every young girl sold against her will into sexual slavery in Southeast Asia also impacts you and me. Each Indian wife tragically set ablaze in what's described as "dowry murder" touches all sentient souls as does the Arab daughter murdered to uphold the fiction of "honor crime" based on the alleged sin of flirting with a young man. These ghastly behaviors directed at suppressing female sensuality taint the pool of shared destiny and harm us all. Their indications suggest the covert presence of Pluto in our midst. And for many women the men we lay next to are in fact bona fide killers. The invisible bloodstains on their hands are the product of legalized killing, the lethal fruit of war. My father, along with several lovers, was baptized in that blood ritual sacred unto Mars. (He served in WWII and retained several bullet hole scars for the remainder of his life; while two intimate partners served in the marines and experienced the jungles of Vietnam.) Rather than blame men called into combat for acting as warriors, it is wiser to modify society so **that war be removed from our lexicon**. I believe it largely stems from that great wound set unnaturally between men and women, a source of never-ending enmity. This first cleavage led to others, a pattern of divisiveness forged on the bases of differences in race, ethnicity, religion, financial status, and so on. We are here on earth to heal ourselves and by extension our world. This process requires our transcending the old definitions. We must stop dragging the chains of yesterday and instead collectively envision a tomorrow based on fresh promise.

Persephone's recurrent return to the light expresses a power that is intrinsically ours. We can make ourselves new. This gift cannot be accessed if we hold onto the past. Just as the poison-wielding snake is forced to molt his skin, we symbolically must do likewise. When poison is extracted from a wound (be it physical, emotional, or of the soul) healing begins. That magical process may require us to recognize where our blind spot or zone of resistance lies. This key factor often eludes the conscious (logical) mind's basis for inquiry; yet there are unique ways to access the deeper truth or root causes to what ails us. Although I approached the following modality with skepticism, I opted for a "soul-retrieval" session. First Radavi (the facilitator) asked me to write down the three most traumatic events of my life. Then I was directed to lie down on a massage table. The room in which she conducted the healings resembled a circular womb. It was cocoon-like and set deep into a forest. Although I lay there with eyes closed and never once felt her touch me, my body shook intensely as she waved a Native American feather over me. By a power allotted to her from an Indigenous teacher she used this technique to dislodge from the electronic grid (aura) surrounding my physical form those layers of trauma long stored there. She took me back to the age of six when my natural mother left. As I recalled intense memories she assisted my letting go of these deep imprints that were not visible, but nonetheless impressed upon the "atmosphere" of my being. By the end of the session I had a strong urge to urinate. As I rushed off her table, I looked down at my feet and noted they appeared to be those of a six-year old child! She had indeed taken me back, and my consciousness had not yet fully returned to present time. I recognized the value of this experience when months later I encountered a painful emotional test. Instead of reacting from the full weight of past trespasses, I was **present** to the immediate challenge. It was liberating, as I could feel myself responding to the moment without bringing unconscious residue forward. I recommend soul retrieval; but must caution readers that practitioners vary in their levels of honesty, integrity, and expertise. Many claim to be healers and channels, while few have worked out their own issues, thus their spiritual balance (not to mention professionalism) may be questionable. The vast majority has no business playing with these forces. Make sure you obtain a bona fide referral from someone you trust before putting yourself in the hands of the unscrupulous. *The Bible* warned there would be many false prophets in this time of transition. *End Times* exist for those who can't see beyond the flat-earth's horizon! An astute trance medium related to me why the notion of Tribulation is embraced by millions. He explained, "Many want oblivion, an end to it all." Pondering his statement I understood that persons leading lives of quiet desperation are not apt to throw the precious gift of human life back at Creator. Rather than improve their human frailties their authoritarian beliefs mistake for God's will what they project onto Creator in the form of false prophecy: That His will commands a destructive worldwide Apocalypse. By placing their faith in a call to arms, they court Armageddon and then mistake the evidence of spiraling levels of violence for God's will! The only "god" this life-negating homage possibly serves is Mars. However, the self-fulfilling prophecy has countless followers and is becoming all too dangerous for those who see beyond its blind rage and blasphemous conjecture.

Before Pluto's discovery in 1930, Mars was considered the ruler of both signs Aries and Scorpio. The powers of death and rebirth are linked to these signs. It's ironic that fundamentalists who readily support the Middle East Inferno also identify strongly with the unborn fetus and work diligently to block legal abortion, their motto being "Right to life." The legendary firebrand Granny D explained that the fetus symbolized the cramped lives lived by those persons who'd opted to follow others' rules. In the unborn they see a reflection of the hopeful innocence they lost, and unconsciously mourn their own forfeiture of freedom. It's been said that if men got pregnant, there'd be no abortion debate at all.

Great numbers of people seem to wrestle with a collective death wish. It's evident in the legions of addicts who use dangerous substances to deaden themselves to life while still in bodies. Whether the chosen vice is alcohol, street drugs, food, cigarettes, promiscuous sex, gambling, or gaming, addictions are often masked death wishes. Some souls may be drawn to darkness to conversely recognize the value of returning to a life immersed in light. Resurrection was not just the story of Jesus. It symbolizes the efforts of Orpheus, who in search of his beloved Eurydice (her life cut short) ventures deep into the underworld. So luminous was his courage, so faithful his love that the fates presented Orpheus with a powerful test. If he could exit the dark world without ever turning back, his lover would follow and be restored to him. Tragically, upon hearing the sound of footsteps behind him, Orpheus succumbed to curiosity and turned to make sure his beloved was there. This simple human reflex defeated his promise and he was forced to watch as her shadow faded away. To love someone held hostage by an addiction feels something akin to Orpheus' challenge. A being of light cannot remain long among those given to darkness, which is to say those immersed in life-negating behaviors. Edgar Cayce explained that bars attract discarnate spirits. In such places earthbound spirits can feed their craving for alcohol by attaching energetically to people who fall "under the influence." I rarely enter such places due to my innate empathy. Clearly at this final phase of the Piscean Age millions wrestle with a host of addictive behaviors. Until the addict makes the personal decision to fight his demons, loved ones have little choice but to stand by. It takes strength of will to walk away with the hope that living a life-affirming example will draw the addict away from the undertow of his self-destructive behaviors. By a process of self-determination each must elect to leave the underworld behind. Then the gradual process of taming the inner nature begins with its goal a return to the light. People can only hide from themselves so long. Whatever issues we fail to clear or balance during our current lifetime will follow us into future incarnations.

Our discussion of Scorpio is not complete without looking into the experience of birth. Years ago "rebirthing" was all the rage. Rebirthing facilitators instructed workshop participants to lie down on comfortable mats. Then through hypnotic-style suggestion coupled with special breathing techniques, they led participants back to their actual birth experiences. Some people readily tuned into the exercise and recognized how their parents **felt** at the time of their births. Suppose a father was especially keen on having a son, but instead confronted the fact that a daughter had been born? (The technology for discerning gender prior to birth has only recently been made available.) The newborn female begins her life aware of her father's disappointment. A friend who recently participated in a rebirthing session told me she learned that her mother was upset about being pregnant and tried to hide her status by losing weight. This friend believes her own struggle with chronic obesity stems from her mother's attitude during the prenatal period. I don't discount such a factor; however rather than place cause on our parents (or worse yet, blame), we must realize that our birth experiences reflect the indications of our astrological charts. What we qualitatively encounter functions as part of a larger plan. Our parents are actors in the scripts our souls have taken on for the purposes of learning. Karma's call for rectitude figures into this inviolate equation. It's enlightening to ask ourselves what lessons we elected to accept in being born to our specific parents. Examine their varied gifts and weaknesses and relate them to this particular lifetime opportunity.

It would be great if every child was warmly welcomed into our world, guaranteed the nurturing love of two emotionally healthy parents. That fate (if it exists at all) extends to a very small percentage of human beings. How we leave this world is also important. While I was working on the final edit of this book I lost my father and stepmother. Saturn-Chronos, arbiter of life cycle changes, was transiting Leo where it would first hit my sun (Yang/father) and then my moon (Yin/mother). Both died at home in their own bed. Since I am firm in the conviction that life is everlasting, that we drop our bodies while our spiritual identities remain roughly intact, it made their passages easier to accept. I believe we retain contact with those important to our destinies in life after life; and that dreams can act as conduits for communication between this world and whatever lies beyond it. Birth is not an accident, nor is death a final act. We are made of the energy of light which can neither be created nor destroyed. We do however pulse in and out of corporeal states just as Persephone appears in spring only to disappear in the autumn.

The Hindus believe that we have many bodies. Foremost we note the presence of the dense physical body, however it's integrated with our emotional, mental, and higher frequency spiritual bodies. To accept as Truth only the evidence drawn from our limited senses (these have evolved as devices specifically adapted to the physical world) is to deny a more spiritually inclusive reality. Things invisible cannot be measured with orthodox tools. Sexual magnetism serves as an apt example. This indisputably potent force cannot be readily measured or defined; and yet as a device of karma, it yokes together those with lessons to complete. Plus on a biological scale every living being urges towards reproduction to ensure the continuity of its clan. Powerful sex can take us "out of this world," and as one friend enthusiastically put it: "It's a straight shot to God!" In honor of *Moon Dance*, perhaps she meant the Goddess Persephone? Curiously the same body portal that facilitates reproduction provides us with a means for releasing wastes. A Shiva-Vishnu parallel is demonstrated through our own physiology. If we observe the glyph that symbolizes the number eight, we note that one circle represents what is yet to come, the procreative urge, while the other circle signifies that which has been spent or destroyed and rendered into detritus. These twin components express as creation and destruction. Entwined they reflect the energetic projections of Yin and Yang, that everlasting life force that ushers in cycles of birth and death, endings that eventuate in new beginnings. All life echoes this sequential pattern.

Persephone's gift to mankind is the sure knowledge that we each are equipped to change, heal, and grow. We need not remain prisoners of a changeless past. Aiding and abetting the process of personal transformation are significant planetary alignments. These are inlaid into our life plans and set to go off like alarm clocks. One such passage is represented by "Saturn's return." It occurs at twenty-nine year intervals. During our twenties we feel free to explore life without much restriction. Once we turn thirty, most find themselves tethered to jobs, new families, or limiting mundane constraints. Between the ages of forty and forty-two, every one of the outer planets conflicts with the original position it held in our natal chart. The result is a sense that life in its present form no longer fits or feels viable. It's as if we're walking in someone else's moccasins. Then between age fifty-eight and sixty, Saturn's second return occurs. Many people radically alter their lives in part because they realize they have entered the autumn phase of their sojourns here on earth. It's time to put into motion that last vital dream! Our solar system is encoded by and through cosmic clockworks. Creator designed this comprehensive system to assist our ultimate evolution. The capacity for rebirth is offered to each and all; there are, however, intervals specific to birth charts that best support its promise.

Do you know Persephone? Is there a friend, lover, or associate who has undergone a bona fide rebirth? Someone who has virtually traveled to Hades (hell) and back, an individual who has recovered from an unspeakable loss? Has a relative beat the medical odds and healed a presumably incurable disease? Who do you know that has completely re-invented herself? And wittingly or otherwise, she exudes natural sex appeal? She's also endowed with natural rhythm and proves it on the dance floor.

Persephone in Love

Perhaps to the scorpion, it is better to sting than to be stung. One way Scorpio marks its lovers is leaving as imprint the kind of sex that simply proves unforgettable. You are thus rendered immortally theirs! This often silent, mysterious sign seldom shows its full hand, and often covertly tests any potential partner's fealty. Persephone's daughters and sister souls tend to live up to their sexual reputations and observe few taboos. They intuitively gravitate towards the body's secret erogenous points, and can render sex a weapon that enables them to control the objects of their affection. In particularly twisted cases, S & M will be practiced. Ending a tie or affair with a Scorpio is seldom a painless matter. Clients tell me that in divorce settlements, the Scorpio's legendary stinger tends to exact a significant financial wound. Lovers from Persephone's realm acquire grace by practicing the difficult art of forgiveness. A willingness to do so within an intimate tie can make love grow... eternally!

Activities that Accord with the Season of Persephone

Have you ever considered a past life regression session? How about a visit to the mummies at The Metropolitan Museum of Art as an unconventional prelude? Stretch your imagination to envision the mysterious rites of Initiation. The ancient Egyptians were a people that believed in the continuity of the soul. They designed elaborate tombs and rituals expressly for the purpose of returning to claim what once was theirs!

This is the season ripe for exploration into soul retrieval. Light incense and candles and prepare to consult the Runes, or get advice from a skilled Tarot reader. Dare to purchase your own Oracle. The Medicine Cards or Cartouche (by Murray Hope) are two of my favorites. Neither requires long schooling for obtaining immediately accessible prophetic insights.

Write a letter (even if you don't intend to mail it) to someone who has hurt you. Explain how you felt, and tell them you now are prepared to bless, release (the painful event), and forgive them. Burn the letter if you like. This act can function as your own "truth and reconciliation" ritual.

Embark on a three-day juice fast to clear your body of toxins.

Visit a Reiki healer.

Choose to produce less waste by becoming more conscious of the products that you use. For instance, when you take a cloth bag to the supermarket, you don't add to the refuse of plastics now dominating the landscape when not sweeping into lakes, rivers, and the grand ocean. There hungry birds take these items for indigenous jellyfish and end up strangled. Purchase biodegradable products.

Prepare a mineral bath and while immersed visualize toxic debris being cleansed from your body.

Also favored are activities directed at remaking, rebuilding, remodeling, rejuvenating, regenerating or resuscitating yourself, or whatever you aim "the force" at!

Prelude to the Ancient Creation Pantheon

During the last twenty-two hundred years while humanity passed through the Piscean Age, polarity has been king. The symbol of two fish swimming in opposing directions aptly reflects a worldview observed through the lens of duality. The Piscean Age operated in part through its polarity Virgo. The result gave rise to highly structured delineations. The first and primary one was wrought on the basis of gender. Bases for division then extended to include race, religion, ethnicity, and class status. These demarcations lent false castigation to specific groups, associating some with goodness, while others were consigned to evil or second-class status. Reinforced for centuries, these value judgments have become part of the collective consciousness, and for many it's nearly impossible to imagine a world without them. Yet envision is what we must endeavor to do that mankind transcend what otherwise appears as irreconcilable division. Through a newly emerging ethos balanced relationships will have room to flourish. We can turn back the pages of time to an era that predated both The Piscean Age and that of Aries, and there note evidence of a more inclusive cosmology, one that represents a departure from centuries of polarized conditioning.

The Greeks and Romans were conscious of the intrinsic relationship connecting the heavens and the earth. Key thinkers of that time concluded that our mortal world was governed by **three** brothers who resided on Olympus. This worldview was imitated by Catholicism in its depiction of the trinity said to exist between Jesus, The Father, and the Holy Spirit. According to myth Jupiter (Zeus) held ostensible rule over Olympus, and his authority extended to include the surface world of earth. His brother Pluto (Hades) was granted rule of the underworld, whilst another brother, Neptune (Poseidon) governed the vast sea kingdoms. This ruling trinity holds a correspondence with human behavior and ultimate destiny. According to Freud, the "father" of modern psychology, human beings negotiate the varied motivations stemming from the interaction of ego, super-ego and id. Another psychological model refers to the interplay between conscious, unconscious, and subconscious dimensions of the mind. Therefore the modern individual's actions reflect a personalized rendition of the legendary "three fates!" To the Ancients these three brothers held high status within the celestial hierarchy. Lesser dignitaries were assigned important complementary functions. Modern astronomers have retained much of the legacy drawn from myth as seen in the naming of the planets within our solar system. Only seven planets were known to the Ancients. The discoveries of Uranus, Neptune, and Pluto occurred in the last two centuries. (India's practitioners of Vedic astrology still don't acknowledge these influences at all! In that Capricorn tradition-based society the worldview seems to stop at Saturn.)

Before we can fully appreciate the nature of the personae that govern the next Zodiac signs we must revisit that powerful phenomenon known as the precession of equinoxes. Since our sun revolves around yet another central sun, the entire solar system continues to move in accord with an extended orbit. Astrology was conceived at a time when wise souls observed earth's journey in relation to the **fixed stars**. These represent "demarcation points" on heaven's circular compass. Since the Zodiac's inception occurred centuries ago the position of our sun relative to the fixed stars has moved by nearly an entire sign. In other words the actual signs no longer align with their original positions! It can be said that the energetic imprint of Aries, the warrior, now overlaps Pisces, the gentle fisher of men as portrayed by Jesus, teacher of peace. I did not include this complex topic in the discussions of all previous signs because it extends outside the intended focus of *Moon Dance*. However, the influence is too dynamic to ignore in the last Zodiac signs.

Returning to the cosmological perspective appreciated by our ancient ancestors, since Jupiter rules the earth plane his influence is easily seen and noted. This planet therefore represents basic consciousness. Brother Pluto, given his affinity with Hades, guides souls to that world believed to exist beyond this one. It signifies the mysterious zone approached at the time of death. Pluto represents processes of consciousness that remain buried or hidden. He qualifies as guardian of the subconscious. Finally Neptune, lord of the sea kingdoms, holds sway over aspects of life neither solid nor tangible. His realm is that of dreams, fantasy, imagination, and escapism, states suggestive of the unconscious mind. Resulting from the precession of equinoxes, Saturn, natural ruler of Capricorn has come to envelop Sagittarius, sign-realm of Jupiter's intended dominion. To the astrologer it's quite clear that archetypal energies suited to Capricorn have "bled over," and now impact the Sagittarian nature. In a sense, Saturn and Jupiter have morphed into one hybrid principle that directly shapes religion, ethics, and morality for the vast majority of persons. Jupiter is associated with gain, prosperity, luck, faith and opportunity, while Saturn is linked to loss, personal tests, fear, and cynicism. *The Bible* has long served as the basis for Western morality. Its dual Testaments project diametrically opposed qualities, ones suitable to Jupiter and Saturn. *The New Testament's* homage to faith reflects the character of Jupiter; while the teaching "as ye reap, ye sow" points to the law of karma which characterizes Saturn's chief mandate. Its harsh message is projected throughout *The Old Testament*. The polarized perspective essentially fueled by Biblical scripture remains a legacy of The Piscean Age. Its dueling antithetical spiritual philosophies have been yoked into one spiritually schizophrenic whole! Hypocrisy, prejudice, illusion, and countless massacres have generated from its basis in contradiction. *Moon*

Dance can't solve the problems of history, nor quell personal religious doubts. Instead it provides thinkers with a broader intellectual basis from which to draw their own spiritual conclusions. As has been noted the qualities of Jupiter and Saturn have found their way into the moral teachings of the Bible. This pair profoundly influences Western civilization as a result. Olympian brothers Neptune and Pluto also have ostensible roles to play in leveraging mortal affairs. However, it bears noting that the one planet curiously unspoken for, a status made conspicuous by its absence is Uranus, the rebel. Known for crashing the party and disrupting the status quo, could these behaviors explain why Uranus was not given a respectable place among the ruling powers of ancient times, nor is it essentially represented today! Uranus speaks for all dispossessed voices, and as ruler of Aquarius, sign of the new age (a phase of dominion that will last for two-thousand years), this long-silenced Divine principle now prepares for a liberated expression!

There is a karmic reason why the ancient astrologers were limited to an awareness of only seven planets. From their perspective, Saturn signified the last cosmological horizon and functioned as something of a guardian. Personified as the old god Chronos, Saturn holds the proverbial hourglass. His role resembles a celestial accountant allotted the authority to appropriate the time extended to our various appointed purposes. Reflect upon Saturn's magnificent rings for a moment. Could these bands of frequency represent the symbolic tests each individual must master before being permitted the freedom to move beyond the lord of karma's restrictive yoke into higher spheres of self-expression? On a collective scale, each "new" planetary discovery has coincided with a profound breakthrough that significantly altered life for mankind. Uranus is tied to the development of electricity, Neptune to the deployment of oil and fossil fuels, and Pluto to nuclear power and laser technology. Responsibility attaches to every human development on both individual and communal scales. As the arbiters of law and order, Creator has assigned to Saturn and Jupiter the tasks of rendering the lessons necessary to prepare souls for incremental levels of consciousness (via inner development). A new phase of enlightenment began when each of the three outermost planets were first recognized. The first one to burst the grip of Saturn's legacy to end its status as outermost planet was Uranus discovered in the 1850's in synch with a historical cycle featuring revolutions and mass rebellion. It rules Aquarius, the sign I've linked to the archetype of Artemis. The long silence of the Divine daughter will at last be spoken for as Aquarius takes its turn rising into celestial prominence. Artemis is an appropriate symbol for the zodiac's rebel-sign in that her newly awakened claim to Divine equality shakes the whole Olympian status quo and the male "bubbas" that managed to retain it for many millennia. As women embrace the place in ourselves that challenges the chokehold of old patriarchal rules and traditions (the fundaments established by Saturn/Jupiter) we act as midwives to this nascent age. Preparatory work is required. Just as the student is expected to prove mastery before progressing onto more challenging skills, the soul through elected action must demonstrate its understanding and respect for Divine law. This Logos is constituted by and through the cosmic curricula embedded into the first seven planetary spheres. To venture into wider spheres of co-creatorship without sound spiritual ethics in place to govern our choices can set back our own progress, while potentially harming the evolution (or trajectory) of other souls. A healthy respect for the law of karma combined with a responsible use of that faith-based faculty known as "setting intention" prepares the individual soul for grander expressions. The master piano player who rides off into jazz improvisation makes his craft look easy, but he first had to train his fingers by practicing redundant scales!

The Aquarian Age governed by Uranus and its radicals is dawning. The case was previously made for Apollo as Divine son (the Christ). It is only natural and fitting that his twin sister, Artemis would represent the opposing sign kingdom, Aquarius. The onset of the Aquarian Age signals the time has come for humanity to regain balance and a more enlightened, inclusive understanding. This requires a new quest, that of rediscovering harmony between the Lovers. Without this spiritual reconciliation our broken Eden cannot survive. Mankind must learn to navigate utilizing both oars: the Divine masculine and Divine feminine expressions of Creation. The wisdom gleaned from ancient myths is not passé since what

Sioux Rose

motivated the Olympians also functions as a timeless reflection of human nature, which itself remains contemporary. Caught in an undertow between what is sublime and what passes for gross impulse, our mortal state compels us to look to the heavens for inspiration (not to mention understanding).

Chapter 9

Sagittarius: The Realm Of Pan-Zeus Awakened
Tapping the Interior Wellspring of Ultimate Joy

Positioned directly across the zodiac dial from Gemini's twins, Sagittarius is a sign also marked by inherent division. Three of the Zodiac's four mutable signs, Pisces, Gemini, and Sagittarius all reflect a dualistic character. The exception is Virgo; the sign that's bound to reveal new mysteries once its true ruler is discovered. When this astronomical event occurs Virgo will no longer be tethered to Mercury, sharing that status with its current cosmic cousin Gemini. The mutable signs have been celestially allotted the chameleon-like capacity to change to suit altering circumstance. This gift of inventive camouflage, equivalent to a karmic double-edged blade, can work for or against the bearer's best interests. Shape-shifting functioned as a powerful protective device for the tribal shaman (a subject we will cover later in this chapter). However for modern individuals that behavior tends to compromise integrity to the point that genuine authenticity easily gets lost. Sagittarius, like its mutable cousins, experiences profound inner duality when confronted with free will's ultimate gift, that of choice. Of course every human being faces the election process, but it holds greater moral resonance in the lives of those born with either sun or moon in a divided sign. The karmic implication of this conundrum suggests the soul lived a set of behaviors that ran counter to her basic truths in a former incarnation. Adaptation of this sort is not surprising given the number of purges and inquisitions deployed throughout the ages to separate "believers" from "heretics." And while most birth charts hold at least some planets in mutable signs, the need to resolve inner dissension proves strongest in those born with a mutable moon or sun (sign). Although there is no research to support this contention, it's probable that a good percentage of persons diagnosed with schizophrenia or bi-polar disorder have key birth-chart planets in the mutable signs. Imagine living in a room with four stereos all relaying different messages at the same time? The scientific community uses its own measuring devices to conclude that these aberrations are biochemical in nature. However, the brain generates biochemistry that reflects the emotional state (which may be driven by belief structures) of its host. I recall reading about an unusual individual who exhibited the physiological symptoms of asthma; but this particular person also suffered from a "multiple personality disorder." When their "alternative inner persona" took over, the same body no longer tested positive for asthma! This is but one example that lends credence to the power of the human mind. Faith, prayer, and visualization have been shown to engender undeniable effects. The Christian Science Church stresses the importance of these approaches. People have often overcome conditions science has taken for impossible. Negative or limited thinking is associated with the lower mind, while expansive, "sky's the limit" perceptions align with the higher mind. Just as primary education and its related learning channels are associated with Gemini, greater intellectual expansiveness is assigned to Sagittarius where universities, publishing, religious theology, and exposure to foreign cultures come into play. These opportunities spur the growth and related evolution of human understanding on a grand scale. Mankind now having arrived at the end of the Piscean Age, long programmed to view life and its variables through a dual lens, must overcome the entrenched legacy of those bi-polar fish along with its embedded perceptual division. Much of the work that human beings face involves weaving back together what false ideology has torn asunder. Meanwhile, each of us faces mundane choices every day of our lives, and our personal election processes consist of choosing the high or low road. Edgar Cayce advised seekers to search their souls before making critical decisions, and determine foremost: "Choose ye which master ye shall serve."

Conventional astrology connects the sign of Sagittarius with Jupiter, also known as the famed Zeus who presided over Olympus. Children of Sagittarius are believed to be lucky due to this fortunate designation. A true understanding of the Sagittarius nature requires us to momentarily return to that powerful phenomenon known as the precession of equinoxes. This covert, cosmic influence has profoundly transformed the naked, nature god Pan, who was formerly content to play music freely in the wilds, into something else entirely! Sagittarius, the sign of opulence and plentitude recalls life in the great garden where fruits appeared naturally, no human efforts were required. Jesus Christ reflected this form of prosperity in that he owned no prized possessions but manifested whatever was needed. Pan's endowment sprung from the abundant relationship that freely existed between human beings and the benevolence of nature, its kingdoms there to fulfill mankind's every need. When people acted like better neighbors, less driven by the modern model of rabid resource depletion, nature was a better neighbor in return. As the centuries advanced, the earthy, materialistic realm of Capricorn gradually came to pass over Sagittarius, and a very different basis for wealth emerged. It was one based on property ownership, the paving and fencing of paradise, added to placing all of nature's precious assets on the unsavory auction block. During this era, men also came to recognize the role they played in conception. While a child's mother is largely indisputable, that certainty hardly extends to the father. Thus at this juncture in human evolution men demanded control of birth-lines by laying claim to women in ways that rendered them virtual possessions, property. The belief in ownership of the "gentler sex" extended from women onto Mother Nature. Across the centuries men have observed the ways their fathers have treated their mothers, and a chain reaction fueled by unequal perceptions of inherent worth has evolved. Furthermore, patriarchal teachings have actively expunged all feminine deities (apart from Mother Mary) from sacred ritual. And here, too, Jupiter proved all too willing to seize control of what ultimately belongs to the great Goddess, Demeter. So began the epoch cycle wherein human law departed dramatically from true and balanced Divine principle. And as nature was placed into bondage rather than respected as humanity's partner, the priceless (and irreplaceable) was forfeited, traded for transitory paper wealth! Today's children are routinely corralled into shopping malls or plastic theme parks while the awe rightly reserved for the wonders of Demeter's kingdoms is instead directed at pay-per-view entertainment or managed play. Native American youth (along with those born to indigenous cultures worldwide) learned survival lessons directly from the source. In the wilds they might dance under the stars, collect the precious falling rain, sit long hours among the trees, or observe the movements of animals and sense their own innate bond with the primal forces that comprise the web of life. They were taught to respect the sacred ecosystems woven strand by strand in order to sustain a vast array of species. Initiation ceremonies tied young persons spiritually to the land and her cycles. Today Demeter's patiently crafted organic webs face utter collapse. Since Pan, protector of nature's myriad sources of wealth essentially morphed into Zeus, as chairman of the board, people have increasingly come to interpret the quality of their lives on the basis of false criteria such as their net worth or what they **own**. Every resource is up for sale! Human beings are so far removed from the wisdom and sentience of nature that the vast majority has no idea what's been lost. Today's children probably deduce that food grows **in** the supermarket! Jupiter is celestially tied to the promise of prosperity; but is there a state richer than living free, true to the law of one's inner being? When Pan morphed into Zeus, a vast transition of values occurred. The abundance freely derived from the Divine Mother as intended sustenance for native populations was instead made to answer to rules formatted to suit an authoritarian father god. This felonious shift opened the door to monetary systems founded in homage to greed. The basis for a hierarchical society was born and generated legions of have-nots. A hunger for status drove ambition in the strong, and much of it was founded on mere self-interest. Over time dark Machiavellian motivations (more suited to the kingdom of Saturn-Chronos) twisted Pan-Zeus and drew him away from the truth borne of his natural (nearly forgotten) instincts.

Pan, as symbol for Sagittarius, pre-dates the Judeo-Christian era. God of the forests and wild places, he wielded sacred magical powers that were derived from elemental alchemy. The trees were his cathedrals as animals sang songs in praise of Creation, with insects offering the background rhythm and percussion that human beings later learned to emulate through drumming. Portrayed as the Centaur, this half-human/ half-animal depiction recalls that Sagittarius will always remain in part a creature of the wilds, untamed by civilization and its authoritarian creeds. No persona of the Zodiac better expresses the blending of traits that results from the precession of equinoxes, as sign comes to overlap sign. Today's Zeus seems far removed from the free and nature-loving Pan. He's effectively morphed into the persona of a corporate C.E.O. and acts like a Capricorn. Pan-Zeus has grown too comfortable with the amenities of ownership and modern principles of wealth. This transposition of values exacerbates the split reflected in his dualistic nature. Having largely forfeited his love of freedom he's become earthbound and newly tethered to materialism. The historical merger between church and state (which America's unique plan of governance has sought to ingeniously transcend) has once again become a threat. Jupiter and Saturn as the planetary custodians of law and order, compel populations to adapt to established rules. These protocols are generated from government and religious agencies. Yet human society has not always marched to the beat of a singular god. When pantheism flourished ceremonies of worship took place outside and drew populations into exquisite synch with the primal forces of nature. Pagan rites were later shaped into religious rituals as advocated by the church-state. The Christmas holidays fall on the cusp between Sagittarius and Capricorn and it's no accident. This time of celebration was offered to the people as something of a consolation. It was designed to ease their transition away from polytheism into the new monotheism. Conformity largely occurred at gunpoint, or upon threat of death. Any who wished to honor the old ways paid a high price. Later those given to practicing the old rites were castigated as witches or heretics and brutally burned at the stake. This barbaric policy hardly marked a short synapse of history; it was sustained for generations to effectively wipe out not only the alternative voice of more humane Gods and Goddesses, but also the entire historical record of practical skills utilized by early herbalists and healers. The transition from free engagement in pagan rituals to orthodox religious conformity coincided with power becoming centralized. Rigid authoritative bodies wielded their self-proclaimed Divine right to control all aspects of human conduct. Nature-based religion, which featured a reverent respect for **the spirit** of God in all things, was replaced by a narrow-minded orthodoxy that demanded adherence to a plethora of new and often complex rules. Freedom was not to be tolerated by the nascent church-state apparatus. Significant to the process of mass conversion was a turning away from the lunar calendar to instead worship a sun-based count of time. Prior to modern times Pan-Sagittarius was a very different entity. He looked first to the moon to observe the passages of his life. Over the course of history he's lost the freedom to express his true self. By adapting to his modern role Pan-Sagittarius inadvertently advocates on behalf of unnatural mores. These ensure that the vast majority of persons will be made to forfeit intrinsic liberties. Pan-Zeus and Saturn-Chronos function as two sides of the same philosophical coin.

The word January derives from the god Janus, a two-headed entity that looks both forward and backward simultaneously. This symbol suggests tension between opposing perspectives. One signifies the past and its tradition, whilst the other represents the future and its progressive possibilities. It's an apt signature to connote the merger between Pan-Jupiter and Saturn-Chronos. A "changing of the guard," takes place at the juncture between any two signs, but it's most significant in anticipation of the New Year. This season of celebration demarcates the end of one year and the hopeful beginning of the next. Where Sagittarius ends signals the onset of Capricorn. However since the essences of these two signs have melded together, differentiation is no longer clear. The paradoxes indicated by the polarized perspectives of the Bible's two texts are reflected in the natures of these two signs. In addition, their respective ruling planets (Jupiter and Saturn) act as custodians of mundane law. Astrologers recognize the authority associated with these two planetary heavyweights; however, they examine the entire Zodiac circle to obtain accurate insights. Inside its circumference the Initiate discovers those living codes drawn from a sacred geometry. This perspective casts apparent irreconcilable opposition into a different light and paves the way towards reconciliation. The astro-logos is a reflection of law writ directly into the heavens, and conceives in these constituent eternal verities proof of a Divine Order. This reference system takes us beyond the notions devised solely through twin portals of perception. Mankind's place in time (arriving at the cusp of ages) prompts a transcendence of established thought processes. It is time to discover new truths, a more holistic way of looking at the experience of life in a human body. Every natal chart can be analyzed with respect to aspects made between Saturn and Jupiter. How these arbiters of personal ethics and morality configure with the entirety of the chart would go far in defining the nature of the individual in question. If astrology were allotted due credence then public officials would not be asked to pass urine tests before being granted high authority; rather their astrology charts would be reviewed for proof of inborn integrity. Those charts evidencing problematic "dialogs" between Jupiter and Saturn would be passed over to make room for those whose charts demonstrated a better balance between these key arbiters of ethics and sound judgment. Only in a world sworn to Mars rules would war go unquestioned while a view from the heavens (which teaches so much about ourselves) remained the silent taboo.

Since everyone is a living portrait of the heavens as crystallized at the instant of their birth, each must account for Jupiter and Saturn as positioned in their natal blueprint. If the pair harmonizes, it's a good indication that you've mastered (in prior incarnations) lessons related to personal ethics and a balanced outlook. Life is a mixture of pain and joy, increase and loss. These rhythms cannot be denied. Jupiter, the largest planet, is associated with cycles of growth and abundance; Saturn is conversely related to periods of loss and diminishment. Events occur to prompt periods of intensive soul-searching. Each human being must negotiate Jupiter's voice of faith, optimism, and joy with the shadow cast by Saturn given its association with fear, cynicism, and personal testing. Both planets (and their related attributes) inevitably impact the overall fabric of human life. What's fashionable today in a cultural climate led by "Calvinistic spirituality," is a Saturn-Chronos call to personal responsibility, conjoined to an inflated expectation of Jupiter's promise that you can have it all. New Age books offer readers a variety of recipes that allegedly allot the acquisition of happiness, wealth, health, and the "right" partner. This premise differs only slightly from the marketplace mantra that everything is available for the right price. It's the modern equivalent of the church of the Middle Ages selling Indulgences! Today's New Age gurus coach followers in the ways and means to write "successful affirmations," believe themselves deserving, act as if, visualize desired outcomes, and set firm intention(s). These are powerful tools; but the spiritual question is whether these manifest manipulations simulate white magic? Jesus taught, "Not my will, but thy will be done." To the Buddhist, deploying such methods to produce a personally coveted outcome sets up a karmic boomerang. In other words, the soul that lays claim to what has not been genuinely earned is effectively taking what is not his. Such action constitutes a subtle form of theft. With today's marketplace the undeclared temple of worship, the obscenely rich are idolized as celebrities, Washington's ubiquitous lobbying firms have compromised the ideals this nation was built upon, and greed has been given a sexier facelift. The love of money has been identified as the root of all that's evil, yet modern society dangerously conditions members to take sacred things like human life and sexual intimacy for mere commodities, things to be gotten. The premise that we can "have it all" presupposes that there is no greater force than human desire at work; that karma can be discounted (perhaps at the price of our very souls). Contrast this banquet of avarice with The St. Thomas admonition that states: "to the one much is given, much is expected." How any individual utilizes her various assets counts on karma's universal ledger. What we learn in any given lifetime becomes our truest legacy. It is what sets into motion the conditions we will meet when next we enter a body. Temporal wealth, on the other hand, does not follow us past the grave. Interestingly enough, when one enters the tunnel of time to observe the mummies on display at New York's Metropolitan Museum of Art, the messages inscribed into the sarcophagi reveal a naïve attempt at establishing a system of eternal banking! Buried along with their riches were elaborate markings intended to direct discarnate souls back to the treasures they left behind! Too bad we human beings tend to reincarnate in different lands and lose contact with the language patterns previously spoken! Nice try, Egyptians! In today's climate of instant gratification, too many people make their life journey a quest after all the right toys. They may accomplish that goal via ethical or compromised means, but the thing of real value, the edifice of character risks neglect if one elects foremost to embrace transitory idols.

Sagittarius governs the ninth sign on the great cosmic dial. As previously noted this sector corresponds with higher education, universities, religion, law, publishing, and long distance travels. The sign was designed to value wide, expansive learning experiences, those that grow the soul on the basis of its exposure to other cultures, customs, and convictions. Regardless, the twin perceptual portals associated with Jupiter and Saturn keep too many minds deadlocked. An intellectual predisposition towards duality sets endless debates over the various quintessential divides. The sharpest minds gravitate to one side of the political spectrum or the other. Intellectual acumen is conditioned to behold life through the polarized prism where good versus evil, the conservative challenges the liberal, the Black citizen remains marginalized from "White" cultural events, and so on. Many Sagittarians pursue the practice of law as their mutability enables them to deftly argue either side of an issue. They may make brilliant cases in the courtroom; but most fail to question the patriarchal constructs that form the underlying basis of their arguments. Since our complex lives force us to confront numerous questions, there is no shortage of debatable issues for alert minds to grapple with. Yet arguing from the standpoint of irrevocable paradox offers no resolution. Logic can only take us so far. Mercury, the archetype of reasoning was given wings for a reason! True enlightenment comes when the mind is ready to transcend its conditioned either-or orientation, a product of prior thought processing. Openness to intuition is the new requirement. And for those who consider themselves atheists, consider that more likely you are rebelling against the incongruities encountered in the religious practice(s) of your family of origin. Imagine a different conception of a Creator, one that exists beyond the limited scope and context described by the old religions. If enough souls woke up to a higher, more encompassing Truth, where would the elite owners of established power find themselves? Little wonder they work overtime to silence their critics. The castigation of heresy has never gone out of style.

Previous sojourns spent in Indigenous cultures are the likelihood when natal planets are found in Sagittarius. This sign frequently compels its benefactors to yearn for sacred rituals. This hunger may lead such persons to lay down their sleeping bags under the stars, hike or dive in remote wildernesses, or search for signs sent by emissaries of the natural world. Sensitive souls set out on personal pilgrimages in search of ways to connect with Divine Presence. Given Sagittarius' link with the centaur, individuals with natal planets found in the Zodiac's 9th kingdom often experience an unquenchable desire to run, stretch their muscles, or distinguish themselves in athletic venues.

Books have arrived on the modern scene that introduce present day urbanites to the mystical rites of shamanism. Its basis for sentience has never been lost. The Green (environmental) movement is composed of persons of conscience who recognize that manmade laws that work against nature can never lead to long-term sustainability. Such persons identify with the natural world as an extension of themselves. Likely they spent past sojourns as members of Indigenous tribes. Their commitment to ecological conservation comes from an inborn connection to the land, and it is galvanized when they're forced to witness industrial giants usurp and desecrate the great Mother's kingdom. Charismatic musician, Jim Morrison, was a Sagittarian and noted for his poetic depictions chronicling modern man's penchant for ecological destruction. Since his untimely death uncontrollable fires have burnt out west, and a recent killer tsunami in Asia took thousands of lives in seconds. Clearly violent storm activity is on the rise. Guess who picks up the tab along with the unfortunates living in the paths where an angered Demeter takes aim? Insurance companies. According to author Gore Vidal, these entities serve as piggy banks to the big corporations. Once upon a time Demeter closed down the harvest systems to show Zeus who was boss. To this day She maintains dominion over nature's assets, the source of natural capital, not to mention the key to human survival. Perhaps Demeter is preparing to instruct Zeus yet again? Since ours is an evolutionary universe, heavens' eternal personae could very well evolve in synch with the progress shown by citizens of the mundane sphere. Zeus, however, is not entirely comfortable with the new authoritarian role he has been prompted to play as a result of the transition of Ages. This might explain the mischief he's wreaked by disguising himself as an animal in order to gain cover while pursuing contact with the lovely maidens of earth. And even when he wears the corporate suite and boasts a wedding band, part of him remains the horny bachelor preferring to dance naked in the wilds. He has been trapped by the appendages of the patriarchy and leads a double life as a result. While his true nature resonates with Pan, he may vote in favor of over-development even while just then making out a generous check to Green Peace! Identifying with the corporate Saturn-Chronos aspect of his inwardly divided nature, he champions prosperity in the form of quarterly profits. In Dhyani Ywahoo's book, *Voices of Our Ancestors*, she identifies the "beauty path." It represents the formulation of decisions based on the true costs apt to be incurred by future generations, rather than what proves profitable right now. Those who possess an affinity with Pan are found on every continent. They live closely with nature and retain magnificent rituals that honor the Earth Mother.

Since Sagittarius signifies the realm of religion and higher awareness, shamanic rituals designed to guide minds beyond existing parameters fall under its aegis. Carlos Casteneda's education by Don Juan (associated with the Toltec Path of sorcery) uncovered unimagined possibilities. Some take his work for a fiction, I think it qualifies as much more. The chronicle of his adventures challenges the worldview of Westerners who have been programmed to respect far more orthodox educational channels. On one occasion Casteneda waxed eloquent in the language of meteorology when Don Juan suddenly burst into laugher. Although Casteneda had learned a thing or two about the sophisticated measuring devices used to predict weather patterns, the Indian understood the more mystical forces that lent life to these phenomena. What Indigenous seers readily note has been denigrated in the same manner that astrology's profound understanding of universal cycles has been discredited (neither having been honestly studied) by modern academia. Don Juan offered his simple elegance: "You confuse the world with what people do." He showed Casteneda the powerful forces that live in the elemental kingdoms. Extending an instruction pertinent to the art of controlling dreams, he provided Casteneda with access to powers few human beings ever touch, no less acknowledge. Similar feats are routinely practiced in India where gurus and adepts shape shift, enter other dimensions, and readily perform what the uninitiated take for magic. Don Juan explained that when people enter this world they immediately fall into massive socialization processes that trap and limit their senses. The cognitive zone of consensual reality he termed the "tonal." Don Juan further explained that sorcerers make use of the realm of dreaming where very different "laws of gravity," not to mention "cause and effect" apply. The sorcerer's realm he referred to as the "nagual." It is a fact that modern mankind uses only a small percentage of its brain. What powers or unique forms of sentience await discovery in those uncharted cerebral territories is yet to be seen. A more down-to-earth understanding of the mechanisms that shape perception is offered by the intellectually-renown author and scholar, Sagittarius Noam Chomsky. His academic studies elucidate how consent is essentially manufactured. The United States prides itself on upholding the ideal of liberty, a status precious to Pan-Sagittarius. Yet the nation's founders readily understood that a viable democracy (one prepared to allot key freedoms to its constituents) relied upon eternal vigilance. When the civilian population is kept in the dark or intentionally misinformed, dangerous political maneuvers can and do occur. America now faces this fate. While editing this book I viewed the film classic, *Easy Rider*. In it two longhaired free spirits (very Sag-like) take off on motorcycles and pass through the Deep South where they hook up with the savvy street-smart attorney played by Jack Nicholson. The trio was not warmly received in small town rural U.S.A. because its members didn't look like (or act like) the natives. Nicholson prophetically uttered the words, "They talk to you a lot about freedom, but a really free person scares them; and when they're scared, they're dangerous." The film bears a tragic ending that lends credence to the young attorney's darkly prescient observation.

Freedom is a precious thing; but we cannot be free as individuals in a society that champions fear and inflates suspicion of others, particularly when the corridors of justice close off to ordinary citizens, and rule in favor of moneyed interests.

We now recognize why and how Saturn-Chronos morphed into Pan-Zeus. This relatively new hybrid can be observed enjoying the popular game of golf. Whilst the Pan nature adores the great outdoors and instinctively seeks out its "verdant temples," Saturn-Chronos is inwardly propelled to answer to the all-important work ethic. Both prospects are satisfied on the grand golf course where big deals occur among powerbrokers against the backdrop of the emerald horizon. Men sworn to achievement must feel at all times that they are mastering a skill or pursuing a viable goal. The golf ball sent sailing over gorgeous terrain seems to satisfy such quests. For Pan, nature serves as the ultimate cathedral. If enough people abandoned their offices, classrooms, workstations, and cash registers Pan could conceivably quit Wall Street and lead us back to the fields with his melodic flute song. Our senses long for ecstasy expressed through ancient dance. Currently ecosystem after ecosystem shows signs of overkill while corporate powerbrokers conduct trades for yet greater profits, ignoring the natural holocaust their bankrupt morality has fostered upon our common earth-home. Earth Mother Demeter can be restored. She has the power to return to beauty, balance, and bounty. The grand magician Merlin related a timeless (and relevant) lesson to King Arthur, that "the king and land are one." How power elects to govern with respect to its use of natural resources impacts the entire life equation. Choices made regarding the distribution of necessities figures substantially into Merlin's mundane formula. Human beings must respect their sacred covenant with the earth and all her sentient beings, for at heart, we are all children of nature. In this shared connection may we rekindle our love of Eden, that we, as champions of the Great Green Goddess, prove her salvation.

In closing it's worth noting that the root of the word joy derives from Jupiter, also known as Jove, purveyor of joviality. Richard Bach suggests that we humans are intended to be the otters of the universe. Our bondage to manmade rules of mercantilism and materialism drains our lives of the very qualities worth living for. We will next examine Jupiter's antithetical counterbalance Saturn-Chronos in the chapter that follows.

Do you know Pan-Zeus? Is a friend, relative, or associate an avid athlete on one hand, yet fully able to play the corporate nine-to-five professional on the other? Does this lucky superman/woman win brownie points climbing the corporate success ladder while strategically easing away office tensions through biking, hiking, or running the marathon? Do you know someone who takes off on exotic quests to foreign lands, and never can read enough books, especially those penned by astute philosophical authors? Is s/he a closet musician?

Pan-Zeus in Love

The following adage was no doubt inspired by a Sagittarian: "If it's one's horse set it free. If it is yours, it will return to you; and if not, then it never was." Few archetypes more truly require spaces in togetherness than Pan-Zeus. Recalling his inwardly divided nature, a portion of the Sagittarius psyche readily conforms to tradition (such as matrimony), while an equally represented aspect requires the opposing need to be free. This sign's affinity with the centaur suggests genuine physical stamina, and this asset naturally benefits intercourse. No other sign is quite as apt to pursue its own version of the "sexual Olympics!" The magic of free, wide-open spaces turns them on. Children of Pan are at their erotic bests while outdoors or off exploring exotic locations. Pan-Zeus may find himself spontaneously aroused while hiking, biking, boating, skiing, or camping. Invest in sporting goods, take off together, and allow nature to do the rest! Her night creatures wait to serenade lovers!

Activities that Accord with the Season of Pan-Zeus

Sagittarius rules the thighs, and that probably explains why this sign is directly associated with running as well as other athletic feats. The Olympics reflect the spirit of Jupiter, and are named after his own personal domain, Olympus! Sagittarius holds a passionate appreciation for sports. Today's near worship of the big arena and its various ballgames suggests a new "opiate of the peoples." If you like the old ballgame, the season of Sagittarius invites you to join with other countless spectators whose spirits are vigorously fueled by endless competitions over "who gets the ball(s)."

Breathe under the stars. Camp out. Set a campfire and roast marshmallows.

Visit the local Humane Society and take a stray animal home.

Write a check to Green Peace, or choose another environmentally conscious organization for your largesse.

Take a day off from work to picnic in the park. Walk through the trees and listen closely for messages on the wind.

Go feather hunting, or gather smooth rocks on a riverbank. Make your own oracle by painting symbols on the stones collected. Devise clever messages to accompany your markings, and then place these stones into a decorated bag. Ask and ye shall receive. In this case, your own insights (messages directed from your "higher self") will be called forth (based on the stone selected) at the appropriate time.

Accept that trip you've long put off. Lunch and shop in an ethnic neighborhood. Draw in the novel scents, sounds, and textures of life as others experience it. Buy a cookbook that features exotic, foreign dishes and indulge your senses.

See a foreign film.

Sponsor a beach cleanup or similar community drive oriented towards the restoration of your local environment.

Begin a community garden.

Rescue your wilderness self.

Study a second (or third) language.

Light candles and invoke a unique personal prayer ritual.

Skinny dip under a full moon (preferably without getting caught)!

Chapter 10

Capricorn: The Realm Of Saturn-Chronos Awakened
Discovering and Honoring One's Purpose

The tenth Zodiac sign sits at the top of "the cosmic dial," and is represented by Capricorn. Traditional astrology appoints Saturn, the undisputed "lord of karma" as governor of this sign-realm. Corresponding with old Chronos (or father time) from myth, it is Saturn's role to partition the chapters of our lives to accord with "a time for every purpose under heaven." Just as Chronos holds the hourglass through which pour out the sands of time, specific intervals direct the life plan and purpose of every individual. In fact Saturn plays a profound role with respect to our maturation cycles. A rudimentary etymological examination of the word chronological takes us back to its root: the entity Chronos. And he depicts something fascinating about time: that discernible "season" changes conform to a regular order. After all Chronos has been allotted the power to measure out (or regulate) specific intervals extended for our intended purposes. These allocations circumscribe our fates and compel us to put our precious time to good use. Once the sand runs out of the hourglass the ending is near. This covert process determines the durations of our relationships, jobs, and even life spans. Who can argue effectively against Chronos when their designated time is up? The mortal aspect of human life makes Saturn's powers fearsome. In the Western world people relish youthfulness and work assiduously to deny "the gravity" of the aging process. Good plastic surgeons are booked months in advance as people endeavor to hold back the hands of time's passage.

In the film noir classic, *The Seventh Seal* directed by Ingmar Bergman, a man's final hour arrives as seen in the approach of sinister lone dark horseman. This clear symbol of death rides up to claim the unfortunate man who as it turns out is not prepared to readily relinquish his life and thus argues compellingly for a reprieve. A compromise takes shape as he's given the chance to challenge death to a chess match. If he loses, the marked man must forfeit his life. It's a compelling wager. Ancient Mayan temple ruins in Mexico recall a time when sports teams fought vigorously, as if their very lives depended on it. Indeed the losing team would face slaughter! Saturn-Chronos warrants genuine fear because human beings have no control over mortality. Due to religious conditioning, many believe God's judgment day awaits them upon death. It so happens that Saturn-Chronos is linked with judges here on the mundane plane. Acting as complement to Jupiter (Pan-Zeus), both planetary principles influence jurisprudence along with the manner by which law is interpreted during each era. Legal determinations tend to change to suit whomever wields power. Voting access extended to women and Black Americans constitutes a relatively recent advance. Not long ago what freedoms did exist were assigned primarily to white males. Constructs of law largely derive from faulty, limited interpretations of *The Bible*, the purported word (law) of God as drawn from an entirely patriarchal thesis. Saturn-Chronos is the personification of *The Old Testament*. Its major teaching, "As ye reap, ye sow" reflects the law of karma. Where Jupiter promotes the consciousness of faith and the expectation of plentitude, Saturn-Chronos prompts prudence and the realization that one must be prepared to face scarcity. Given the rotary nature of the wheel of cosmic time, key planets continually cross the realm of Saturn-Chronos to foster cynicism and misanthropy. It is no hardship to maintain faith when life's circumstances flow effortlessly, yet quite a different matter when one feels tested. *The Book of Job* presents a vivid recollection of the trials attributable to Saturn, the planetary arbiter of karma. On a worldwide scale many will soon face tests of their own as Pluto, the planet of endings that lead to new beginnings, advances across Capricorn. This phase will last nearly two decades. The U.S. economy has been stretched past fiscal sanity in pursuit of a war of choice while jobs have bent sent overseas. Tax and tariff policies have allowed wealth to aggregate dangerously upwards without the requisite "trickle down" to support a consumer-based retail economy. Climate change threatens humanity while there is talk of "the end of oil." Without time (or in some cases the will) to invest in alternative energies the engine of the industrial world might come to an abrupt stop! While in a democratic society a plethora of interests ought be represented, corporate lobbyists have congressmen on dubious payrolls, and too often dictate public policy. Plus infrastructure suitable to a surveillance society has been ominously implemented. Mankind is positioned to face profound tests in coming years.

Pluto's transit of Capricorn aligns with the final phase of the Piscean Age. Neptune, its ruler, began a once in 165-year transit of Capricorn in **1984**, the year chosen by George Orwell to signify his prophetic account of looming government encroachment over human rights. Was this elected title the product of coincidence or eerily prophetic? Neptune is the planet of deception, and Capricorn signifies government and those structures that solidify established power. Neptune remained in Capricorn, Saturn's domain, from 1984-1998. During a portion of this interval Saturn also crossed Neptune's kingdom, Pisces (March 1993-April 1996). The "mutual reception" thus engaged favored government deploying arts of deception formidably. One noteworthy thing that emerged was the growing merger between church, state, and corporate interests. A critical and related astrological event owning far-reaching implications occurred on January 15, 1991, the exact date the first Gulf War began under the direction of George Bush, Sr. It was the date of a solar eclipse in Capricorn, nor was this any ordinary eclipse. Throughout history eclipses have portended change to the political landscape. Shakespeare penned his tragic tale of *Caesar* beginning the storyline with an eclipse. The eclipse occurring on January 15, 1991 involved a veritable cosmic congress convening! No less than seven of the zodiac's ten planetary principles met in Capricorn on that fateful day. Given Saturn's influence over important political events that shape history as well as doctrine, the decisions volleyed among heaven's dignitaries during that conference are apt to hold sway for twenty-nine years! (In other words until Saturn's orbit 'round the sun completes this cyclic phase.) Saturn-Chronos' support of conservative values may therefore yoke humanity for the duration of this cycle. Battles aimed at regaining lost human liberties may wage until 2020 A.D, the year of the next meeting (these occur at twenty-year intervals) between Saturn and Jupiter. The "law and order duo" will unite right on the cusp of the far more liberating and progressive sign of Aquarius. It's evident that recent and substantial traffic across Chronos' domain has paved the way for Pluto's visit to Capricorn. Pluto tears down in order to make space to rebuild. It is divinely mandated to replace dead wood with new growth. However it also is associated with death and violence. Governments worldwide will be radically transformed over the course of the next seventeen years. Since Saturn-Chronos retains power by suppressing liberties, the weight of restriction set against individuals will eventuate in a bursting point. That may very well take shape as a worldwide revolution beginning in 2020. This trend may have been anticipated by elites. The marketing of a "war on terrorism" serves as ingenious cover; it sets up a basis for effectively suppressing dissent. Loose legal jargon marks no clear distinction between the peaceful protestor, environmental activist, and the genuine terrorist who's a real threat to citizens. Surveillance of domestic populations in purportedly democratic nations is now routine. As *Moon Dance* asserts time is non-linear, therefore human beings once again return to that symbolic point in our shared destiny where Moses must lead his people out of pharaoh's captivity. Today's pharaohs are the global corporations that have turned the world's working poor into virtual slaves. The only discernible difference in the status of today's tethered masses is in the extent to which they are free to shop. Capricorn is the sign of human ambition and is a champion of business a/k/a "free" enterprise. Yet free trade is anything but free. Its invisible costs are passed onto Earth Mother Demeter generally without the slightest reverence or regard. While nearly everyone partakes of her bounty, it is She who has paid the price and picked up the check across the long centuries of abuse. The worldwide market devices that encourage America's profligate lifestyles while Demeter (like any overworked Mom) demonstrates paroxysms of climatic overload are criminal, if not insane. With dead zones extending past continents, violent storm systems becoming annual events, and global warming sending species into toxic shock, the natural world cannot supply growing populations with an endless supply of mostly superfluous (if coveted) objects. These have already taxed Demeter's ecosystems to the max. Capricorn, domain of Saturn-Chronos, is the sign of consequences. Where do our inordinate appetites lead? The Tarot offers an apt response in the form of the devil card. Said to represent Capricorn, its image reminds us that human beings are bound not only by greed, but also by their addictive appetites. Mastering the lower self by summoning the self-discipline to follow the dictates of our higher spiritual selves is the quintessential task every human being must eventually face. Since it so happens that Mars (the principle of rash self-interest) is exalted in patience-oriented Capricorn, the premise "he who conquers himself is greater than he who conquers a city" is emphasized. *The Bible* refers to a significant moment where Satan (Saturn) tempts Jesus by offering him unlimited access to the riches of this world. Jesus responds, "Get behind me Satan." His choice conveyed an enlightened appreciation of more lasting riches, those of the spirit drawn from "the kingdom within." Christ went on to advise followers to abandon earthly temptations, and instead "Seek ye first the kingdom of God, and all else will be added unto you." Jesus pursued a wealth of the spirit, rather than a desire to hoard objects. The sure knowledge the universe will support one's true needs is lost on Saturn-Chronos, who is motivated by fear and never feels he has enough. During the past two decades as the entire Zodiac cast (including the outer planets) crossed Chronos' domain, the lust for objects of status has given greed a virtual facelift. Being filthy rich could well qualify as the newest aphrodisiac. The media lays its hosannas before captains of industry. Many of these celebrities endure falls from grace as their self-serving Machiavellian sins are aired in public or the courts. No sign brings to mind the adage, "What profiteth a man to gain the world and lose his soul" more than Capricorn. Saturn-Chronos, signature of father time, is rigid. He is not given to trusting human nature, nor is he any friend of liberty. Therefore as powerhouse Pluto begins its long transit of Chronos' kingdom we are apt to witness a tightening of controls over citizens' rights. In America rightwing judges have already been placed into important positions. Their determinations will strongly color Pluto's passage through Capricorn. The use of fear to invoke citizens to willingly entrust their safety to uniformed guards answering to one branch of the military or another is ominous.

History shows that once a population forfeits liberties, these treasures are not easily regained. Dread, panic, and trepidation prove reliable sources of population control. Fundamentalist religions prey upon the security needs of their followers. Authoritarian by nature, these organizations use manipulation tactics to shape the behaviors of their congregants. The presumption that following strict rules leads to lives of privilege and prosperity is patently false. To the uneducated, the threat of "hell and damnation" remains a time-tested device known to elicit conformity. When people are taught to think, act, and believe alike, any basis for a democratic society is lost. Uniformity is anathema to nature. It insults life as expressed by Demeter's countless diversified communities. The beliefs in sin and hell have held minds hostage for centuries and essentially disabled that key intrinsic, autonomous mechanism known as **instinct**. Given this loss, individuals have looked to outside authority figures to tell them what's real or false. Human beings either learn to internalize Saturn by owning autonomy and facing their personal lessons (the spiritual equivalent of growing a solid backbone); or they fall prey to externalized sources of authority all too ready to assume control over their intimate lives. Saturn-Chronos is depicted as old and stern because his role is a tough one. The Zodiac's boot-camp sergeant, he demands that we face our tests in order to spiritually mature. What the soul learns becomes its permanent legacy; and hard won experience is arguably more precious than gold.

Moon Dance articulates the expressive voices of all members of the Divine circle. Each of its twelve inlaid positions is perfectly calibrated to harmonize with the others; but when any intended voice is silenced spiritual symmetry unravels. This phenomenon has apparently occurred as Mars has come to singularly define far too many aspects of human life. With the great plan thrown askance, the Mars principle of violent force, exalted in Capricorn, has been given free reign. Typically the army (along with the entire military) serves the nation-state's leaders. Ideally there should be a bona fide reason to deploy its deadly powers. Just war is the determination that force must be utilized for self-defense. When instead the military steps out of this role to assume the shape of conqueror, then naked aggression fuels leaders' ambitions of expanding empire. This

253

dark objective has entire societies bowing down in homage to its ends. Once war is undertaken then generally civil liberties become suppressed. The Geneva Conventions cite war of aggression as the supreme crime against humanity for good reasons. Yet America under the deadly influence of a massive military-industrial complex recently initiated a war of choice begun on faulty pretexts. Once war is initiated, the president may argue (as did our 43rd chief executive) that as commander-in-chief, his powers exceed those established by the U.S. Constitution. The nation's founders, having seen tyranny firsthand, designed a unique system of governance precisely to avoid that outcome. Checks and balances would naturally result from the interplay of three **co-equal** branches of government. The founders recognized that power can't be trusted; indeed absolute power is known to corrupt absolutely. Unfortunately a good percentage of persons conditioned by old traditions prefer a strong father figure. Working together an insidious group of "Conservatives Without Conscience" (as author John Dean referred to them) recently devised the term "Unitary Executive." Through it they endeavored to deliver to the U.S. president powers never intended by our Constitution. The use of "signing statements" by former President George Bush sidestepped the authority of congress and the courts and set a dangerous precedent, that which is conducive to authoritarianism, if not totalitarianism. These trends resonate with Pluto's long transit of Capricorn, a cycle that began in concert with Saturn transiting letter-of-the-law Virgo (2008). When power becomes consolidated, by whatever name we term it, tyranny results. The dictionary defines fascism as: "A system of government characterized by rigid one-party dictatorship, forcible suppression of the opposition (unions, other parties, minority groups); the retention of private ownership of the means of production under centralized government control, belligerent nationalism and racism, glorification of war."

Having established that Mars represents the army and Capricorn, the centralized power of the state, it is useful to recall that every ocean wave must turn under itself to gather forward momentum. A similar process ensues with respect to historical cycles. Capricorn's celestial influence will not last. The recidivistic trends currently surfacing via fundamentalist movements in the United States (as Christian theocracy), the Middle East (as Islamic fundamentalism) and Israel (as Zionism) all demonstrate homage to Saturn-Chronos, an often-punitive god. These belief systems foster fear and lead to separation. Not only do they adamantly argue in favor of retaining ancient tribal designations, they also inflame deep-seated antipathies. The result? People remain divided on the basis of their sect, religious affiliation, caste, and nationalistic identity. These delineations threaten to tear our world asunder. National borders are fictions devised by mankind, as are those demarcations that pit person against person. These deep divisions must mend; and the healing process calls for a collective transcendence of previous definitions. A return to the circle, which is to say a teaching of the fundaments drawn from the celestial blueprint designed for our world, could inspire new affiliations. Human beings require a unifying model that makes room for varied voices and perspectives. Global calamity can be avoided if we unlearn hatred for one another. Out of necessity arrives the mother of global invention.

Why do you suppose Creator designed our solar system by setting specific planetary principles into graduated concentric orbits? From a metaphysical standpoint the layout is anything but accidental. The last three planets whose orbs extend beyond Saturn have all been discovered since the turn of the 19th century. Unknown to the Ancients, these revolving spheres have recently led humanity to new communication technologies, advanced energy systems, and greater freedoms. Their various functions suggest the basis for a progressive plan designed for humanity's evolution. Thus while Capricorn, realm of Saturn-Chronos sits at the top of the cosmic dial where it promotes worldly success (and those privileges extended to an elite and "chosen" few), its position anticipates that of Aquarius. The rigid structures resonant with a strict authoritarian father-god eventually must yield to the more egalitarian ideal mandated by Aquarius, the sign that signifies the Divine spark awakened in mortal flesh. Whereas Capricorn champions personal status and hierarchical social structures, Aquarius promotes a truly democratic, just social order. History evidences the ongoing battle between power's apparatus held in the tight clasp of a variety of kings, popes, dictators, and emperors and the fierce rebellions taken up by the masses in pursuit of those inalienable rights writ into the heavens. Saturn-Chronos seeks to preserve social, economic, and political agendas that grant benefit to a few, while holding the vast majority in bondage. Astrology may anoint Leo the sign of kings and queens, but it is Capricorn that favors czars, dictators, and those worldly characters too often intent upon the abuse of power. India is recognized as a Capricorn nation and its caste system follows the Saturn-Chronos model. Vedic astrology (as practiced in India) allots no credence to the latter planetary discoveries. Growth is impeded when individuals are held hostage to old gods, when symbolically speaking Chronos is given the last word or final authority on a subject's unfolding life plan. Capricorn is by nature suspicious of change, antagonistic towards youth, and bent on retaining its hold on authority. Thus Capricorn, along with its varied agencies and structures often acts to freeze progress. When the early church levied its death threats against heresy, it discovered a powerful means for silencing dissent. By ominous parallel as conflicts rage the war state expects conformity of its citizens. Its jingoistic climate encourages too many to mistake blind allegiance for patriotism. Karl Rove, a Capricorn, was referred to as George Bush's brain. He used rumor, blackmail, and calumny to stop political opponents in their tracks. Careers have been ruined or otherwise compromised. J. Edgar Hoover, another Capricorn, used similar tactics. According to myth, don't forget, Chronos was prepared to devour his own children. This act in metaphor strikes up an analogy to another misanthropic Capricorn, the ornery president Richard Nixon. He gave The National Guard the order to shoot peaceful demonstrators at Kent State University thirty years ago. A paranoid leader he sought to subsume the voice of youth as it rose like a fierce tide to challenge his authority. Capricorn is the sign of fear, mistrust, and paranoia. In the excellent film, *The Conversation*, a specialist in surveillance comes to conclude that he is being spied upon. Tortured by the suspicion that now he is on the receiving end of clandestine violations to his presumption of privacy, he comes unglued and tears his home apart looking for "the elusive bug." Karma has its own ways of coming full circle. *The Bible* relates, "Judge not that ye not be judged." No doubt timeless advice, given we often end up walking in the shoes of the person(s) we judged in order to develop empathy.

Returning briefly to the Tarot's depiction of the Devil card we notice it features two figures chained to a hooded figure, and thus held in bondage. Today's work ethic enslaves people. While corporate chieftains have seen their fortunes grow by obscene proportions, the minimum wage has essentially been frozen for a decade. Housing and auto prices have meanwhile tripled. At the closing phase of the Piscean Age oil wars have been waged to regulate prices at the pump (or, as some surmise, to maintain the dollar's hegemony over global trading in black gold). People are so busy trying to keep up with the costs of living that a great many don't realize the extent to which they've lost contact with nature, spirituality, or true freedom. Quiet desperation has never been louder! Aquarian firebrand Granny D in her nineties still offers impassioned speeches that stress the importance of personal liberty. She's ingeniously unmasked the displaced projection that fuels the fundamentalist crusade to protect unborn fetuses. Masked grief she calls it for lives that have never been lived on account of followers' strict conformity to the stale rules of others. Many people walk lockstep as they robotically follow rituals forced upon them by the "old gods." Just as governments bent on repressing civil liberties rationalize such initiatives by stating they are done to protect the people; religions do likewise. Assuming the role of moral custodian, religions (and sometimes government) act in pre-emptive ways to battle the evils that presumably lurk deep in the human soul. Thus adherents are expected to honor the dictates issued by religious authorities. Clearly great minds and theologians have long debated whether evil is inborn to the human experience. Perhaps it has emerged in response to unfair, often unjust constraints levied against too many persons century after century. The Black slave who sought to run away and had to fight off the abuse of "his master," was hardly evil. Today's Iraqi insurgent who battles American soldiers occupying his nation is portrayed as evil by American media; but the truth is he seeks liberation for his homeland and elected lifestyle. Although the United States in its imperial overreach, assisted by an obscene arsenal of weapons, purports to know how other nations and their people ought to live (a notion utilized as cover since the ostensible motive is exploitation of other nations' resources), the contention is patently false. Naked aggression cannot be masked when it takes shape as a blatant trespass against international treaties and a sovereign citizenry's rights. The U.S. record of imperial hubris calls out for karmic blowback, and it's likely to take shape during Pluto's upcoming opposition to the United States July 4 sun-sign. (Peak begins in 2012.)

What then becomes the price of our fears? The U.S. military has admitted that the cost of stockpiling weapons (for five decades) now far exceeds their initial production costs! Industrial profits derive from a complex infrastructure that is itself dependent upon phenomenal amounts of coal, oil, and nuclear power. Without these energy sources the engines of power would come to an abrupt halt. Although utilized for forty years there remains no safe technological means for storing the radioactive detritus produced by nuclear power plants. Meanwhile the Pentagon recently acknowledged that global warming poses a greater threat to citizens than terrorism. Yet captains of America's corporations energetically thwart investment in renewal energies such as solar and wind power. It's not like this avoidance comes cheap, either. Climate events have grown in severity and dramatically impact the U.S. year after year. Seven hurricanes hit Florida (2004-2005); Katrina wiped out New Orleans, and massive heat waves accompanied by drought have put Atlanta on notice. California properties risk rapidly spreading fires on a recurrent basis. These events cost insurance companies, which happen to come under the purview of Saturn-Chronos! Since Capricorn is the realm of consequences (foreseen or otherwise) it's far more cost-effective to change energy gears instead of remaining on our present course. Recycling technologies must be engineered at the onset of all industrial processes. Teaching conservation rather than rabid consumerism makes sense given the fragile state of the natural world and the imminent collapse of interlocking ecosystems. As Dr. Seuss's *Cat in the Hat* came to realize, it's far more expensive to clean up an escalating mess, than to avoid one. A related premise operates in the holistic health field where instead of focusing resources on treating a wide array of diseases, we might learn better ways and means to prevent them!

Capricorn as the last of the Zodiac's three earth signs is practically born with a gene for sound business; plus its mythological counterpart Chronos supports the modern marketplace culture. Since profits direct priorities, money is not often enough spent on what's actually good for people. Note the degree to which the tentacles of the insurance industry reach deep into health care cutting off access (and sometimes necessary surgery) to too many people. Businesses are often forced to cut costs and sometimes that directly compromises safety. The airline industry must do its best to contain costs in order to maximize profits. When safety protocols considered optional are bypassed it means a plane has a greater chance of crashing. In the wake of such a calamity millions of dollars are spent in heroic attempts to recover the elusive black box. Great effort is expended to determine what went wrong while that same money is seldom earmarked to prevent disaster! What is the logic here? According to astute author Naomi Klein, we've entered into an epoch of "disaster capitalism." In her view crises are seen as excellent business opportunities. Sometimes these occur on their own, while insidiously, at other times they are helped along. The city of Key West, Florida incorporated in mid-January and therefore qualifies as a Capricorn entity. It utilized this enterprising approach way ahead of its time. At the turn of the 20th century this tiny island city was one of the wealthiest regions of America. Putting its own version of disaster capitalism to work, its chief industry was the wreckers! Crafty enterprising pirates set up lighthouses that intentionally lured ships to dangerous reefs where their seaworthiness would inevitably become compromised. The wreckers wasted no time in jumping aboard the sinking vessels to steal the goodies. Designing dire fates for others is hardly a sound or moral basis for enterprise. Yet it's fast become the new model of empire, a fierce extension of global corporate capitalism without conscience. There is nothing progressive about the sign of Saturn-Chronos or its use of surreptitious strategies to maintain its ends. Saturn functions to sustain the status quo and frequently impedes efforts directed at meaningful, progressive change. This may explain why (as per his myth of origin) Chronos was quick to swallow his own children, the living symbols of the next generation. That's one way to preclude change! But who benefits from keeping the old ways? Established bastions of power lead the charge against new thought. For substantial periods of time esoteric perspectives, which is to say more inclusive ways of viewing our shared web of destiny have been kept off limits. These guardians continue to control mass media along with mainstream education to insure that young minds are kept closed before they have a chance to open.

Following its twenty-nine year revolution, Saturn plays a crucial role in mapping every individual's life cycle given increments specifically built into its orbital plan. The maturation process of human beings is catalyzed in part due to scheduled prompts that occur at seven-year intervals. The Hebrews recognized this natural celestial cycle and wisely put aside grain to sustain them across the inevitable lean times. These repeat every seventh, fourteenth, twenty-first, and twenty-eighth year. Then that same cycle recurs. Ultimately Saturn celestially knocks on our birth charts every seven years; plus it returns to its original position at age twenty-nine, again at fifty-eight, and once more at age eighty-six. At these "Saturn return" junctures we either consciously weed our lives of outgrown elements, or destiny takes a hand in that process. Acting as the persona of father time, Saturn-Chronos recalls *Hamlet's* deceased father, who having been murdered returns in ghostly form to haunt the young man by forever reminding him of his "anointed purpose." Astrologers agree that Saturn's position in the natal chart represents our karma, or zone of greatest personal labor. Like the Bible's *Book of Job*, Saturn (by natal chart position) articulates the area we're most apt to feel tested. As individuals develop their personal histories, often one arena stands out in its power to challenge. It likely conforms to Saturn's sign or related aspects. Because we routinely come up against difficulty a basis for fear gets established. Author Liz Greene's insightful text, *Saturn, a New Look at an Old Devil*, explains the sign where we find our Saturn reveals where we tend to overcompensate. Everyone has Saturn somewhere! As the lord of karma, its sign designation points to where "heavy lifting" will be required! Ultimately Saturn acts as our spiritual coach. A life wasted counts against our karmic account. The Buddhists remind us of the impermanence of human life, and since no one knows when his hour may come, it's important to do what we can today to improve our tomorrow. Part of that process involves facing the objectives demarcated by our birth blueprint, and where possible gaining an understanding of and respect for the plan of our soul's trajectory.

Saturn applauds self-discipline. A healthy balanced individual understands that time is her most precious resource and uses it accordingly. Saturn-Chronos tends towards seriousness, even melancholy. After all it's been noted that depression rates rise around the Christmas holidays, which of course introduces the season of Saturn-Chronos. Winter is cold. On real and symbolic levels human warmth may reach its nadir. The darkest day of the year occurs on the winter solstice, December 21 to usher in Capricorn's month of dominion. I've always felt that celebrating New Year's during this dour hour was rather out of cosmic synch. Thanksgiving, in contrast, works in accord with Pan-Jupiter's season of abundance; and Mother's Day, celebrated during the season of Taurus-Demeter resonates. But to evoke party time when the work ethic of Capricorn asserts its shadow over festivities? The macabre author Edgar Allen Poe was a Capricorn who suffered from depression. Although the product of fiction, Ebineezer Scrooge has taken on a life of his own and aptly personifies Saturn-Chronos. Once his understanding is enhanced by a spirit-guardian generous enough to point out the waste of a life based solely on accruing profits, Scrooge experiences a spiritual epiphany. It's exactly what should befall (if via cosmic express) today's captains of industry! Charles Dicken's novel *A Christmas Carol* ought to be required reading for all government and corporate executives!

Conventional astrology depicts Saturn-Chronos not only as father time, but also as the signature of paternal authority. The role model set by our biological father influences our political sensibilities. Researcher George Lakoff makes a compelling case that those individuals raised in homes with strict fathers acting as central authority figures embrace conservative (Republican) values. Those reared in more liberal climes, following what Lakoff defines as the "nurturing parent" model, identify with progressive values and a similar philosophy of governance. The polarity that operates between these dual political camps reflects the qualitative interplay of timeless principles, each a thematic component of a great design plan that is portrayed through ancient celestial archetypes.

As has been related, all positions hold a key purpose, but these become dangerously compromised when any singular one claims disproportionate power. Pluto's current (and lasting) influence over the realm of Saturn-Chronos will teach mankind difficult lessons. Elite interests aligned with old bastions of power will use overt and covert means to maintain a concentration of power at the apex of the human pyramid. In contrast Aquarius, the Divine expression next to be realized seeks to spread self-determination around. For this New Age Phoenix to "rise" humanity must transcend its old ways and burst the chains of previous forms of bondage. The required process calls for a radical re-examination of established belief systems and the behaviors these give rise to. Saturn-Chronos represents both individual karma as well as that of nations. Aquarian ideals, about to emerge on the wheel of cosmic time, must catalyze human beings to vastly alter the ways they have been living. This subject takes us to the next chapter. There the 11th house principle of synergy inspires groups committed to specific, if dissimilar agendas to work together. The Divine circle of right relations is our invisible ally and magically assists those committed to restoring harmony to our world.

Do you know Saturn-Chronos, someone who seems rather old for their tender years, a person devoted to ambition and at times given to displaying Machiavellian tendencies? Does one of your relatives or associates act as if s/he is Atlas and expected to hold the entire weight of the world on her shoulders? Do you have an acquaintance who thinks of fun or recreational activities as a waste of time? They prefer to devote themselves to entrepreneurial projects or challenging, labor-intensive goals?

Saturn-Chronos in Love

It's been said that the children of Saturn-Chronos loosen up and become **younger** with age. A great many play the role of protector. Often this takes shape as being romantically drawn to or involved with a younger partner. Acting to assist the love interest's chosen career, Saturn-Chronos builds up his partner, and works to substantiate bonds based on mutual respect and affection. This is not to say that the earthy goat is immune to seduction. Capricorn is patient, and that asset adds immeasurably to lovemaking skills. Saturn-Chronos tends to provide protection and security to their loved ones. Their dutiful efforts instill a deep and abiding trust in prospective partners. This tends to invite reciprocation in the form of sexual responsiveness.

Activities that Accord with the Season of Saturn-Chronos

Take off your watch, and while you're at it, take the day off! Live liberated from time's tick-tocking away!

Walk barefoot in the park or at the seashore.

Visit a National park. Hike or bike up a mountain.

Make a pilgrimage to Washington, D.C. to view the Library of Congress and take in its powerful symbols of liberty. Observe the precious documents preserved so that citizens can plainly view the founding ideals that set this Republic and its elegant political design into motion.

Eat at a vegetarian café or health food store.

Observe the Sabbath. Consider what would happen if the whole world took a 7th day pause to allow nature the opportunity to rest and plausibly recover?

View classic black and white movies and note that heroism was conveyed through actions that championed the greater good rather than personal advantage.

Donate to a charity.

Indulge in fantasy. Travel back in time by visiting a Renaissance Fair.

Make a whimsical purchase at a thrift shop. Defy pragmatism!

Take an earnest accounting of all those that have contributed to your life, and where possible, offer thanks or a token of appreciation.

Allow a skilled chiropractor to tune your spine and harmonize its grid-work of chords.

Chapter 11

Aquarius: The Realm Of Artemis Awakened
Honoring Personal Truth

The zodiac's futuristic sign was not born to live in the past or abide by yesterday's outdated notions. Earth, along with our solar system, adheres to an orb that echoes our sun's revolution around a central sun. In accord with these complex cosmic clockworks our current position relative to the fixed stars indicates that a profound era of transition is underway. The Aquarian Age is in its beginning stages, and it prompts a new understanding with respect to the human being's relationship to the larger cosmos. Aquarius is considered a "space age" sign, and as the last expression of the air sign trinity, it moves the soul towards a higher awareness. One that respects the players, friends, and allies integral to the great journey constituted by life, the quintessential adventure. History often is told through the metaphor of the son coming to replace the father, as olds ways yield to progressive change. Aquarius, however, is the sign apt to shock convention while opting to break the rules. Therefore to signify the "changing of the Olympian guard" that's now in progress, *Moon Dance* acknowledges the influence of **the Divine daughter**, Artemis. She connotes the rebel and brings to mind the legendary women of the Amazon. These females reputedly discovered their own powers in feats that set them apart from men. Artemis constitutes the archetype of the self-realized woman, a vital expression of the Divine feminine and apt symbol for the rise of the Aquarian Age. Already basic definitions for masculine and feminine behaviors are unraveling. Gender bending expressions are seen everywhere as a growing segment of the population turns away from orthodoxy to assume gay or bisexual lifestyles. Artemis challenges all traditions, regardless of whether they're codified on the basis of race, religion, nationality, or gender. She signifies the Age of the awakened daughter prepared to lay just claim to her divine birthright; for as twin to brother Apollo, the Divine son (sun), how could both share the same zygote while only one is acknowledged as holy or divine? It falls to Artemis (and all awakened souls) to challenge those standards that have deadlocked women's rights and expressions for centuries. This great heist against the Divine feminine became institutionalized long ago and set mankind on a collision course, where instead of seeing spiritual progress it circles itself. With only patriarchal Mars-rules navigating, our world has come to its present ominous state where a critical task falls to Artemis: that of altering humanity's directional course through a massive vision correction. This feat can be accomplished by raising consciousness and restoring ideals, ones that can help build sustainable, balanced societies. The advancement of the human race rests upon its capacity to transcend prior self-destructive inclinations. The Aquarian Age activates the voice of the divine daughter to establish a new ethos on earth. Awakened women and men everywhere must endeavor to plant the understanding that generates an integrative, as opposed to divisive basis for civilization.

The ever-turning rotary dial of the heavens ensures that a percentage of citizens will be born into Artemis' kingdom, regardless of time period or geographical location. Such persons carry the requisite strength of will to march to their own drummers. They can devise new music as needed, for they are highly inventive souls. Artemis is celestially directed to act from innate integrity. Frequently she will come up against the ingrained injustices of society and feel forced to challenge its protocols and standards. Artemis is unlikely to find personal fulfillment by adapting her life to suit false creeds or principles. Nor was she designed to be a follower. She was born to lead, intended to pave the path to new forms of human expression. Artemis represents the sign-realm of invention, innovation, and serendipity. Her stellar kingdom upholds Truth. Any truly self-realized person, one largely immune to mass media's indoctrination process can prove enormously powerful. A faith in the power of Truth arms bearers to stand up to forces that otherwise would hold back the wheels of progress. Mainstream agencies grant false witness to **what humanity might become on the basis of what it's been**. Over the course of centuries all sorts of indoctrination processes have been utilized to thwart mass consciousness. Human beings have effectively been held hostage to old effete traditions largely through the use of a potent narcotic: that of fear. Just as insanity is explained by doing the same thing the same way and expecting different results mankind cannot sustain old ways (and thinking) and expect anything better than the calamitous redundancy of war. What had been humanity's trajectory will remain unless a cognitive critical mass is reached and galvanizes citizens to explore alternatives in a vigorous discovery process apt to span the globe. It would seem that there are forces seen and unseen intent upon freezing human evolution. The old "gods" are jealous deities that would have no new understanding arise to challenge their claims to sovereignty. They also deploy deception. Yet mystics believe there are higher kingdoms devoted to mankind's evolutionary possibilities. One problem is the vast majority maintains a thought process soaked in centuries of conditioning, too much of it based on deluded ideology. Often the very act of arriving at, no less speaking Truth constitutes a revolutionary endeavor. Although Uranus (the planet believed to govern Aquarius) was discovered in the 19th century, those cast from the mold of Artemis have been born throughout the course of time. These evolved souls founded organizations, and during periods of intolerance and inquisition, initiated secret fraternities that published important books to ensure that the light of truth would never go out despite the darkness of their era. Dan Brown's popular *Da Vinci Code* alludes to this underground. From the perspective of history, once Uranus was discovered, a series of actual revolutions took place. At their core was a common passionate drive to improve citizens' rights. Tension between authoritarian powers and the people's quest for liberty remains a recurrent theme on earth. It is in part attributable to the relative influences played by Saturn-Chronos and Uranus/Artemis on the mundane stage. History demonstrates that tyrants consistently emerge to threaten the precious freedoms citizens seek and fight to preserve. Due to Neptune's conditioning (remnant of the fading Piscean Age) truth is often regarded as inconvenient. Given that life is a struggle for the vast majority, whether they labor for good health, a way out of dead-end jobs, strategies to overcome despair, or a partnership through which to exorcize existential loneliness, most do not find time to pursue personal meaning. Fewer explore the big epistemological questions. Instead most mundane hours are cannibalized by rendering unto Caesar what appears his due.

Aquarius, as the eleventh zodiac realm, represents the power of synergy. Jesus taught that: "If two or more gather in my name and ask, then so shall it be." While attending a Unity Church in the Florida Keys the minister shared an intriguing anecdote. It depicted hell as a sumptuous banquet table where all the seated guests had spoons attached to their wrists. The metaphor is clear: if we set out only to feed ourselves, we cannot enjoy life's delicacies. Heaven is portrayed as the exact same scene except that each diner extends his wrist to feed his neighbor. It's rare in today's world for people to come together in peace without harboring competitive ego-driven agendas. Centuries of conditioning have taught us to resist cooperation and treat one another with distrust. As a result the virtually untapped synergistic potentials of the eleventh house remain dormant, and those problems long confronted by the human race remain woefully intact. The magic of spiritual synergy is left out of our approach to remedying what is wrong. Chiefly due to the insistent ego and its driven self-interest our capacity to break out of self-destructive feedback loops is disabled. One area where the 11th house power of the collective has been permitted to demonstrate its effectiveness is in the ubiquitous Twelve Step programs. These congregations animate the powerful premise attributable to the Zodiac's 11th house: that when two or more enter into agreement the assistance of The Holy Spirit is assured. This transcendental force treats conditions that seem insurmountable. A recovery process of global proportions is needed to summon those still slumbering under Piscean Age delusions into a mass awakening. Aquarius promises to illumine a clearer path to understanding. A cathartic process for mankind is inevitable as Aquarius now begins to rise on the global destiny dial. We are all souls recovering from centuries of duality, paradox, inconsistency, prejudice, and suffering. Along the path of our many lifetimes, we have born witness to (and sometimes perpetrated) unspeakable injustices. Castigation by race, creed, religion, and economic status has led to purges, inquisitions, holy wars, and other grotesque atrocities. Aquarius' genius derives in part from the unexpected. Its methodology goes beyond what those who live "in the box" can imagine. Evolution can happen in a flash if one seizes the moment.

In George Lucas' brilliant rendition of *Star Wars*, it is brother Luke (Apollo) and his twin sister Leah (Artemis) who assemble an ad hoc, colorful group of unlikely allies. Their team is able to effectively locate the singular flaw in the death star (Mars). A small group, they work together to undermine the nearly omnipotent military empire led by Darth Vader. Truly this is the myth for our times! Aquarius seldom elects to meet force with force; instead it joins together those of like mind who use their varied aptitudes to overcome impediments. The world was never flat, and planes could always fly; but it took the imagination of the most evolved members of society to recognize these latent possibilities. The capacity to call forth invention remains a key aspect of human nature. It often falls to the destiny of the Artemis-born to shake things up and rattle humanity's cage by introducing change. Persons who by nature resonate with Artemis may indeed be those who spent previous lifetimes preparing for the experience that now will take them beyond Saturn. In theory, by this point in their personal evolutionary trajectory they should have mastered an understanding of the higher order at work. Ideally they find themselves inwardly mandated to act in accord with its principles. Incremental octaves built into the zodiac as demonstrated by the concentric orbits the planetary principles adhere to suggest that Saturn's rigorous testing is the preparatory work required before a soul may advance to the next sphere (Aquarius). There it is free to assume the visionary zeal celebrated by and through the eleventh sign-realm. Traditional astrology defines Aquarius as the sign of radicals and radical invention. This influence is reflected in the lifework of Aquarian Charles Darwin whose scientific theories regarding evolution still remain posthumously debated by the church. Similar castigation confronted Aquarian native Galileo Galilee, while Aquarius Abe Lincoln (whose conscience was sickened by the unjust practice of slavery) shook up the fledgling United States' economy by taking steps to abolish its reliance upon the dehumanization of human beings. Those who boldly speak of change frequently find themselves up against those status quo forces intent upon their silence. Various and sundry programs have been designed to wipe out alternative voices. This undemocratic agenda has been the predominant strategy used by the patriarchal order to maintain itself. A politics of exclusion is once again being revivified in America as authoritarian institutions assisted by their followers seek legislation intent upon controlling others' freedoms. What Aquarius, and by extension, Artemis endeavor to teach the world is that just because our fathers (Capricorn) did things a certain way does not mean we must continue as thus blindly following along. Repeating costly mistakes is not the best way to honor our ancestors or their traditions. To do so binds our wings.

Marilyn Ferguson's *Aquarian Conspiracy* spells out the countless inroads that humanity has begun to explore in its quest after new models for living. More recently thousands of courageous pioneers met in exotic Brazil for *The World Social Forum*. A colorful cast consisting of rebels, visionaries, social engineers and other dynamically motivated persons collaborate on the ways and means for fulfilling their mandate that: "Another World is Possible." Rabbi Lerner, who publishes *Tikkun Magazine*, champions varied arts, practices, and resources that help to repair our shared and broken world. Indeed much requires mending. The Aquarian Age is slowly coming to life, invoked by courageous pioneers, individuals who see beyond yesterday. These children of Artemis are given to exploration and drawn to the unorthodox. They truly embody a "live and let live, so long as it harms none" ethos. Agents of a new epoch they prompt us to look beyond the boundaries that preserve effete structures based on outdated thinking. One key legacy of the Piscean Age is a set of paradigms that have crippled mankind along with nature! Although scientists as informed messengers have warned of the dangers of rapid climate change, the fossil fuel industry has engendered a public relations campaign intent on muddying the waters. Instead of America using its manpower to refit infrastructure to reflect greener technologies, money is wasted on the delusion of defense through militarism. What kind of model is this? Old institutions built on false principles and held up by fear are fated to collapse. Oppressive values court periodic revolutions as history amply demonstrates. That's because the rigid rules imposed by Saturn-Chronos abrade against the quest for liberty passionately pursued by souls who resonate with

Aquarius-Artemis. Ceaseless friction between these "ideological tectonic plates" leads to periodic progressive breakthroughs. Nation after nation reflects the lesson that populations tightly constricted discover the ways and means to effect their own liberation. Saturn-Chronos may represent the interests of the elites, but Aquarius-Artemis speaks for the people. The agendas consistent with these dueling political forces are a direct reflection of two chief archetypal imprints as drawn from the blueprint of the firmaments.

As those inherently compelled to march to their own drummers know, there is often a price paid for stepping out. The rebel is often socially ostracized or banned from participating in functions sponsored by the established group. Only the strongest are able to stand alone on the pinnacle of principle, while most are shamed into conformity. Societies routinely punish members that challenge their protocols. Note that solitary confinement within the prison community is considered the greatest punitive measure. In times past, the "dangerous" individualist might be banished or sent into exile. Today modern family life plays a powerful role in socializing children to fit in and adapt to the dominant paradigm. Disciplinary measures that border on child abuse await those tender souls that don't march in lockstep with the existing order. The ones that question conventional mores or ask embarrassing questions of authority figures (who too often demand strict obedience to out-dated norms) are often made into scapegoats. Brave souls have often been falsely castigated, branded heretic or criminal by corrupt authority figures that had their own tainted agendas to protect. Frequently such persons are punished for being born ahead of their times, positioned to impart gifts of invention and understanding to others caught inside the fold. Yet often it is when things fall apart, when the center no longer holds, that innovators are called for. Should necessity arise as the mother of invention, the Artemis native is equipped to meet the tasks at hand. Such persons are celestially wired to see beyond yesterday, and capable of ingeniously inventing tomorrow before our awestruck eyes. Luckily, the rotary nature of the cosmos is such that there always will exist "free radicals" born to challenge every era and culture. Saturn-Chronos precedes Aquarius-Artemis on the dial and it's mandated to solidify rules; yet there comes a point where adherence to these dictates blocks progress. It is the task of Artemis to break old effete chains.

Many Aquarians, by virtue of their ruling planet Uranus' association with electricity naturally sparkle. They radiate palpable charisma. Ellen Degeneres and Oprah Winfrey are two examples that effervescently radiate, and almost organically connect with huge audiences. At the time of this writing, Sarah Palin's Aquarian charisma (and in her case, twisted eccentricity) has been given enormous play in the 2008 presidential election. When a person is endowed with irresistibly attractive qualities as Edgar Cayce related such a gift carries a karmic responsibility. Take the gorgeous model that poses for ads that promote cigarettes. Her enviable good looks are utilized to seduce others into a deadly lifelong habit. Cayce explained that one who is highly attractive, thus given the gift of attracting people must be mindful of where their influence leads. Aquarians are often endowed with good looks, plus many are born leaders. They make poor followers since they are by nature compelled to question formal rules and challenge authority. Their cosmic task is to evolve systems, rather than maintain them in present form. Since education in the United States is directly influenced by the corporate model, conformity is sought after on a massive scale. Instead of fostering the boundless imagination that stems from a curious, open mind, the educational system seeks to condition all students to pass uniform tests. This so-called market savvy approach undermines the cognitive resources most needed to maintain America's technological edge. Novel inventions emerge from a place in the collective unconscious very close to where dreams live. Whether a Jules Verne or Rod Sterling, those who probe *The Twilight Zone* often return to reveal new developments to their earthbound peers. Such vision directly benefits mankind. In contrast children forced to manage their minds like so many neat manicured lawns effectively forfeit any basis for innovation. Uniformity is the enemy of imagination. Can the world afford to lose it? Growth tends to happen at the fringes. A certain tyranny attaches to the pursuit of the mean. If everyone aims towards what's average, diversity gets sacrificed. Earlier in our discussion we noted that Gemini operates as the first octave of air and thereby introduces a basis for learning.

Libra, air's second octave, invites the extension of communication to take in the other person's point of view. Eventually this leads to the facilitation of law and those social contracts that enable groups to live peacefully together. When these intentions mature (which is to say solidify in a society) then Aquarius emerges to embody the air element's highest expression. The children of Artemis own a ready access to intuition and it fosters moments of genius, an acute awareness based on a direct inner "knowing."

Souls advanced to the path of Aquarius, the first realm that exists outside the buttressing karmic rings of Saturn-Chronos, begin to directly engage in a co-creative relationship with Divine forces. This perhaps accounts for why so many Aquarians embrace quirky, rather offbeat beliefs. A number of Hollywood's glitterati revere scientology. It's hardly coincidental that these celebrities hold sun, moon, or ascendant positions in Aquarius. When I participated in an enthusiastic *Course in Miracles* group, I met an Aquarian woman who was absolutely convinced she would never die. I agreed that her spirit was immortal, but she insisted that her physical body would withstand death, the great mortal equalizer! I know of another Aquarian who thinks that global warming is a hoax; nor does he believe that astronauts ever landed on the moon.

Having arrived at this juncture of ages where Aquarius is being summoned from the dream zone of Pisces, children of the light are compelled to use their massive creative endowments to invent new paradigms of purpose, passion, and possibility. Previous Piscean Age passivity presumed that a Messiah would come to right all wrongs and remedy all compromised conditions. A great many still wait for a force outside themselves to act as deliverer. But this inactivity betrays the spiritual gift of free will. When Christ, Avatar of the Age of Pisces said "The way to the father is through me," he did not mean that by repeating his name (as mantra) matters would improve; rather he challenged believers to follow his example in how they elected to live and treat their fellow human travelers. His Truth compelled embodiment through action. Aquarius as radical rebel and iconoclast is predestined to become the author of new doctrines. Whatever is genuinely true, i.e. one of the eternal verities, cannot be altered. Mankind must rediscover these inviolate truths. It must realize that its evolutionary path requires other than pouring new wine into old wineskins! The transition of ages is upon us, and that generation born when Pluto (planet of ultimate transformation, in the form of endings that lead to new beginnings) transited Leo (1939-1957) became the flower children. It was their call to resist the patriarchal designs that defined the world up until their mass arrival. For a brief but promising flicker of time a second Renaissance gestated; and while it may seem that its light has gone out, providential seeds were successfully planted. These will bear fruit to stir the nascent Aquarian Age.

In the sixties the Beatles went to India and returned with deep, spiritual wisdom imparted to millions through their songs. Theirs was a call to unity spread round the world. They harmonized "We're all one," while their nemesis, the Rolling Stones intoned *Sympathy for the Devil*. These two inordinately popular bands demonstrated in their musical themes the polarity so instrumental to the Age of Pisces with its two fish swimming in opposing directions. It is now time for mankind to realize that our world is modeled after a great circle. Based on the relationships encoded within its circumference, we discover the means to mend what has been broken, and peacefully reconcile what formerly passed for irreconcilable opposition. In the case of Artemis, a vital part of her identity is projected onto her twin brother, Apollo. Since evidence suggests that twins retain substantial telepathic links, whatever their specific cognitive endowments, the pair must work together on cosmic as well as terrestrial levels to assist mankind in acquiring a more unifying, life-sustaining understanding. Apollo presides over Leo's kingdom of love, while Aquarius signifies ultimate higher mind. The interplay of the two signs (Leo and Aquarius) suggests the need for a communion between love and inspired awareness. True religion (that which exists in harmony with Universal law) calls for an open heart and an open mind. It prompts the individual to inwardly listen for the intimations of her inner soul, and grants the courage to act in accord with universal Truth and Principle. The soul grows when it takes time to note the miracles contained in everyday events, things frequently dismissed or taken for granted. When we realize that our gifts are intended to serve the universe (or greater good), we sense a benign protection, that our needs will likewise be met. Artemis champions behaviors that spontaneously erupt as

273

impulse sprung from a healthy interior wellspring. Her revolutionary perspective inspires humanity (person by person) to take down the walls erected by Saturn's fear-driven conditioning. Walls exist not only on external planes. Their intangible counterparts partition off key portions of our inner lives. Without the power of love, "the greatest of these," guiding humanity's collective course, citizens of the Aquarian Age could find their activities sinking to the depths of Atlantis. That civilization was believed to have fissured from within due in part to its focus on misapplied technological innovation, genetic engineering included. In addition there was an ongoing deadly clash between the sons and daughters of the Law of One against the children of Belial. Due to this virtual attack on the unified field of Divine Essence a veritable tear in the "fiber" of the manifest world (earth) reverberated. There are parallels today as Leo, twin to Aquarius, must act as cosmic counterpart by preparing human hearts for a vast transition. When the higher love is combined with a respect for universal Truth humanity will be freed from its deadly illusions, and collectively pursue a more life-affirmative course.

Artemis is embodied in citizens who boldly elect to live unique lifestyles and act as creative role models for others. They understand that Truth is not served by shadowy behaviors condoned by a consumer-driven media machine intent upon marketing false appetites. Because the promise and possibilities associated with this visionary sign of spontaneous invention have yet to be written, the daughters of Artemis are invited to add their innovative aptitudes to the proverbial mix. That approach is sure to empower your intrinsic Artemis! For many centuries the voice of the empowered feminine has gone unspoken for. Now it is time for the collective consciousness to recognize Her voice and divinity. She speaks for inclusion, and represents **all** disenfranchised groups, those who have long been punished, or told they were excluded because they were not children of the Divine. The Artemis soul altruistically offers her contribution, even if it will be better appreciated after her time when society has had a chance to catch up with her vision, ideals, and understanding. Such awakened ones expand upon and enrich the entire human race. The voice of Truth as personified by and through Artemis speaks through our conscience. It prompts us to ask ourselves, "What does

Divine intelligence warrant of me in this instance? Which is the path that supports the greater good?" As global technology binds mankind together through one gigantic ongoing conversation (via the worldwide web) and planes carry passengers anywhere in a single day, it is wise to regard all persons as fellow travelers, citizens of a singular world. The hour has come to move beyond fiercely competitive ideologies as bases for national identities. Our allegiance must aim at a higher, more unifying set of premises. By looking to heaven's model we note the great circle of creation, and taking the moon's perspective into account, realize that all sentient life on earth is ultimately connected. This all-inclusive understanding inspires us to transcend the artificial boundaries that have led nation into conflict against nation for far too long. Aquarius, signature of the zodiac's eleventh house champions friendship. Situated out beyond Saturn's confining rings it welcomes non-conformity, and invites us to explore new dimensions, even of ourselves. Aquarius does not ask that our friends talk, walk, or think alike. Instead it calls for endlessly innovative initiatives, and asks each to be true to the "law" of her innermost being. Uniformity hardly reflects the truth of creation, so why should human beings fall slave to any authoritarian creeds? Tradition-based beliefs and protocols reflect the power structures effete entities have used to hold mankind hostage; but as the dial of the heavens turns to lend Artemis ascendancy, these restrictive structures must fall away. Artemis, proponent of space exploration, relates the view privileged to astronauts who note our splendid sphere dancing in a silent sea of incomprehensible beauty. Through Aquarius and its upcoming cycle of promise, humanity will expand its previously circumscribed intellectual conjecture, and collectively tune into a new bandwidth on the great universal dial!

Do you know Artemis? Is there a friend, loved one, or acquaintance whose life seems at times to be charmed? She dares to live her dream, does her own thing, and where necessary challenges authority figures? Is there a friend or relative in your circle who, refuses to dye her hair, dress "her age," date someone of the same race, or follow the minuets of protocol that demonstrably undermine

275

real freedom? Is her life utterly unique in its insistence on being lived on her own uncompromising terms?

Artemis in Love

Artemis in love is a free spirit unwilling to be bound by society's conventions. She may be drawn into romantic bonds that include same sex partners. Equally, she finds herself attracted to persons who come from different backgrounds, races, or religions. She is given to nonchalantly turning a friendship into an intimate encounter. Friendship and erotic love work together for Artemis who can be totally present one minute, an electric companion in the best sense; and then suddenly utterly detached. Artemis embodies Kahlil Gibran's advice to lovers, that they should "put spaces in their togetherness." Although Artemis generally refuses to curb her extracurricular activities to conform to a partner's possessiveness, she can be surprisingly demanding of her significant other's fealty in return. To love Artemis is to embrace her offbeat lifestyle and respect her rebel causes.

Activities that Accord with the Season of Artemis

Support a humanitarian agency like Amnesty International, or donate to Green Peace or The International Red Cross.

Participate in a peace march.

Buy green products. Grow your own bean sprouts.

Substitute your coffee with a fruit smoothie each morning; or experiment with aromatic herbal teas.

Invent something.

Shop for unusual clothing items that don't conventionally "go" together.

Honor a friend with a token/gift of your appreciation.

Acknowledge others' contributions to your life. Form a well-wish circle. Invite each member to articulate her hopes and wishes. Every person present takes a turn as the group invokes the powerful synergistic magic associated with the eleventh house. As all affirm aloud the manifestation of that which is desired, the promise of two or more asking reverently in the name of Holy Spirit is metaphysically activated. (I've seen this process work miracles.)

Step out of your routine and pursue the unknown by succumbing to serendipity. Honor the urge to explore by letting your inner muse lead you to wherever.

Run for public office, or support a candidate who champions high ideals and would benefit from your support.

Go wind sailing, fly a kite, or bungee jump.

Stalk the sacred by participating in a vision quest or experience an authentic Indigenous American sweat lodge.

Listen to rebel 60's music.

Visit a health food store and where possible, trade in prescription drugs for their natural, herbal equivalents.

Consult an oracle to call upon the wisdom of your guardian spirits.

The truth, not always consistent with what appearances suggest, is out there. Follow its trail! Push your understanding beyond prior boundaries by reaching for knowledge in an area you never previously pursued.

Consider modifying your diet by consuming more health-supporting organic, vegetarian meals.

Chapter 12

Pisces: The Realm Of Aphrodite Awakened
The Embrace of All

According to myth the sensual goddess of erotic love, Aphrodite, emerged from effervescent sea foams. There is an alternative X-rated version of Her origin that takes into account **why** the seas foamed. Seems as punishment for certain conduct her father's severed genitals were thrown in to create quite a stir! Apt beginning for the Goddess born to mock patriarchal standards by freely choosing from the Olympian cast for her pick of lovers and would-be consorts. Traditional astrology may credit Neptune (a/k/a Poseidon) with rule of the last zodiac sign; but given the implication drawn from its twin fish swimming in opposite directions, **two** distinct voices are better suited to do this complex sign cosmic justice. *Moon Dance* belatedly allots to Aphrodite her rightful representation, and here is why: we first encountered Venus in the persona of Demeter. There she takes on the mantle of great Earth Mother. Venus is also directly associated with "the pleasure principle." Her connection with the zodiac's first earth sign Taurus awakens the physical senses and the rich endowments these promise. Thus Venus, in the persona of Demeter, sensitizes human beings to beauty, exotic scents, thrilling tastes, and when not impeded, unabashed sensuality. Next we encountered Venus in the persona of Hera, wife of Zeus. Governing Libra, the zodiac realm of union and marriage, Hera presides over intimate bonds, and inwardly instructs human beings to live up to the ideal of fair and equitable partnership. Venus directly "rules" the signs of Taurus (Demeter) and Libra (Hera). However she was also allotted honorary status, that of being exalted in Pisces where she lends profound influence to the Zodiac's final sign. This mystical position situated where the circle endlessly returns to meet itself brings all elements potentially into unison. Further, it is intended to inspire the spiritual realization that all sentient beings are inter-connected. As Pisces closes the circle it gives rise to a unified field suggestive of a singular entity. This Zodiac position reveals (if primarily to the spiritual Initiate) the complex web of existence shared by all sentient beings. What holds it together; coheres matter to this great circle? I believe the answer is Love! This Divine realization imparted by Venus in her 3rd manifestation suggests the path toward reconciliation between men and women who were cast into perpetual conflict throughout the long Age of Pisces. A dying phase, it erroneously led mankind to tear asunder what Spirit had joined together. Jesus, the fisher of men and avatar of The Age of Pisces taught peace and reconciliation. Clearly that is not what was furthered in His name. A healing process is now required of mankind, one that calls for honoring the equally Divine attributes of both genders! How human beings negotiate this age-phase transition is critical. Life as we know it has reached a crossroads. The cosmic version of a changing of the guard, a vast transition is upon us. Since history tends to be written retrospectively, as the canoe passes over rapids, it's tough to assess one's course. No wonder so many persons now feel lost.

The earth's cover of water by proportion (75% of its surface) suggests the same ratio present in our own physiology. Water is conducive to feelings, and Pisces is the last of the **water** signs. The spiritual journey completed when the circle closes suggests by extension the sum of all feelings, a direct encounter with the entire emotional panorama that flesh is heiress to. Water is remarkable for the forms it readily assumes. Turning to ice when temperatures fall below 32 degrees, water quickly morphs into steam once temperatures surpass 212 degrees. Water can move earth, absorb air, and put out fire. Its diverse expressions suggest the strength of spirit required to embrace life's vicissitudes while retaining a sense of empathy. Persons born with their moons or suns in Pisces are prone to the experience of heightened empathy on a regular basis. Aligned with Aphrodite's realm they are destined to know firsthand the full spectrum of feelings. Such sensitivity often functions as a double-edged blade. Many prefer to shut down and thereby escape the fate of being vulnerable to ever-changing emotions. Pisces' position on the universal dial represents the twelfth house. It's considered the domain of karma and "self-undoing." Since Pisces rules the feet this connection readily suggests the adage: "to shoot one's self in the foot." The parallel derives from the twelfth house propensity for self-defeating actions. The water element is mysterious given the sea's surface hides whatever takes place beneath. Logic, the purview of the air element and its expressions through intellect, cannot penetrate these obscure depths. The 12th house (signifying Pisces) suggests oceanic depths as metaphor, and points to the farthest reaches (and unseen levels) of our minds, i.e. the unconscious realm. Psychology has noted that a great many people are susceptible to automatic behaviors. One egregious sort takes shape as addiction. Many individuals fall prey to a psychic undertow that subverts their wills. Seduced by substance their lives involve endless struggles to break free. They are trapped from a place so deep inside that rational decision-making does little to offset chronic dependency. Astrologers can discern propensities toward addiction by observing the natal chart. Because the twelfth house and its Pisces' counterparts mark karma, it's probable that behaviors from the past recur to stir the soul's current learning experience. Telling indications show up on our present astrological maps. What individuals prone to escapist behaviors meet is what is yet to be mastered in themselves. Birth chart planets found in the twelfth house or in Pisces raise red flags for potential addictions (as do adverse aspects to Neptune, the sign's planetary ruler). Suppose a person fell to alcoholism in a previous incarnation. Currently they incarnate into a household where one parent is an active alcoholic. Some people approach fire and smelling the risk elect to stay out of harm's way. Others don't understand the danger. By the time they reconnect with their old temptation, it's too late. Once again exposed to that which compromised their experience in a former lifetime, they prove susceptible. It's the equivalent of an ambush of fate. Medical studies reveal that alcoholics metabolize alcohol differently than do those who are not "allergic" to this often-deadly substance. Autopsies done on Skid Row alcoholics demonstrated that their unique body chemistry actually converted alcohol into a molecular structure similar to heroin! Therapists have noticed that children born to drug or alcohol abusing parents carry a greater risk of adopting these self-destructive habits. Evidence further suggests that such individuals are genetically susceptible to alcoholism. Psychology relates these findings, yet karmic astrology explains **why** it is that specific people find themselves grappling with this particular battle of the soul. Without a spiritual basis for assessing the legacy of karma, life's painful lessons appear to occur by random selection, as if some kind of amoral roulette wheel spun out our fates. Mystics believe that karma is an "equal opportunity employer." The complex interplay of cause and effect traces back to the soul and its journey of lifetimes. Surface appearances provide limited data. Edgar Cayce often intoned the truth that, "entity is meeting self," and it makes perfect cosmic sense. Life's tough stuff does not come our way by sheer caprice. The birth chart offers compelling evidence to explain the nature of our personal lessons. If a susceptible individual falls prey to the substance that would consume him, his will becomes entangled in a psychic undertow. Thus "free will" becomes effectively disabled. The Catholic Church has actual protocols designed to fight demonic possession, and these forces are referred to as dark **spirits.** Is it mere irony that alcohol is popularly referred to as spirits? The substance seems to take hold of human souls just like a demonic force. The same holds true for other addictive substances. Sugar, caffeine, and even guns, porn, and shopping could be added to the list of things Americans are increasingly addicted to. At the final phase of the Piscean Age escapist behaviors have assumed epidemic proportions.

Sommerset Maughm spoke of a pervasive "quiet desperation" that stole joy from the lives of the living. In the modern world, a great many wonder what purpose their lives serve. This question is planted in us all for a reason. Many ponder the thesis deeply. Others prefer to lose themselves in collective escapes like sports, television dramas, virtual computer reality, or gambling. Like the twin masks drawn from ancient theater, life presents each of us with both comedic and tragic circumstances. Poets ask would we recognize joy without its contrast felt in sorrow? Our "polarity planet" appears designed for both as literature reflects in a body of works that has spanned centuries. Great minds have long wrestled with mankind's dichotomous estate. Robert Frost encountered two paths in the wood and chose the one less traveled by, a sentiment echoed in Scott

Peck's book by that title. The Bible relates: "Choose ye which master ye shall serve." Pisces' two fish reflect opposed pathways, a problem added to in that water by nature seeks its own level. It's easier for people to surrender to rather than fight the proclivities of their lower natures. The upper Arcanum of the Tarot addresses the tension that exists within every human being as his lower and higher natures vie for command. Mystics relate that the key purpose for taking on a human body is to attain greater levels of self-mastery. When the soul enters the earth plane during a phase strongly influenced by Pisces' planetary positions, (this sign representing the last stop on the grand cosmic dial before the great cycle begins anew with Aries), she will wrestle a dubious privilege, that of feeling what the entire human family is emoting at any given time. Many thus endowed escape into themselves; although a minority wisely seeks communion with the numinous, the place the soul recognizes as its home. Now in vogue is a search for the soulmate. Aphrodite's alluring presence is conjured by the hypnotic call of the legendary sea sirens. Across the centuries millions have been drawn out to sea. What is more romantically compelling than the endless blue horizon? When we swim in the ocean it feels like we "become one" with the waters. Similarly in Tantric sex we can melt into our partners. Our bodies are writ in that code that marries the substance of the male with the substance of the female. It's fair to say that the urge to merge is literally written into our genes! The mating dance is a component of our biological destiny; and it might have led to boundless joy had not the dark powers placed a wedge of sin between the genders to endlessly divide and conquer them.

I was given an amazing experience, something akin to an "Initiation by water" to gain a fuller understanding of Aphrodite's realm. Oddly enough this event coincided with the year's one and only new moon in Pisces rousing Aphrodite back to life for her annual phase of dominion. Along with two of my Leo-Apollo female buddies we made a short pilgrimage to our agreed upon magic spot. With the road increasingly penetrating the deepest secreted places of the Great Goddess, such places of spiritual regeneration are fast disappearing. Nonetheless, what was unique about our find was its placement at the end of a canal that bridged the Atlantic Ocean with the Gulf of Mexico. Due to intense tidal changes recurring throughout the day certain intervals would see sudden and forceful movements through the canal leaving wildly swirling eddies. These whirlpools formed due to an uneven ocean bottom marked by rocks and coral growth. We gingerly walked out onto the reef, and then gently slid into the water allowing the restless tide to carry us onto the swirling eddies. And what exhilarating rides we had! Granted it's a rather dangerous undertaking since one can be drawn downward due to the centrifugal force of the spinning water. Summoning a Zen-like state we didn't fight the flow; instead we surrendered our bodies to this greater force and "rode the current." Rolling up like an embryo I felt taken by the waters, almost as if a powerful invisible lover grabbed my hair and sent me into a primordial spin, an orbit of my own! The sensation was something akin to "a cosmic orgasm" as I was swirled and jettisoned again and again by the circular momentum of those wildly free flowing waters. At the core of this experience was a direct intimation of how it was that Aphrodite emerged from the sensual sphere of water's ancient spiral dances. Simulating the primal source of our origins in the mother's watery womb, conception born of erotic love is welcomed in this medium. And water ever after as primal source of innate sensuality reconnects us with the reproductive means to our own continuity (as a species). The waters give life its chance, and there can be no life without the great Yin-Yang dance!

Aphrodite's realm in numerous ways demonstrates the everlasting truth that all things come full circle. We are born from a circle/womb, and our lives symbolically simulate its trajectory. Those fortunate enough to experience Aphrodite's mystical Tantric embrace know bliss is found when the ego melts away. In the clasp of erotic love barriers between self and the beloved dissolve. At such times nothing seems to lie outside the self. This holy experience invites us to transcend the boundaries of the body. In a sense we become other. Many who suffer from addictions don't realize they are actually searching for a spiritual state of at-onement. They mistakenly surrender their psyches to a substance that can only simulate such contact. Unconsciously all healthy souls seek communion with their Creator. Inwardly they long for their celestial home and source of origin. This places mortal existence into something of a paradoxical state. Across the ages souls have become more and more ensconced in matter with materialism driving dominant belief systems. The spiritual premise, "Seek ye first the kingdom of God and all else will be added unto you," has been subverted. A spiritual impoverishment has resulted. Thus at this final phase of the Piscean Age who is not wrestling with enormous tests? Quite likely these signify our final exams, lessons left pending from past incarnations spent in "Earth School 101." It's useful to make it one's spiritual practice to experience gratitude for the blessings of life. However those who have opened their channels to empathy cannot help but feel extreme grief for what is actually taking place in our world. So much of what passes for leadership is outright fraud and obfuscation. Pisces' essence is depicted by the opposed courses set by two reversed fish. One route makes headway through deception and eludes accountability. Denial of global climate change in the face of catastrophic weather events dulls the clarion call for immediate, intelligent action. Where is the leadership? Why has it not summoned a more responsible ethos of conservation to offset the rabid consumerism that is bringing nature's ecosystems to near collapse? During the closing acts of the Piscean Age inaction in the face of calamitous species loss constitutes a collectivized version of shooting ourselves in the foot. Mass karma can only be altered if allegiance to Mars rules is overcome. The endless call to make war while trafficking in armaments can never deliver to humanity the security falsely promised. It is only the god of death that ends up temporarily appeased. The evils that emerge from the mindset of righteous aggression feed upon themselves and thus endure.

The massive suffering now visited upon citizens of the Middle East (children of Creation's inviolate circle) suggests a great wound with over a million persons rendered unwitting martyrs. Catholics are told to patiently bear their suffering. Hindus are promised a reward in the next life, while unfortunate young Islamic suicide bombers believe virgins await them on the other side. Jews hold a heritage for being cast aside to play the unfortunate role of society's scapegoats. The Age of Pisces has resulted in an extended phase of martyrdom. Its contents, paid in the collateral of suffering, imprint every culture. Thus as global destiny unfolds in increasingly dangerous rebounds of past hostilities it's useful to remember that significant portions of our beings remain immortal. Ultimate spirits we take on mortal bodies for the purpose of learning lessons specific to the earthly sphere. Pisces as the last Zodiac sign represents the final experience generated from the great cosmic time dial. Likely it symbolizes (by virtue of the type of karmic scenario we find ourselves currently wrestling with) a synopsis of the lives we've each lived. If we could gaze back far enough into time we'd realize that we've all worn many moccasins. Therefore the tendency to judge others on the basis of their present status is spiritually shortsighted and places unnatural boundaries between persons. In contrast compassion unites. Given that all of us are struggling with tough karmic challenges sensitivity for others is warranted. It need not require unspeakable tragedy for human beings to put aside their differences. Better to recognize each other's fundamental humanity and thereby endeavor to act cooperatively. As the structural integrity of long-established paradigms comes asunder, we face the opportunity to act collectively. The hour has arrived to design systems supportive of growth for future generations. To embrace these necessarily novel approaches means transcending much of Pisces' erroneous conditioning. A good place to start is with the countless millions virtually hypnotized by a wide array of false religious teachings, some on a par with those espoused by the late Jim Jones who shared lethal Kool-aid with obedient followers. Sadly many people seem to want oblivion, an end to it all. Instead of throwing the gift of life directly back in Creator's face, these darkly faithful harbor extreme angst and project their death wish onto Creator. How? By embracing the heinous fiction that Holy war (a/k/a End Times or Armageddon) represents God's will! Remember, the only god this model lays homage to is Mars.

Astrology's timeless capacity to translate the celestial sign language offers several compelling analogies that help explain this historical era. Oil, which is the remnant of organic debris slowly dissolved into sea-beds over time constitutes the treasure directly gotten from Poseidon's realm. This resource fuels the industrial engines of the modern world along with its labyrinth of complex technologies. Arab leaders refer to oil as "a soft loan from Allah." Fascinating the influence oil holds over our epoch as it pretty much constitutes the "Holy Grail" of our times. Oil is "governed" by the sign of Pisces, as is Florida having incorporated in late February. Deceptions R'U.S. style, high-placed officials were able to undermine the vote count, and therefore the presidential election of 2000. This electoral deceit placed a warrior into power who, as a variety of inside sources later related, fixed the case to go to war in Iraq. Lies have run rampant at this karmic juncture. Note the influence of the following Pisces persons on current events: Ralph Nader, Osama Bin Laden, Russ Feingold, and Israel's Sharon. For those wrestling with doubts about *End Times*, astrologers offer the more optimistic perspective of a massive Age phase transition. There are among us many who still fight the notion that the earth is not flat. For such types "the end" supports their belief in finitude. Yet often what appears as final represents instead a fundamental change to the thing's previous form.

Earth has long served as a spiritual school. Souls must demonstrate competence with respect to its lesson plan before being freed to move onto new levels of expression, those waiting on other vital spheres. Pisces' "proof of passage" calls for individuals to show their willingness to extend compassion. Too many hide behind labels of righteousness while acting with utter disregard for the painful circumstances of others' lives. They often prove too quick to fan the flames of enduring tribal antipathy. Such behaviors reveal an absence of spiritual growth. Quite possibly in our everyday walks of life we are already experiencing The Judgment Day. How each of us treats his friends, family, and fellow earth travelers becomes the great test. Pisces, where the circle meets itself, reminds us that we are all connected; that the circle knows no sides. To be without prejudice is to recognize the face of Creator on everyone. Mystics refer to this state of awareness as the "at-onement." An astute treatise on reincarnation, *The Wheel of Rebirth* offers the remarkable life-to-life journey of an individual given its content in a vivid series of recollections. Edgar Cayce's numerous recorded trance-readings reference this same life-to-life continuum, however its language is abstruse and often difficult to follow. In *The Wheel of Rebirth*, the "over-soul" offers lucid commentary at the conclusion of each life-chapter. In this way a profound explanation is presented for where the individual gained spiritual grace and conversely created new karma. A bond with the subject's twin-flame figures prominently in the evolving storyline as this significant other is encountered in several recalled lifetimes. Another writer who passionately pursued the premise of a life-to-life continuum featuring enduring human bonds is Dick Sutphen. By using hypnotic suggestion to regress enthusiastic groups of people he accumulated data strongly suggestive of the ongoing essence of love. Spiritual sources relate that conjugal love serves as a springboard or stepping stone. Spiritual evolution does not stop when lovers attain a blessed state of temporal paradise; rather the experience of love is intended to expand like a living web to embrace the entire human family. Sadly this type of love is all too rare in our world.

Major factors now coalesce to produce a radical shift in values. Climate change, the karmic blowback of war, and reckless fiscal policies operate in concert to hasten a collapse of the dominant paradigm and its inherently unbalanced founding principles. Life as we've been experiencing it is due for a radical revision. For one thing, Neptune will soon enter its own sign (Pisces) for its first homecoming in 165 years. This event occurs in 2012, the year designated for a massive transition according to ancient mathematicians who devised the Mayan calendar. In anticipation of its return Neptune now passes through Aquarius, the last most evolved of the three air sign kingdoms. This 14-year phase begun in 1998 coincided with the burgeoning popularity of the worldwide web, a virtual reality sphere that hosts millions of simultaneous conversations. A good number of people now live almost exclusively through computer interactions. Some engage in the cyber realm to the extent there's minimal actual human contact. In a sense, the projection of their virtual selves has come to replace who they in essence are. Perhaps this mass phenomenon is a critical step, one that paves the way for a sentience not limited to dense physical reality. If prophecies of violent earth change hold true, then millions of souls will rapidly cross over. The sudden tsunami that ravaged the shores of Asian nations just after Christmas 2004 took a quarter of a million lives in a flash. Remnants of Pompeii remind us how quickly a thriving city can be reduced to volcanic rubble. The modern ruin of New Orleans brings to mind what the wise Buddhist sages relate: that human life is impermanent. Life may appear ordinary one moment, and completely eclipsed in the next. Yet the soul embodied as a spark of Creator is by nature infinite and remains intact. The mortal body in contrast cannot know when its final hour will arrive. It's therefore wise to live by the precept of Grace even during this challenging juncture. The path alluded to by the "fish less traveled by" requires an awareness not confined to the limitations of the transitory physical body. Inevitable mortality must be reconciled against the sure knowledge that the essence of the self will be preserved given its inviolate bond to the numinous.

The late Dr. Seuss was a Pisces, and he exhibited the sign's capacity for marked imagination. Akin to a modern shaman, his books shared powerful spiritual lessons. In my early career as a junior high school English teacher, I designed a class project where students were asked to choose a book and read it to an elementary school class. I was to grade them on their expression and verbal delivery. What was fascinating about this project was what was revealed in the books selected. Each seemed to indicate the exact lesson faced by the person choosing it. A particularly pretty Pisces student selected, *I Had Trouble In Getting to Solla Sollew*. In this Seuss classic a creature is bound and determined to make his way to a city where nothing is purported to ever go wrong. The quest to reach this desirable location is frustrated by repeated setbacks. When at last the creature arrives at his longed for destination he learns he must yet earn the key to the city! And when this task is completed, darned if a "key slapping slippard" isn't stuck in the very lock to render the apparatus useless! Seuss lays waste to the notion there's a perfect place, a veritable Shangri-la where one can escape their intended lessons. This particular classic imparts a major reality check to those given to escapist tendencies! Another student, a wise Aquarian remarked, "You take yourself wherever you go." And in that same class was a Capricorn, struggling with that sign's failure of imagination who chose, *On Beyond Zebra*. In this Seuss masterpiece a young fellow creatively envisions animals thus far not seen in any zoo. Dr. Seuss married humor with wisdom to instill in children the understanding they are unlikely to find nirvana on this plane, yet they can explore the world and make their own wondrous discoveries. Even in the seemingly nonsensical tale, *The*

Cat in the Hat, Seuss carefully pointed out that no one is free from the law of consequences. Unfortunately a great many people defy that understanding and make it their life stories to learn by default. That's where the Zodiac's 12th house of karma comes into play along with institutions like ashrams and spiritual retreats that encourage inner reflection. Where self-undoing occurs on a massive scale, society is compelled to supply places for contemplation and healing such as jails, mental institutions, and hospitals. These facilities come under the umbrella of 12th house "rule." Trapped in secluded settings individuals are prompted to take a fearless moral inventory. For some such efforts lead to life-altering spiritual epiphanies. With less dramatic fanfare this journey is extended to every woman on a regular basis since the moon makes a crossing of her 12th house once a month. This phase corresponds with poet Robert Frost's sentiment expressed as the wish "to get away from earth for a while."

Perhaps the dream of transcendence explains why we dream at all. These departures from ordinary reality serve as salvation to some souls, escapism for others. Imagine what the prisoner's fate would be were he not transported through dreamtime to more liberated locations? Traditional astrology places sleep and dreams under the dominion of Neptune (Pisces). Across the ages all sorts of authorities have sought to explain these nighttime reveries. Just as one cannot read a newspaper under water since the print will readily dissolve, the terrain of the unconscious mind is not adequately understood by or through the conscious intellect. Don Juan, earlier mentioned, explained that the human mind divides into dual perceptual portals consisting of the Nagual and Tonal. One key facet of sorcery is the art of dreaming wherein the mystical apprentice must learn to control his actions on the dream plane. Mastering skills on this intangible plane allots access to the Nagual. There laws depart substantially from their operations in ordinary reality. The sorcerer's training leads to heightened perceptual acuity and unique forms of power. While the Tonal relates to the collective experience of consensual reality, the Nagual opens the door to what most never fathom (and probably wouldn't believe). These twin zones of sentience are mirrored in functions specific to each brain hemisphere. Dual aspects were explored in Mercury's chapter where we encountered the mindsets resonant with Gemini's twins. Now we meet them again as Pisces' two fish speaking through the unconscious portion of cognition. The left-brain favors rational problem solving and supports the masculine bias of linearity/logic, whereas right brain stimulates imagination, feelings and intuition. Those who own the capacity to harmoniously integrate both realms of sentience tend to be the wisest. Likely they are also old, advanced souls. On a global scale, it is time for mankind to utilize and balance both cognitive oars. Rather than veer uncontrollably off course under the direction of warrior Mars' cold logic of winner-takes-all (M.A.D-style aggression), we must deploy the counterbalancing right brain so that compassion and universal caring right our global course! Edgar Cayce imparted useful lessons drawn from the legendary continent of Atlantis. Whether actual history or fable, its cautionary implication in the form of a sunken civilization bears significance to modern times. According to Cayce a great trespass against nature took shape as Demeter's gene-banks were mined in order to engineer hybridized creatures capable of enormous labor. Images of half human/half animal beings derive from this epoch. This ancient civilization fell into something akin to a civil war, its state of divisiveness severe enough to unsettle matter! The spiritually enlightened of the times recognized a "law of one," and knew that at essence all sentient beings are connected. Their nemesis, the children of Belial lived for self-interest alone. The ideological schism between both "camps" eerily resembles the rift currently underway in America. Rabid rightwing conservatives talk about "god" while eliminating social service programs designed to protect the needy. They support policies that enrich the wealthiest through war and champion high incarceration rates of fellow citizens. Spiritually aware persons in contrast commit to building and sustaining a just society where the "pursuit of happiness" falls to everyone. *The Bible's* story of the Great Flood, referenced in Plato's ancient dialogs, relates that civilizations risk the fate of being washed away if Divine law is not followed. It has happened before. Is mankind courting the same fate that befell Atlantis? Trance-channel and author Pat Rodegast was asked, "Will there be a nuclear World War III?" The answer she offered over a decade ago was: "Divine Intervention will not allow it." I hope the statute of limitations has not run out on those words, since current events suggest that leaders have either gone mad, or are headed there!

Pisces' two fish also represent the swirling forces of Yin and Yang. Either they confront one another antagonistically or blend into magnificent unison. It's time that the great lovers first encountered in Eden rediscover the power of truth and reconciliation. It's plausible that your present gender represents what's needed to balance the experience of prior incarnations. It's probably a departure from the gender experience of recent incarnations. Men who take on the mask of machismo may be rather new to this thing called maleness! Given the fierce history of the world Jesus presciently advised: "Be kind to one another." That basic recipe, along with turning the other cheek, could go a long way towards facilitating the mass healing our ailing planet requires. Recall the Greek and Roman worldview where power was shared among three brothers, each given a specific sphere of dominion. Since we generally sleep eight hours every night, one-third of our lives comes under Neptune's rule. Pisces, aligned with the 12th house of self-undoing also makes use of a treacherous instrument: that of the too often-subtle ambush of fate. These beguiling traps seem innocent and attractive enough at the onset since the dangers they pose are not revealed until one is caught like a fish on a lure! The very premise of seduction is embodied in Venus-Aphrodite. Perhaps she designed the original Venus Fly-Trap plant! How often is it that the thing that allures also presents the path to our undoing?

Earlier we experienced Venus in the persona of Hera where governing Libra she champions the lesson of balance. If one is centered, she is less susceptible to temptations (in the form of tantalizingly dangerous persons, pleasures, or things) that might derail her course. Without self-possession these "items" and the sensations they give rise to can fast become addictive obsessions. It is no accident that the final zodiac kingdom compels us to tame our egos by acquiring the discipline to transcend self-destructive behaviors. Most must fall into the sea before they learn to swim. Through honestly facing our selves in karma's mirror we summon the strength to overcome those fateful flaws that led to our periodic turns round the wheel of time. All beings run the risk of remaining locked into their own perceptual paradigms, blind to their chief flaws until graced by an epiphany they at last can transcend themselves. This feat may constitute the work of many lifetimes. Pisces can delay the liberation of souls by utilizing its weapon of deception. That includes the self-deceptive sort. Acting as the human equivalent of the chameleon, Pisces adroitly takes on semblances. Its tantalizing array of camouflaging devices thrill, delight, and sometimes destroy. A master of that art was the writer Anais Nin who kept diaries of her sensual conquests. A Pisces and daughter of Aphrodite, she appeared to take delight in destroying the confidence of men who fell under her trance-like spell. Raw sexual magnetism can draw people to behaviors that may seem inviting, but can cost them their bodies, minds, and souls. Countless women have lost their lives to jealous boyfriends or husbands. Others have been disfigured or emotionally battered, and recovery often involves walking through the valley of the shadow of death until at last one arrives at personal resurrection. Ultimately every ill can serve a purpose if and when darkness is brought to light. Recall the grain of sand that lodges inside the oyster aggravating, irritating, and wounding until a pearl is formed. Pisces as portrayed by the two fish offers the soul a choice. One road promises to feed the physical senses. The other constitutes the higher path and it calls for a self-disciplined spiritually oriented lifestyle. Such a commitment suggests the road less traveled by. As a society we fail to nurture our inner spirits, that aspect of ourselves that aches for contact with its numinous source. The ensuing emptiness in turn attracts a wide array of mood managers, many in the form of self-medication.

The terrain of the twelfth house can prove treacherous. Many don't recognize their weakness until they fall under its thrall. In addition, motives generated from Pisces' deep watery domain bypass those "guardians" that stand watch at the gates of intellect. Regardless of our varied cognitive endowments, everyone struggles with a twelfth house influence. It indicates where compassion (even for the self) must come into play. Scripture states one must forgive in order to be forgiven. That spiritual formula when put into practice balances karma. It may even invoke grace. Universal law is not designed merely for those who wrestle with ostensible addictions, although the vast majority finds itself addicted to something as the Age of Pisces with its attendant escapisms runs out the cosmic clock. Remember, it is when two or more gather together that the power of the Holy presence can intercede on their behalf. We need each other, and have come into this world to learn to get along. Humanity cannot afford to remain seduced by the greatest deception of all, that which has torn apart the family of mankind as if all branches (or tribes) do not stem from the same primal tree of life! Individuals have come to the place in their shared evolutionary journey where it's vital that each now recognize herself as a member of the great circle that never ends. To maintain homage to Mars rules will court global disaster. Thus we are now challenged to reassemble the Divine circle and thereby draw forth the profound balancing powers of Venus. Intentional acts of Divine integration will transform our world. Or put another way, we must lay down arms to join hands!

Our *Moon Dance* journey now returns to where it began to fulfill the law of cycles. As sentient creatures we exist within a vast celestial sea that rocks and rolls to the unseen currents of time. Moving on a sphere through space our journeys accord with the rotary nature of the heavens as we, too, spin, turn and dance along with the heavenly bodies. Aphrodite yields once more to the fires of spring where Mars-Aries takes dominion upon the grand cosmic stage.

Do you know Aphrodite? Is there a woman in your circle who's so attractive that she presents a veritable danger to others' marriages? Is there someone who sends mixed signals, enticing you to come closer, while simultaneously doing her utmost to ensure you won't succeed in getting too close! Do you have a relative or associate who plays victim in order to win another person's sympathy? Using this method she subtly gains access to whatever resources suit her agenda? She may have a tendency to load on the perfume, but she sure knows how to choose sexy shoes!

Aphrodite In Love

The Aphrodite native was born into the swim of things. She intuitively senses her connection with others, and may be quick to note their weak points thanks to a developed intuition. Her seduction strategy includes either playing her own weaknesses to gain control of another's strength (shades of The Biblical Delilah who cut off Samson's hair); or she can reverse poles to enact the role of comforter. She encourages others to become dependent on her good graces and thereby leverages control. Adroitly she assumes the role of femme fatal in order to attract the type of male who sees himself as a strong protector. However she can also deftly deploy compassion to draw hard luck types her way. Due to the symbol of the two opposing fish, the Pisces native can either exhibit supernatural beauty like Aphrodite-born Liz Taylor, or its opposite. She is a master seductress; yet if she finds herself paired with a genuine soulmate, she's capable of true devotion to him and his cause. Otherwise she can toss men like fish right back into the sea without evidencing the slightest shade of conscience. Naturally empathetic, she wins others' trust; but due to her intrinsically mutable nature, her own loyalties are neither firm nor consistent.

Activities that Accord with the Season of Aphrodite

If you've never tried it before and wish to overcome a stubborn habit, book a hypnotherapy session. Transcendental forces may help you break free.

Walk barefoot on the sand.

Invite a friend to share a rich bottle of wine and make a gourmet pizza from scratch.

Mix exotic oils and become your own scent-ual apothecary. A gypsy I encountered long ago took a shine to me and mixed up a version of *Love Potion # 9*. It consisted of positively sinful doses of vanilla, patchouli, and amber. Absolutely sensuous, I suggest you try it!

Like Pisces native Sarah Jessica Parker from *Sex in the City*, lift your spirits by shopping for shoes! Could that prove the antidote (or ad hoc therapy) for the Zodiac's shoot-yourself-in-the-foot sign?

Visit an aquarium, take up snorkeling, or enroll in a deep sea diving class.

Grow bean sprouts. Dance in the rain. Paint with watercolors.

Swim in an exotic sacred place.

Prepare seafood if you dare!

Pay a visit to someone hospitalized, or consider joining an organization that lends comfort to those that are ill and alone.

Make peace with the earth and your fellow travelers here. Adapt a lonely loving pet from an animal shelter.

No one can remain lost long if they look to the heavens above and follow the arc of the moon as writ into the firmaments. She constantly changes, is always going through phases, but ultimately she knows where she's headed. As you acquire finesse in the art of *Moon-dancing*, you shall too!

Thank you for opening yourself to the great *Moon Dance*, a legacy that belongs to every woman, for each is a daughter of a Goddess!

Final Words

There is a story within this story and how it came to be. Much like the moon and her journey through all topographies that we are destined to follow, since the inception of this work in 1991, life has taken me through enormous phases. The work began when by sharing my daily life with a partner I witnessed clearly my inner changes projected onto him also noting how the tenor of the bond altered. I began to see the pattern emerge and given my background as an astrologer, realized I had discovered a tool that could be of enormous service to others. In its original inception, the ideas this book presented were certainly unique, but not yet entirely defined. However the work attracted attention from Inner Traditions Publishers. Eventually they passed on the project recognizing they had no editor with enough astrological knowledge to adequately groom the manuscript. I did my best to encapsulate its intriguing theories by writing short versions for **Ms. Magazine** (which found no resonance with then editor, Marcia Gillespie), and several women's glossies. They too passed on the subject matter. Only *Dell Horoscope* (and its editor, Ronnie Grishman) had the courage to publish my work on this novel topic.

When my second daughter left home for college in 2000 I found myself drawn back to the manuscript and began a rewrite. It was interrupted first by the death of my father, and then my stepmother. These sobering events synchronized with my firstborn daughter bearing first a son, Phoenix, and then a daughter, Chloe. Thus *Moon Dance* has traced the major episodic changes of my personal life. Several time-consuming edits followed once I was able to root and dedicate my efforts to the fruit now in your hands. It's been an Initiation writing it, and a weight off my mind to at last produce it. And it is my sincere hope that those drawn to this new way of looking at time will grow in relation to their own investment, that is in observing and coming to respect their own *Moon Dance* cycles. The themes of time reside quite truly on the inside and impart to us the capacity to feel all that flesh is heiress to.

Bibliography/Notes

Part I

Alan Oken, *Astrology: Evolution and Revolution,* pages 131-133, Bantam, New York, 1976

Noel Langley, *Edgar Cayce on Reincarnation*, pages 179-186, Warner Books, 1967

Naomi Klein, *The Shock Doctrine*, Picador/Henry Holt, New York, 2007

Richard Wilhelm (translation), *The I ching: Book of Changes*, page 68, Bollingen Foundation, 1950

Kahlil Gibran, *The Prophet*, pages 11-16, Knopf, New York, 1979

Robert E. Lane, *The Loss of Happiness in Market Democracies*, Yale University Press, 2000

Margaret Mead, *Coming of Age in Samoa*, William Morrow, New York, 1928

William Pollack, *Real Boys: Rescuing Our Sons From the Myths of Boyhood*, Macmillan, New York, 1999

Marion Zimmer Bradley, *The Mists of Avalon*, Ballatine Publishers, 1984

Talisha Abelar, *The Sorcerer's Crossing*, page 51-53, Penguin Books, 1992

Bron Malinowski, Sex and Repression in Savage society, Routledge Classics, London 1948

Rajneesh, *Tantra, Spirituality and Sex*, The Rajnessh Foundation, 1977

Anais Nin, *Fire: A Journal of Love*, page 163, Harcourt & Brace, New York, 1995

Carlos Casteneda, *The Teachings of Don Juan*, Ballantine Books, New York, 1968

Part II

Dr. Alberto Villoldo (various tapes and lectures)

Robert M. Sapolsky & Lisa J. Share, "A Pacific Culture Among Wild Baboons," 2004

Wilhelm Reich, *The Function of Orgasm*, Orgone Institute Press, 1942

Leon Uris, *Armageddon*, Doubleday, New York, 1963

Jack London, *The Star Rover*, page 290, Valley of the Sun Publishing, Malibu, California, 1983

Rajneesh, *Tantra, Spirituality and Sex*, page 13 and 31, The Rajneesh Foundation, 1977

Richard Wilhelm (translation), *The I ching: Book of Changes*, page 166-167, Bollingen Foundation, 1950

Emmet Fox, "The Mental Equivalent," (pamphlet)

Jean Shinoda Bolen, *Goddesses in Everywoman*, Harper & Row, New York, 1984

Jean Shinoda Bolen, *Gods in Everyman*, Harper & Row, New York, 1989

Susan Faludi, *Backlash*, page 238, Crown Publishers, New York, 1991

Dr. John Gray, *Men Are From Mars, and Women From Venus*, Harper Collins, New York, 1992

Gordon Michael Scallion, *Notes From the Cosmos*, page 112-113, The Matrix Institute, New Hampshire, 1987

James Lovelock, *The Revenge of Gaia*, Penguin Books, New York, 2007

Yogananda, *A World In Transition*, page 5-7, The Self Realization Fellowship, 1994

Amory Lovins & L. Hunter Lovins, "Natural Capitalism." Article from *Mother Jones*

Dhyani Ywahoo, *Voices of Our Ancestors*, page 3, and 57-59, Shambala, 1987

C.G. Jung, *The Archetypes & the Collective Unconscious*, Bollingen, Princeton University Press, 1959

The Course in Miracles, Foundation for Inner Peace, 1975

Paul Brenner, M.D. *Life is a Shared Creation*, Devorss & Co, California 1981

Jane Roberts, *The Nature of the Psyche*, pages 113-114, Bantam (Prentice-Hall), 1984

George Lakoff, Moral Politics: *How Liberals and Conservatives Think*, University of Chicago Press, 2002

Carlos Casteneda, *A Separate Reality*, Ballantine Books, 1968

T.H. White, *The Once and Future King*, Berkley Publishing Corporation, 1939

Richard Bach, *Illusions: The Adventures of a Reluctant Messiah*, 1977

Elizabeth Haich, *Initiation*, page 47, George Allen Ltd. London, 1965

David Korten, *The Great Turning*, Berrett-Koehler, 2006

Gloria Steinem, *Moving Beyond Words*, Simon & Shuster, New York, 1995

James Caroll, *The Boston Globe*, July 4 essay published in 2005 or 2006

Louise Hay, *You Can Heal Your Life*, Hay House, 1984

Kahlil Gibran, *The Prophet*, page 11-16, Knopf, New York, 1979

H.K.Chaloner, *The Wheel of Rebirth*, pages 160-164, Theosophical Publishing House, Illinois, 1976

Charles Fillmore, *Keep a True Lent*, page 152, Unity

Gregg Braden, *The Divine Matrix: Bridging Time, space, Miracles and Beliefs*, (Audio CD)

Julia Cameron, *The Artist's Way*, Penguin/Putnam, 1992

Diane Stein, *All Women Are Healers*, The Crossing Press, 1990

Dr. Robert Mendelsohn, *Confessions of a Medical Heretic*, page 51-52, Contemporary Books, 1979

Sherill Sellman, *Hormone Heresy*, Get Well International, 1996

Gerald Jampolsky, *Love is Letting Go of Fear*, Celestial Arts, 2004 (with Hugh Prather)

Vistera Parham, *What's Wrong With Eating Meat*, Ananda-Marga Publishers

George Orwell, *1984*, Penguin Modern Classics, 1949

Jamie Sams & David Carson, *The Medicine Cards*, Bear & Company, New Mexico, 1988

Shere Hite, *Women and Love*, page 395, Alfred A. Knopf, New York, 1987

Susan Faludi, *Backlash*, page 238, Crown Publishers, New York, 1991

Gordon Michael Scallion, *Notes from the Cosmos*, page 112-113, The Matrix Institute, New Hampshire, 1987

Dr. Seuss, *The Cat in the Hat*, Random House, New York, 1957

Dr. Seuss, *On Beyond Zebra*, Random House, New York, 1955

Dr. Seuss, *I Had Trouble in Getting to Solla Sollew*, Random House, New York, 1965

Liz Greene: *Saturn: A New Look at an Old Devil*, Samuel Weiser's, 1976

Dan Brown, *The Da Vinci Code*, Doubleday, 2003

Marilyn Ferguson, *The Aquarian Conspiracy*, J.P. Tarcher, Los Angeles, 1980

Noam Chomsky, *Necessary Illusions: Thought Control in Democratic Societies*, South End Press, Boston, 1989

Edgar Evans Cayce, *Edgar Cayce on Atlantis*, pages 66-69, Paperback Library, 1968

Pat Rodegast, *Emmanuel Speaks*, Bantam, 1985

About the Author

Sioux Rose began her career writing horoscopes for newpapers and magazines in Puerto Rico. She graduated to a weekly television spot on the island's only English language station; and then once relocated to Key West, Florida, Sioux landed her own weekly live television program. "Astrology and the Divine Order." Quite popular with locals it aired for seven years (1986-1994). During this phase Sioux's work was retained in glossy Spanish magazines, and a new column, "Celestial Fine-Tuning" began for the prestigious Lear's Magazine (New York). Sioux was an esteemed guest on numerous radio programs in Florida, Chicago, and New Mexico. She co-authored "Starmates" with Zolar (Simon & Shuster) in 1989, and then "The Alchemy of Fusion: Planetary Pairings in Signs" for The American Federation of Astrologers (2000). "Neptune and the Final Phase of the Piscean Age" was self-published at Iuniverse (2004) along with a channeled novel originally submitted into a national contest sponsored by Ted Turner. "Evolving Toward Eden: The Divine Promise Restored" was reborn and is now available at Iuniverse. Sioux's astute and humorous astrological allegory for children of all ages, "Cassandra's Tale", will soon be available as well.

Having spent her entire adult life pursuing mystical subjects, counseling clients utilizing astrology, tarot, and numerology, Ms. Rose now presents a powerful spiritual tool intended to guide readers to their "place in time." Likely the book she was born to write, "Moon Dance: The Feminine Dimensions of Time" is a unique amalgam. Drawing upon astrology, Jungian archetypes, and mythology it uncovers the mysterious rhythm structure of time. Sioux has also written six movie scripts, two now published as novellas, while a number of novel projects wait in queue.